CIVIL WAR
SOLDIERS

CIVIL WAR
SOLDIERS

Reid Mitchell

V I K I N G

VIKING
Published by the Penguin Group
Viking Penguin Inc., 40 West 23rd Street,
New York, New York 10010, U.S.A.
Penguin Books Ltd, 27 Wrights Lane, London W8 5TZ, England
Penguin Books Australia Ltd, Ringwood, Victoria, Australia
Penguin Books Canada Ltd, 2801 John Street,
Markham, Ontario, Canada L3R 1B4
Penguin Books (N.Z.) Ltd, 182-190 Wairau Road,
Auckland 10, New Zealand

Penguin Books Ltd, Registered Offices:
Harmondsworth, Middlesex, England

First published in 1988 by Viking Penguin, Inc.
Published simultaneously in Canada

LIBRARY OF CONGRESS CATALOGING IN PUBLICATION DATA
Mitchell, Reid.
Civil War soldiers.
Includes bibliography and index.
1. United States. Army—History—Civil War, 1861–
1865.   2. Confederate States of America. Army—History.
3. United States—History—Civil War, 1861–1865—
Causes.   4. United States—History—Civil War, 1861–1865
—Social Aspects.   5. Soldiers—United States—
Attitudes—History—19th century.   I. Title.
E492.3.M58 1988   973.7'42   87-40565
ISBN 0-670-81742-2

Printed in the United States of America by
Arcata Graphics, Fairfield, Pennsylvania
Set in Sabon
Designed by Fritz Metsch

for
E. T. Mitchell
and
Joseph G. Tregle, Jr.

Preface

This is a book about the soldiers who fought during the Civil War. It uses the most personal of documents, their letters and diaries, to re-create their wartime experiences. It is also a book about the meaning of the Civil War, written in the belief that establishing what the war meant to that generation will help us decide what it means for us. The war is central to our past; we can turn to it as an image of what it means to be American, what it means to live within the dreadful rigor of history—what it means to be human.

I have been called a "post-Vietnam" historian, the implication being that my perception of the Civil War has been shaped, maybe distorted, by the moral questions generated by that later war. I don't know why it would take the Vietnam War to raise issues inherent in the tragedy of Americans killing Americans in a conflict over the meaning of democracy and freedom. In any case, if I am a "post-Vietnam" historian, I am also a "post–Civil Rights" historian—let me be exact: I am a post–desegregation-of-the-New-Orleans-public-school-system historian; I am a Southerner fortunate enough to have gone to school with my fellow Southerners, white and black.

So I come to the letters and diaries left by Civil War soldiers with the questions I would have asked the writers if they had been alive. Why did you fight? What did you think of your enemy, your American enemy? How did you feel about slavery and race and all the unfinished business that means in some way the war you fought is still not over? What was it like to be in battle? Were you frightened; how did you overcome your fear? How did you face death— how did you give meaning to violence and destruction? How did you accept that you yourself were a killer? What did you take home from the war? What legacy have you left us?

These are my questions, but I have not willfully imposed them on the soldiers of the 1860s; they were their questions too. They knew they were caught up in great and troubling events; they sought meaning for them. They were no simpler than we are, no less intelligent, no less human. If I am not always satisfied with their answers, it is not because I am so smug as to think I can give better ones. But the questions are not ones on which we can stand neutral—they represent the moral dilemma at the heart of our past.

Acknowledgments

I want to thank those whose teaching, friendship, and encouragement have contributed to my career in history and to the writing of this book. At the University of New Orleans, Warren Billings, Jerah Johnson, Joseph Logsdon, and Gerald Bodet of the history department supported my efforts as a student and welcomed me back as a colleague. I owe as much to the English department there, particularly to K. Raeburn Miller, Margaret Maurer, Robert Bourdette, and my good friend Julie Jones. And many thanks to Mahaptos. At the College of William and Mary, Cam Walker, James J. Thompson, Jr., and M. Boyd Coyner all encouraged my interest in Southern history; Lawrence Goodwyn taught me to respect the people I study and to listen to what they have to say. It is hard for me to imagine this book without the courses I took at the University of California, Berkeley, particularly those from Charles Sellers and Winthrop Jordan. I also want to thank my friends in Berkeley, who did their best to keep me out of trouble: James Oakes and Deborah Bohr, Richard Boyden, Maddy Powers, Bryan Lelong and Mary Hartfield, Joseph Franaszek, Christian G. Fritz, Marlene Keller, Gloria Fitzgibbon, James Kettner, E. Wayne Carp, Paula Shields, Lacy Ford, and Juke Joint Johnny.

I also thank the University of California for funding part of the research for this book. The U.S. Army gave me a grant for research at the U.S. Army Military History Research Institute. E. T. Mitchell and Martha Reiner provided most of the financial support for this book. Friends and family who invited me into their homes helped my research while making the process so enjoyable I almost wished I could slow it down—thanks to Tom and Clarice Mitchell, Joe

Auciello, Drew McCoy and Betsy Gittel Kleinbaum, Dave Navarre, Liza Buurma, Cam Walker, Charles Royster, E. Wayne Carp, Bryan and Patty Mitchell, and Bob Korstad.

This book was originally a dissertation done under the supervision of Kenneth M. Stampp; these thanks are hardly adequate. An independent scholar himself, he promotes independence in his students. Robert Middlekauff, James Oakes, James McPherson, Earl Hess, and Frank Smith all read the dissertation and offered suggestions for turning it into a book. I am indebted to Charles Royster not only for his comments on the manuscript but for cigars, conversation, and the example of his scholarship. Jan Lewis provided me with the closest reading of my manuscript, from which I benefited greatly. During the final revision, Peter Hegeman and Liza Buurma each took time, the one from his fine novel, the other from her excellent playwrighting, to try to make sure I wrote not academic jargon but readable prose.

I dedicate this book to the two men most responsible for my decision to study history: my father, E. T. Mitchell, and my professor and dear friend, Joe Tregle.

My greatest debt is to Martha Reiner.

Contents

CIVIL WAR
SOLDIERS

ONE

Wars for Freedom

During a scout near Cheat Mountain, Virginia, in the fall of 1861, a squad of federal cavalry approached a group of mounted men. The men turned and fled. The Union soldiers fired and one man fell off his horse, struck by four balls. The Union soldiers rushed toward him and he—in accordance with his rebel "brutish instincts"—pulled his revolver but was too weak to fire. With his last words, he begged for water. The Union soldiers tended him but he soon died. Examining his corpse, the soldiers learned he was Lt. Col. John A. Washington, "the great-nephew of George Washington *Shot in the back* in the very act of treason against the government his great ancestor constructed."[1]

That same autumn Maj. Paul Joseph Revere was taken prisoner by Confederate soldiers and confined in Richmond. He and his brother were among the officers held hostage for the crew of the ship *Savannah,* who were being threatened with execution as pirates by the U.S. government. Revere wrote home that should they be executed, they would die "as becomes *Christians and gentlemen.*" Major Revere was not executed, but exchanged. Upon his death in 1863, his regiment delivered him a tribute; they proclaimed him a "cheerful and dauntless christian soldier," one worthy of the name of his grandfather, the Revolutionary hero Paul Revere.[2]

The Civil War proved curiously filled with echoes of the American Revolution. The patriotic past and the Biblical past were the two great historic memories by which Americans measured their present. The events and the very places of the Revolution reappeared in men's memories throughout the war years. The Revolutionary War had created the American nation. It also created American

1

nationalism, for a sense of national identity is dependent on history and myths. A people require symbols to bind themselves into a nation; the Revolution provided them. Thus the men who fought the war for the Union—the nation that the Revolutionary generation had founded—believed that they embodied the principles of 1776.

But the Revolution did not simply create a new nation; it sundered an existing empire. Southerners did not repudiate the Revolution in 1861; they did not renounce the legacy of 1776. Confederates saw themselves as the true Americans. The sectional conflict and the Civil War were in some ways a conflict over the meaning of shared past.

Whatever caused the Civil War, it was fought in the name of freedom. The generation of 1861 regarded liberty as their heritage. This liberty, bequeathed to Americans by the fathers of 1776, was a fragile thing, always embattled, always threatened by a hostile world. By the time rebels fired on Fort Sumter, Americans North and South believed their liberties were most threatened not by the despots of Europe or the Indians on the frontier but by one another. The men who marched away to war in 1861 did so in the name of freedom.

In 1861 the differences between North and South were many and profound. An economy largely dependent on slavery was radically different from one that relied on free labor. The defense of slavery had led to an ideology in the South that attempted to reconcile democratic and liberal values with racial hierarchy. But whatever the differences between Northern and Southern economy, ideology, and culture, they had a common history that united them, a history that influenced them even as they made war on one another.

This history was a potent force. It was not, however, the only thing North and South shared. Both sections had the same political institutions—whatever their ideological differences they both participated in a common political culture. And it is easy to exaggerate their ideological differences. Furthermore, Northerners and Southerners often shared the same evangelical Christianity. Providence was seen in human events. A great revelation of their common history and culture was the willingness to use war as an instrument of policy—and to see the Hand of God in war itself.

In short, the men of 1861 went to war as Americans. Literal cases of "brother fighting brother" were rare, but the war revealed that shared national identity does not always prevent conflict—and conflict of the deadliest sort. Loyal to their political institutions and beliefs, thousands of men volunteered to defend Southern rights while thousands of others volunteered to preserve the Union. The decision to become a soldier could represent long thought and the most deep-rooted convictions. On the other hand, it could be the result of popular pressure or even a mere moment's indiscretion. But whatever a so-called blundering generation of politicians may have done, no matter what Southern conventions decided or Northern governors proclaimed, the Civil War could not have taken place without widespread popular commitment. Neither the United States nor the newborn Confederacy possessed the power to force the American people into large armies or to gather the taxes necessary to support them without mass support. Nor were politicians in the two democratic societies, North and South, able to create war simply from their own ambitions and prejudices.

In one sense the story of American men at war in the 1860s is an old story told once more; some aspects of war are near-universal. And the Civil War experience encompassed far more people than those men who made up the armies. What that conflict has meant to the United States may never be fathomed to its depths. Nonetheless, an understanding of why men, North and South, went to war, how they fought and killed and died, and what happened to them is crucial to understanding the war's meaning for America.

Confederate volunteering went hand in hand with Southern secession. Even as politicians predicted a short war or no war at all, Southerners joined local military companies and prepared to be heroes. There was a heady quality to the days between Lincoln's election and Fort Sumter. Secession probably generated far less enthusiasm among the mass of Southern whites than the war itself did. The prospect of Yankee invasion united the white South. The Northern army was real and concrete, compared to the phantoms that the fire-eaters had raised. Furthermore, while a Southern white man might deplore secession as a policy, he resented any attempt on the part of the North to tell the South—tell him—what to do. The invasion was a threat to his community, and he quickly rose to meet it. Even though Southerners tried to dissolve the nation their forefathers had helped to create, they still insisted they were loyal to the founders' vision. Confederates cast themselves as the true heirs of the generation of 1776. In particular, they saw themselves as defenders of the Constitution, a document that protected Southern rights. One soldier expressed the sentiment that motivated the majority of Confederate volunteers when he wrote, "I reather die then be com a Slave to the North."[3]

The reasons that men gave for enlisting in the Confederate army reveal some crucial aspects of the Southern mind during the crisis of the Union. Racism and the fear of slave insurrection motivated some volunteers. Others fought to defend a South they saw as a land of opportunity; their motivation was in part, and perhaps indirectly, economic. Still others thought the South possessed a culture so distinct from the North's that it required a separate nation. And a great many went to war because they hated Yankees.

Such seemingly disparate individual reasons, however, formed a reasonably coherent ideology; no one factor could realistically be divorced from the others. Economic opportunity and the South's distinctive culture both rested on the fact of slavery. The Yankee was feared because he threatened to destroy the South's prosperity by restricting slavery. But Southern whites hated the Yankee primarily for racial reasons—first, because they believed he might encourage the slaves to rebel, and, second, because he might try to impose equality of the races on the South.

North Carolinians, for example, grew excited as their state neared secession. Men flocked to join the volunteer companies being raised. Some companies apparently functioned as vigilantes as well. In Shelby the vigilance committee hung a man "for giving a runaway negro a free pas, and playing the Devil generally." The slave himself was not hung. The company was after abolitionists. One Georgian decided to enlist after hearing of a slave insurrection scheme, said to be led by white men in the area of Kingston. A slave, who was later hanged, revealed the details of the plan, which, as was always the case when whites recounted black plots, included the selection of wives for the slaves among the white ladies of the community. Another Georgian, who had supported the Union until his state's secession, proclaimed himself "ready to Start any time to fight Abolitionists." He would not see the South "governed by a negro." Mansfield Lovell, a Democrat and a Southerner who lived in New York City at the outbreak of the war, thought that Unionism was simply a cover-up for Black Republican goals. In April 1861, as troops left New York for Washington, he commented, "The 'nigger' has been rolled up in the Stars and Stripes until he is completely hidden."[4]

Southerners exaggerated the immediacy of the threat to slavery—the Republicans had promised only to put slavery on "the road to ultimate extinction," not to abolish it the day after Lincoln's inauguration. One cannot accuse an entire society of paranoia, but it is hard to avoid concluding that the events of the 1850s, particularly the unsuccessful slave revolt led by John Brown, had created a great fear in Southern whites. They were ready to believe the worst. It is not clear how secession would eliminate all Northern threats—antislavery propaganda and even the next John Brown could be smuggled into the South; runaway slaves would now find haven in a North no longer bound by the Fugitive Slave law; the Western territories would be forever denied to the South—but secession at least defied the Northern enemy. It was a panacea that would not bear much scrutiny.

Examples of racism and Confederate loyalty are straightforward and easy to understand. Men who desired the perpetuation of slavery and who wished to keep blacks under white control withdrew from the Union when the North became increasingly hostile to slavery. But racism can operate in more complicated ways. In some men it twisted and deformed even their greatest virtues. For men like William Johnson Pegram, Confederate loyalty was compounded of admirable qualities and the worst brutishness.

After the war Pegram would become one of the boy heroes of the Lost Cause. The bespectacled, shy student was one of Lee's finest artillerists; his death in the arms of his adjutant satisfied all the demands of Victorian notions of friendship. "I bent over and kissed him and said, calling him by his name for the first time in my life, 'Willie, I never knew how much I loved you until now.' He pressed my hand and answered, 'But I did.'" Those who watched Pegram in battle agreed that the reserved and pious young man came to life in those moments.[5]

During the months after Lincoln's election, Pegram reluctantly supported secession, even though he found the prospect of disunion terrible and feared civil war. The Constitution had proved worthless to protect the South; Lincoln was the South's enemy; and the vice-president, Pegram thought, was half-black. The peculiar degradation of a black vice-president was symbolic—it mattered little what Hamlin *did* as compared to what he *was,* a black man who would preside over the Senate. And, of course, Hamlin was not black except in Southern imagination.[6]

Pegram's ferocity in battle was matched by the ferocity of his racism. He approved, unreservedly, the wholesale slaughter of black prisoners at the battle of the Crater as a matter of policy, and he welcomed the Northern use of black troops precisely because it refired the combativeness of the weary Confederate soldiers in the trenches around Petersburg. Even after witnessing the murder of one prisoner, Pegram, whose piety was quite real, described the battle of the Crater as "a very brilliant day," given to the South by the "merciful kindness of an all & ever merciful God."[7]

Racism and fear of abolition were in some ways negative expressions of the Confederate vision. The slave system demanded a South free from Yankee interference. Secession had a positive content as well. The progress Confederates preached was not always easy to distinguish from the dominant American dream of economic prosperity. But as the future Confederate economy would be based on black slavery, the man who dreamed of prosperity inevitably was threatened by the nightmare of emancipation or insurrection. Some Confederate volunteers were fearful visionaries.

Rufus W. Cater of Louisiana, a Breckinridge Democrat, believed the widespread rumors of abolitionists incendiarism in Texas, thought the South had done everything possible to prevent war, and welcomed secession, as he loved liberty more than the Union. Its Northern enemies, he wrote in June 1861, were motivated by no virtuous desires, but by "sensualism and rapine." Abolitionists were godless fanatics who wished not simply to end slavery but to exterminate the Southern people. Against his visions of the ruin that would overrun the South if it did not resist Northern encroachment, Cater erected a vision of the great nation that the Confederacy would become if it successfully prosecuted its war for independence. His letter to his doubting cousin Fanny grew as rhetorical as a Fourth of July oration as he celebrated the nation to be:

> Have we not all the elements that go to constitute a great nation. A soil that yields a hundred-fold to the hand of industry a climate which none can surpass in salubrity resources that might well be compared to the wealth of a Croesus, all this is ours. What an extensive Sea and gulf coast indented with safe and capacious harbors! What great facilities for transportation in the deep and broad rivers that irrigate our beautiful country. And what is better than all this a brave and enlightened people. A people who with amazing rapidity change a wilderness to a smiling garden, who maintain themselves with one hand and with the other clothe the world. A people who build fair temples to science and decorate them with a Knowledge which is the experience and the results of the labors of age.

Clearly this son of the planter class entertained no purely agrarian visions. He looked forward to Progress as blissfully and as confidently as any Yankee millowner. Nor were the virtues of the Southern people that he chose to celebrate aristocratic. Cater prided himself on his people's industry, commercial enterprise, and science—stereotypical Yankee virtues. His dream of the future left out the slaves whose toil clothed the world. The Confederacy he predicted was as much an enterprising region as the New South for which Henry Grady would later call.[8]

Some men's loyalties to the South were based on appreciation of its economy; some men's loyalties to the newfound Confederacy were based on hopes of an even wealthier future. The South had provided white men sufficient opportunities for social mobility that even nonslaveholders might fight for slavery. No other agricultural region of the United States had matched the prosperity of the antebellum South. If a man wished to farm and to earn wealth and had no objections to slavery, the South offered the best return on his investment of labor and capital. And this was accomplished without undue concentration of wealth in the short-staple cotton regions. To some, this alone made the South and its political embodiment, the Confederacy, worth defending. Robert Patrick, a Confederate soldier, expressed his feelings for the South by quoting a song: "To the South, to the South, to the home of the free. . . . Where a man is a man if he is willing to toil/ And the humblest may reap the fruits of the soil."⁹

Nonetheless, during the decade immediately preceding secession, the South began to show signs of an economic and political crisis. Its social structure was growing increasingly rigid. In parts of the South good land was getting difficult for poor men to acquire, and farms were becoming fewer and larger. Slaves were relatively more expensive, and the proportion of the white population that held slaves was decreasing. Indeed, some historians have explained secession as an attempt by slaveholders to protect slavery before nonslaveholding whites became an overwhelming majority in the South. In any case, it was getting more difficult for "the humblest" to work their way to wealth.¹⁰

Southern men turned to expansion to solve the economic predicament of their region. Cheap lands lay to the west. If Southerners could spread their institutions westward, the chances for prosperity and upward mobility would not be lost. But there, at the borders of the land desired by Southern society for its very existence, stood the Yankee. The Yankee would prevent the expansion of the slave society and doom the South to stagnation and worse. Secession seemed to be the answer. As one Confederate volunteer explained it, the South could not be part of a government "where cotton was not king."¹¹

The Yankee was the symbol of all that the South hated. He was, of course, the abolitionist. Even the nonslaveholder, who may have resented the planter, very rarely had love for the slave. He too could be stirred by tales of abolitionist incendiarism. For those Southerners who saw the future of the South in terms of prosperity and economic development, the Yankee was a villain who resisted Southern progress. At the same time, ironically, the Yankee also embodied the capitalistic values that those troubled by economic transformation had come to fear. Finally, after the war began, the Yankee became the invader. The usefulness of the Yankee as an ideological symbol lay precisely in the fact that he could represent all that threatened white Southerners, no matter what their politics.[12]

Hatred of the Yankee led some Southerners to believe in the existence of two cultures in America. They volunteered to defend what they saw as the superior civilization of the South. H. C. Kendrick did not fear that "a degraded set of Northern people" could triumph over "a noble and respectable squad of Southerners." Confederates were "men that are fighting through a pure motive." New Orleanian Francis Ruggles, who was born in Massachusetts, believed the North and the South to be two different peoples. "Their institutions, feelings, sympathies, and actions are quite different." He wished to be forever free of "the avaricious, bigoted, unprincipled people of the North."[13]

A young Mississippi lawyer observing the parades of the soldiers marching off to war felt emotions that were "conflicting and nearly overwhelming." What made him want to volunteer was not love of his country or any other noble feeling, but "a kind of vindictive spirit" that shocked him. He envisioned a North justly laid waste by a war it had started; Washington itself would be leveled. Nothing less would do. "I feel that I would like to shoot a Yankee, and yet I know that this would not be in harmony with the Spirit of Christianity." He restrained himself from August 1861 to March 1862, and then joined the Confederate cavalry.[14]

Some men would volunteer only after they had become convinced the conflict was funadmentally sectional. A Virginian, an officer in the regular service, wrote a friend who chose to stay in the army that he felt compelled to follow his state into secession, although he believed it suicidal. Up until the time of Virginia's secession, he had thought the war was indeed a war for the Union, in which case he was willing to fight for the old flag. When his own state left the Union, he reinterpreted secession and decided that the war was simply a conflict between the two sections. He concluded, "I must go with my people."[15]

In some cases, men did not go with their people. For example, Henry E. Handerson, an Ohioan of New England descent, was employed as a private tutor on a Louisiana cotton plantation. Because of his Northern birth and education, he thought Southerners had nothing to fear from the election of Lincoln. Nonetheless, when Louisiana seceded, and a home guard formed "to maintain order among the Negroes and other suspicious characters," Handerson joined, and he later enlisted in a Confederate company raised from the Red River area. Secession may have been unnecessary, but once accomplished he threw his lot with the South, as his present and future interests lay with that section of the country. He explained to his father in 1865 that whether or not Louisiana had a right to secede, it certainly had a right to rebel. And, as he confessed when he wrote his memoirs in the 1890s, he was caught up in the popular enthusiasm for volunteering in his neighborhood. He was indifferent to the moral question of slavery; it was a "disadvantage to the South, but no *sin*."[16]

Thus, a man's birthplace did not always determine his allegiance. The Confederacy's ideology—white supremacy, economic opportunity, resistance to governmental interference—appealed to men who had been born and raised outside of the South and even outside of the United States. The fact that men from the North could comfortably live in the South before the war and willingly fight for the South during the war once again suggests the commonality of American culture North and South. The Mason–Dixon line was no Berlin Wall. Ambitious men who had gone South to seek their fortunes had a great deal to lose from the threatened destruction of slavery.

The Confederacy invoked the highest American ideals to summon the men of the South to war. On the day New Orleans's elite Washington Artillery was to leave for the seat of war in Virginia, the Reverend B. M. Palmer addressed them from the steps of City Hall. He told them that the war they left their homes to wage was perhaps the most holy in all of human history, "a war of civilization against a ruthless barbarism which would dishonor the dark ages, a war of religion against a blind and bloody fanaticism." They would fight "the despotism of the mob, unregulated by principle or precedent, drifting at the will of an unscrupulous and irresponsible majority." The Confederacy fought to vindicate the right of self-government. Palmer blessed the flag of the Washington Artillery—literally. The Washington Artillery left New Orleans with considerable enthusiasm. Then two men on board the train died of the heat; their bodies were shipped back to New Orleans, and depression settled on the new soldiers experiencing their first deaths of the war.[17]

Union soldiers at Gettysburg discussed the causes of the war with one of their Confederate captives. They justified their part in the war with several arguments, all of which the Southerner rejected as "puerile": the Confederates' firing the first shot at Sumter; the supremacy of the federal government over the states; the federal government's ownership of states formed after 1789. "But when all else failed," the Confederate wrote, "they relied defiantly upon that most miserable and destructive delusion, 'The Union must be preserved.'" Such, he concluded, was "the shibboleth of their faith."[18]

The Confederate was in a sense right when he implied that Northerners professed the value of the Union almost as an article of faith. The Union represented two interrelated things to them: the political and moral principles that set the United States apart from other nations, and the power necessary to defend those principles. One of the best expressions of Northern ideology came from an unusual source. A "Mr. Kellogg" of the 38th New York Volunteers was taken prisoner at Bull Run and confined in Libby Prison. There he wrote a play, *A Stirring Incident of the Federal War, 1861,* which he and his fellow prisoners performed. The production reminds one of mirrors reflected within mirrors. The play's heroes are Union soldiers, captured at Bull Run. George W. Ward, a stalwart young Northerner, lamenting the federal defeat, caused by overwhelming numerical superiority on the part of the Confederates and by their loathsome trickery in firing from behind trees "like so many Indians," persuades his fellow prisoner Phalen, a good-hearted, comic Irishman, to escape with him. After they manage to flee the prison, they are recaptured by a typical Virginia family: a farmer, his sixteen-year-old son Will, Will's sisters, one of whom is a loyal Unionist, and Cole, a humorous black slave who is terrified of Yankee "Bobilitionists." Fortunately, after the capture permits Ward to make various patriotic speeches to the Southerners, a patrol of Union scouts rescues him and Phalen. But the strongest lines are given to Mary, the sister who refuses to celebrate the Confederate victory at Bull Run. She will not support the Confederacy "against the Constitution our forefathers fought to raise," and the heritage of "Washington, Virginia's noble son." Instead, she predicts a Northern victory and a perpetual Union; echoing Lincoln in calling on the American Revolution, she insists, "You can't devide with equal right a heritage of graves."[19]

This heritage was the legacy of the Revolution. Union soldier Caleb Blanchard explained his enlistment by reference to the Revolutionary fathers. He wrote his wife, "Freedom is just as dear to us now as it was to our forefathers in revolutionary times." Freedom could be protected only by a strong Union. "You do not want to see this union and all our liberties taken from us and I stand by and not lift my hand to save it. . . ." Despite the fact it was "a sacred duty" for him to volunteer, he found it hard to do so, as he believed "no man loves his wife better than I."[20]

The issues of the war, soldiers insisted, went beyond the borders of the United States. Samuel Storrow enlisted after the failure of the Peninsula campaign and Lee's invasion of Maryland. He explained his decision in terms that anticipated Lincoln's Gettysburg Address. "If our country and our nationality is to perish, better that we should all perish and not survive to see it a laughing stock for all posterity, to be pointed at as the unsuccessful trial of republicanism." The cause of the Union was the cause of liberty throughout the world. Abolitionist and officer Henry H. Seys saw the American flag as a "beacon of hope to the nations of the world." One pious Yankee believed that high enlistments proved the justice of the Northern cause. He asked, "what would induce so many to leave their homes if Providence did not move upon their minds their must be an overruling hand in this thing." He did not, however, reflect on the reason for Confederate enlistments. Even those who may not have had strong feelings about the Union's significance for mankind's future were still appalled by the South's apparent repudiation of the American political system. How could the South rebel against what Northerners liked to call "the best government ever organized by man"?[21]

Some soldiers found additional confirmation for their decision to volunteer in the land itself, its physical beauty and fertility. An

Ohioan observed the countryside from Columbus to Cincinnati from the platform of the last car on his troop train; it called to mind the sacrifices his forefathers had made for this land and strengthened his resolve to defend his country and its institutions.[22]

The threat posed by the Southern slavocracy to Northern access to the land had been a major theme of the Republican Party. In much the same way that the Yankee became the symbol of all that the South hated and feared, the slaveholder came to represent the greatest enemy of personal liberty. The fear that the slavocracy of the South would undermine Republican institutions was strong in the North before the war. Secession appeared to confirm Northern fears about the extreme lengths to which the slave owners would go.

Like Southern apprehensions about the Republican Party, these Northern fears came in part from internal factors. The outbreak of emotion in the North following the South's secession cannot be judged solely by the threat the South—or the slavocracy—offered to the Northern people. The Confederacy, after all, did not plan to invade the North. Northern society at the eve of the Civil War felt tensions analogous to those that helped produce the secession crisis in the South. For example, the appeal of free soil may have been in part the result of a decline in personal independence for some Northern men. In the Midwest, to which men went seeking the small farms that had been the foundation of America's republican order, land became increasingly hard to obtain during the 1850s, and tenancy rose. Certainly, the rise of the factory system and the decline of the artisan made individual economic independence difficult to maintain. In the case of men like Blanchard, this lack of economic independence made them sensitive to threats to their political independence. In peacetime Blanchard had been a mill hand in Connecticut. He was uneasy about his place in society back home, but was determined not to let himself or his family feel inferior to anyone. He wanted his family to feel "as good as enybody and to be independant." His fight to protect republican freedom began not at the front but at home.[23]

A fear of declining personal independence helped fuel the emotion with which Northern men went to war against the rebellious slavocracy. Many viewed the conflict as a Southern attempt to subvert their liberties. A Pennsylvania soldier assured his wife that if the Confederates won, she and their children would become "perfeck slaves," and that all their property would be seized by the rebels to pay their Confederate debt. Just as Southerners who feared enslavement to the North enlisted in the Confederate army, some Northerners volunteered because they believed Southern tyranny threatened them. Both sides used the word "slave" to designate the condition they most abhorred.[24]

Hatred of slaveholders did not necessarily imply love for the slave. The Civil War was a war to protect freedom before it was a war to extend freedom. But there were some volunteers in 1861 who joined support for the Union with abolitionist sentiments. For these Union soldiers, freedom for white men was not enough. Only a small proportion of the Northern army in 1861, antislavery soldiers, wished to turn the war for the Union into a war for emancipation. They went to war believing that they had history on their side, that any war against slaveholders had to become a war on slavery itself. They were right.[25]

Most Union soldiers, however, did not support emancipation. Abolitionists were not always regarded with favor. A. C. Wilcox wrote his cousin that she had been misinformed when she said their mutual acquaintance Henry Wooten had been "accidentally wounded." The truth was that a man in his own regiment had shot him for advocating abolition. In repeating hearsay, Wilcox may very well have been wrong about the manner of Wooten's wounding, but it is significant that he accepted such an explanation as plausible.[26]

Rufus Mead, Jr., who took advantage of his regiment's presence in Maryland to discuss slavery with local blacks, hoped that the war would strike "such a blow" to slavery that it would "never rise again." Nonetheless, he did not think it was quite yet time for slavery's abolition, and his fellow soldiers of the Fifth Connecticut were "very touchy on the Slavery Question." The Reverend Mr. Bullard of Boston gave the Fifth Connecticut the watchword "The Sword of the Lord & of Washington." Neither, apparently, were emancipators.[27]

One veteran would later recall that in 1861, as his regiment passed Mount Vernon with uncovered heads and the ship's bells tolling, slaves came to the shores of the Potomac or threw open house doors to watch the Union troops go by. He said they regarded the passing soldiers with wonder, but in their "simplicity," few of them considered "what the conflict was likely to do for them."[28]

Whatever passed through the minds of those slaves along the Potomac River that day, it seems likely that most slaves had thought a great deal about what the war might mean to them. Even this same soldier said that when his regiment reached Virginia, in March 1862, the blacks welcomed Union soldiers and "the prospects of the new life which they hoped the war would give them." The Union soldier's assumption that blacks had not considered the war's significance to them would contribute to the belief that blacks were entitled to no political rights other than freedom, and that emancipation was a gift, presented to a possibly indifferent people by the virtuous volunteers of the North.[29]

The hostility of the average Union volunteer toward antislavery sentiment should not be exaggerated. If he had no love for trouble-making abolitionists and much antipathy toward blacks, he also had no fondness for slavery. Slaveholders had disrupted the Union; they were perceived as self-styled aristocrats marring a democratic society. To say that men would not go to war to end slavery is not the same as saying they desired its perpetuity.

In June 1862 Virginia Unionist Henry J. Johnson was disgusted to realize he and his friend had eaten dinner at a hotel table with "that infernal abolitionist from Illinois Owen Lovejoy." But by the time the Emancipation Proclamation went into effect, Johnson was for it "heart and soul," even though his family contemplated moving to California to get away from the freed people. Johnson pledged devotion to "the noblest inheritance ever given to mankind." He condemned those in his regiment and in his home county who opposed the creation of West Virginia from the loyal counties as "Butternuts."[30]

As was the case with the Confederate army, a Union soldier's allegiance was not always determined by his place of birth. South-erners who were devoted more to the Union than to the South would fight with the federal forces. And Unionism drew particularly on those alienated from Southern society: those who were geo-graphically isolated and remote from the market economy and those who were enslaved. Most Southern Unionists did not act as isolated individuals rebelling against the community from which they came. In general, like Northern Confederates who lived in the South, Southerners who fought for the Union received encouragement from the community they lived in. The majority of Southern white Unionists came from a specific geographic area: the Southern highlands. In one sense, they represented the nonslaveholding South.[31]

Southerners in the Union army could find themselves in uncomfortable positions, particularly when those around them equated Unionism with Northern culture. "A tall, raw-boned mountaineer in a first lieutenant's uniform" was ridiculed by Northern soldiers for his uncouth habits; he said, "I belong to the Sixth East Tennessee, and I'll fight Secests as long as I got a har on my head." This answer caused the soldiers to substitute cheers for their former insults. But the contempt initially displayed for the odd-looking, funny-talking man does indicate the general contempt many soldiers felt toward Southern culture. Northerners perceived loyalty to the Union not to be simply a matter of ideology, but a matter of regional identity. An Arkansas man who left his family to join an Illinois regiment was described by a fellow soldier as "formerly a southerner." The Northerner did admire the Southern-born soldier's "grit." A foraging expedition brought him back to his old home; "he saw his younger brother standing out by the fence and he cursed his Brother and called him a d--d purty sesesh." He refused to enter the house to see his mother and father and then he told his fellow soldiers "to go in and take what ever they wanted for he said that he knew they were rebs for they wer his parents."[32]

The Arkansas soldier was exceptional; most volunteers had the support of their families and friends. Local loyalties were a crucial part of Union and Confederate voluntarism. Northerners and Southerners alike saw themselves as belonging to some larger community, one that extended both in time and in space. But the smaller communities which men lived in also helped determine their response to the crisis of 1861. Loyalties to families, townships, and counties influenced men as much as their allegiance to states, sections, and abstract principles. In fact, one advantage the Union possessed was the fact that Northerners could simultaneously fight for the Union and their local communities, whereas Southerners generally had to choose one over the other. An Illinois soldier remembered how indignant the people of his neighborhood felt upon secession. Public meetings were held at churches and farmhouses to discuss the proper response to secession, where speakers "blew the fife & beat the drum & exhorted the men to rally 'round the flag." The men of his company "left home burning with desire to wipe treason from the earth."[33]

Recruitment in Theodore F. Upson's community had leaned on the patriotism of schoolchildren: in April 1861 the children had presented a tableau of the hanging of Jefferson Davis to encourage enlistment. But other community pressures inspired the sixteen-year-old Theodore to enlist in April 1862. People hinted that Upson's father, who helped lead the recruiting drive, "was a lot more patriotic about other men's sons than his own." Upson spared his father when he broke the news to him, telling him he was enlisting to save the Union "your ancestors and mine helped to make."[34]

Family honor was a powerful incentive for enlistment, North and South. Men frequently spoke in terms of going to war to protect their families. The generation of 1861 did not respond to the national crisis in atomistic terms. They volunteered not simply as individual Americans, but as representatives of their families. On one hand, soldiering was an extension of the masculine role from the very origins of the family; a man defended his home. On the other hand, Victorians, having divided the world into masculine and feminine spheres, recognized that both were essential to civilization. Only as a representative of the family—father and mother, brothers and sisters, sons and daughters—could a man fully embody those values for which he fought. As men served, their own companies and regiments became imbued with a sense of family. Officers thought they acted as fathers to their men. One's fellow soldiers became one's brothers. Generals Joseph Johnston and W. T. Sherman became known as Uncle Joe and Uncle Billy. Lincoln was nicknamed Father Abraham—father to an entire people. Robert E. Lee, ironically, was "Marse Robert"—patriarch of a plantation. The Union itself, a mystical body inherited from the founding fathers and cemented with the blood of patriots, was in a sense the family writ large.

Fighting was a man's responsibility—if one did not fight one was less than a man. Men may very well have fought during the Civil War for reasons having less to do with ideology than with masculine identity. One Illinois soldier bragged to his mother that his "coming into this war has made a man of your son." C. E. Taylor, who had been described as a "wild—reckless and disipated Son," joined a Mississippi regiment in order to reconcile himself to his father by bravery in battle. He hoped that by proving himself a hero he would earn a return to his family's affection.[35]

A Southern soldier tried to explain why the prospect of a fight cheered him. In battle one attempted to become a hero; the soldier felt "that he is a Man and that he is in a man's place." His explanation also reveals another motive for men's service in the army. Going into battle dissolved acrimony among the men and made them all part of "the one great Cause," each one dependent on the others and each with a duty toward the others.[36]

Perhaps the men of 1861 needed a "great Cause" in the face of the divisive forces of the modern world. Perhaps the sectional conflict had gone on so long that men could no longer stomach the never-ending process of compromise. Perhaps men preferred to emulate the generation of 1776 which fought so bloodily and so successfully for American independence. In any case, it was not difficult in 1861 to enlist Americans to kill other Americans in the cause of Southern independence or the Union.

The crisis produced by Fort Sumter offered an escape from the political process. No longer would men indulge in compromise, in wheeling and dealing. And no longer would the party dominate men's loyalties and demand all their affections. Now the nation— either the Union at the North or the newborn Confederacy—would be paramount. Men's old partisanship could be forgotten in the heat of new patriotism. The war would destroy the old, temporizing, divisive ways of the past forty years of politics, and return Americans to the emotions of 1776. Enthusiasm, not calculation, would rule.

When Americans North and South raised regiments for the army and sent them to war, they saw the soldiers off with almost identical ritual and celebration. The population at large wanted their soldiers to believe they represented all of them. The soldiers of 1861, after all, were volunteers—independent and rational citizens freely choosing to defend American ideals. In a sense, the soldiers' reputation would become the home folks' reputation as well. Nothing made this clearer than the ritual of flag presentation observed North and South. Customarily, particularly in the early stages of the war, the ladies of the community would get together to sew a flag for their boys, which would be presented to the hometown company in a public ceremony.

This ceremony became stereotyped early in the war—a speech given by a leading citizen, a reply by the company commander, and perhaps a picnic or banquet. Confederate Col. C. R. Hanleiter's acceptance address, while perhaps slightly more rhetorical than some, was typical of the genre. "Their defense of this Flag—the insignia of our Nationality, and the contribution of warm hearts devoted to the cause of our section," the colonel proclaimed, "shall attest how well the 'Jo Thompson Artillery' acquit themselves in the momentous struggle." He promised those who made the flag that it would "be cherished by us as one of the most sacred mementoes of *Home*; and when it waves over far distant fields, it will remind us of the loved ones left behind." The men of the regiment would "plant this Flag on the field of carnage" and maintain its honor always.[37]

Hanleiter's address reveals something of the significance of this often repeated ritual. The flag itself was the emblem of the community that sent companies and regiments into the field. These units were almost always composed of men from a single town or county; in a very real sense they represented their communities. Their flags linked them to their homes.

Furthermore, the flags tied the soldiers to an element of society they had left behind when they marched to war. The flag, made by the women of the community, was something to be protected much as they thought their wives and mothers should be protected. If the men left their communities to protect their homes, as many of them insisted they did, they brought something of their homes with them into battle. The flag was the physical tie between the homelife they had left and fought for and the war into which they were plunged. In Civil War battles the importance of advancing one's flag and defending it from capture—and, conversely, capturing enemy flags—indicates a devotion to flags far beyond what military rationality might seem to demand.

Finally, the importance of the individual flag, presented to men by their friends and families, takes on additional meaning when one considers how often men's patriotism was expressed not in terms of political discourse but simply in terms of the flag. Many a Northern soldier said he went to war to fight for the flag, the emblem of a nation. Philip A. Lantzy announced his enlistment to his parents by saying, "I am Gone to Fight for the Stars and Stripes of the Union. . . . I think it is gods will that the Rebels Should be made come under our Stars and stripes[.]" Whatever these men were fighting for seems to have been better expressed in material symbols than in reasoned discourse.[38]

When Fanny Pender offered to make a flag for a company from Salem, North Carolina, her husband's response was testy. He hoped that if she made a flag, it would be "a nice one," but she should do so only as "a work of love" and not of utility. Every company that arrived at the North Carolina camp came equipped with more flags than it needed. By April 28, 1861, Dorsey Pender was "sick of flags."[39]

Pender's comment is that of the soldier who is tired of the high-flown rhetoric and sentimental ignorance of the civilians who send men off to war. Pender was prematurely disillusioned. Most of the volunteers of 1861 saw war as a glorious prospect and victory as a certainty. The flag presentations, the patriotic speeches, the parades all celebrated the war, and they were all elements of a political culture common to the North and the South.

The most important reference point for this political culture was the American Revolution. Both the Union and Confederate armies kept the Revolution before their eyes in systematic fashion, by celebrating its past events at appropriate times. Soldiers were reminded of their Revolutionary heritage, the heroism and purity of their forefathers, and their own duty to emulate them. Both armies customarily observed Washington's Birthday, when the Farewell Address was sometimes read aloud to the assembled troops. But the most significant holiday on both sides seems to have been the Fourth of July.[40]

In 1861 the federal forces at Fortress Monroe and the Confederate forces facing them simultaneously celebrated the Fourth of July. In the latter camp three regiments—totaling three thousand men—held a general muster. One admiring soldier said after seeing this display, "It appeared to me we could whip the whole combined forces of the North." A year later the federal troops in New Berne were assembled to hear the Declaration of Independence read aloud. Later that afternoon the officers had a collation, and in the evening the entire camp enjoyed fireworks and band music.[41]

Men in the two opposing armies, on the very same day, less than a mile apart, could hear the same documents read aloud, documents held to be fundamental to American nationality. They could celebrate the same accomplishments, in much the same way—with feasting, drinking, military display, patriotic oratory. The two halves of a divided nation could simultaneously perform civic rituals originally designed to hold that nation together. The soldiers who participated in these rituals would soon be killing one another in the name of the heritage the rituals celebrated.

The reliance of the Confederacy on traditional American symbols was almost embarrassing. For example, Jo. Augustine Senaigo composed a patriotic air, "The Land of King Cotton," to the tune of "The Red, White, and Blue." He proclaimed Dixie, "the home of the brave and the free," "the terror of despots," and its states "champions of freedom." Taking his cue from the song whose tune he had appropriated, he apostrophized the new nation, saying, "Wherever thy banner is streaming/ Bare tyranny quails at thy feet." Confederates could not imagine patriotic self-congratulation in terms not already familiar—nor did they wish to.[42]

A Confederate soldier copied another patriotic song while in camp in 1864. This song not only used the tune of "The Red, White, and Blue"; it relied upon the fact that those were the colors of the Confederate flag as well. The dual nationality of these colors led to some confusion in the song: at Bethel, where the Confederates won, "victory perched on the red white and blue," and after the Seven Days, the Yankees retreated "with their degraded banner of red white and blue." The Confederate singer in the end promised to "stand by the colors of the red white and blue"—an ambiguous promise indeed.[43]

Indeed, Confederates created their most distinctive symbol—the battle flag—because of the confusion that their first official flag caused. The earliest Confederate flag, the "Stars and Bars," looked so much like the U.S. flag that in battle, troops carrying it were mistaken for Union soldiers. The army had to adopt the battle flag, then, to prevent possibly fatal misapprehension; their decision to do so presumably relieved Union commanders as well. But if the flag served as an emblem of that which men fought to preserve, the Confederate flag was an image of how much the Confederacy shared the common American culture.

It would be going too far to say that the South lost the Civil War because of its inability to create distinctively Confederate symbols. In general, however, Confederate symbols were pathetically reminiscent of the old American symbols, just as the Confederate constitution copied the United States constitution, and as Confederate ideology was a parody of American ideology. It is quite understandable that Confederates, with their common American heritage, should continue to use the old symbols, but the power of borrowed symbols to compel loyalty is severely limited. However, the Confederates had no choice: they had to use American symbols because they regarded themselves as the true Americans. And historically, their claim to American symbols was hard to dispute.[44]

By 1865, of course, there was a potent Confederate mythology, and its hold on the Southern mind increased as time went on. Just as the war hallowed the battle flag, it created heroes, both specific— Lee, Jackson, Stuart, the gallant Pelham—and stereotypical—the loyal slave, the superior Confederate soldier, the dashing cavalryman, the lady on whom was placed the whole burden of running a plantation, the high-spirited, Yankee-defying belle. All Southern families suffered during the war; few did not lose a father, son, or brother. By the end of the war, the South had a history powerful enough to tie its whites together, a history distinct enough from the North's—and so much in opposition to the North—to sustain a regional mythology of incredible strength and longevity. But this was not the case in 1861.

What there was in 1861 was a pervasive American identity, shared by soldiers North and South. Both sides viewed war as purposeful and controllable—a fit instrument of policy. Both held up fighting for the right as the highest expression of patriotism.

Both referred to the heritage of the American Revolution to sanctify the call to arms. And both sides fought in the name of freedom.

In the less than one hundred years since Washington's victory at Yorktown, Americans had reached the point where their common history not only did not prevent conflict, but actually encouraged it. The legacy of the Revolution was ambiguous, upholding both rebellion and union. One might paraphrase Bernard Shaw and say that the North and the South were two regions separated by a common culture.

Self-evidently, the North and the South did not share an identical ideology. The Civil War, as tragic as it was, was not simply some ghastly mistake. The issues of 1861 were very real: secession and Union, slavery and freedom. No set of issues more fundamental to the republic had been raised since the Revolution. But the very similarities in the way the two sections went to war, the way they fought the war, and the things their soldiers said they were fighting for suggest that the two sections agreed on far more things than they differed. A shared culture is no guarantee of peace and harmony. And American culture, which placed so high a value on freedom and which suspected that enemies to liberty were almost universal, was particularly likely to generate conflict.

Furthermore, embedded in the legacy of the Revolution was the notion that the preservation of liberty required the willingness to fight, kill, and die. If men's freedom was threatened—and men felt very threatened in 1861, although they could not always identify the forces that threatened them—their patriotic response must be to go to war to protect it.

If 1776 had demanded that Americans kill Britons to protect liberty, 1860 made a more onerous demand—Americans must kill Americans. This new burden was eased by the fact that Americans were accustomed to the notion of killing to protect their liberties and that Northerners and Southerners had already begun to see one another as strangers. The soldiers of 1861 went to battle convinced they fought an enemy that was un-American, somehow foreign—a savage enemy.

TWO

Enemies and Savages

Americans had learned the meaning of war in conflicts that occurred long before the Civil War. From the time of the initial settlements, white Americans had battled a people they regarded as savages—the Indians. Barbarism and civilization, they believed, had confronted one another in the wilderness of North America. Civilization inevitably won, but the savages had been awesome foes.[1]

The savage was only one of the images available for Americans to use in picturing their enemies. Another traditional foe of the republic had threatened American institutions. He was the regular soldier, the pliant tool of despotism. While the savage was wild and uncontrollable, the regular was obedient and disciplined.[2]

Just as the Revolutionary War provided the images that defined freedom, it also illustrated how tyrants could use savages and soldiers against freemen. The British army, in the American imagination, had been officered by aristocrats and filled with British regulars and German mercenaries. The British had fought alongside Indians. Indeed, the Declaration of Independence accused the British army of "cruelty and perfidy, scarcely paralleled in the most barbarous ages"; and Britain's Indian allies were described as "savages whose known rule of warfare is an undistinguished destruction of all ages, sexes, and conditions."

The haughty aristocrat, the subservient automaton, the lawless savage—Americans combined all three images when they contemplated their enemy in 1861. Despite the logical contradictions, Confederates proclaimed the Yankee mercenary and lawless fanatic, and Unionists called the rebel both savage and regular soldier.

The savage, the aristocrat, and the regular soldier were perhaps the three psychological types most inimical to republican institutions.

Each side identified the other as savage from the very earliest days of the war. In June 1861 the story spread through the Northern army that the women of Richmond wore ornaments made of the bones of Union soldiers. The First New York Mounted Rifles heard that when two of their men were wounded and taken prisoner, the rebels took their coats and jackets and then kicked them. Union soldiers burying the dead at the Williamsburg battlefield concluded that many "had evidently been bayonetted by the rebels, after they were shot down."[3]

Early in the war many assumed that to be captured by the enemy meant certain death. The surgeon of a New Jersey regiment insisted on staying behind to tend the wounded at First Bull Run; his colonel soon thought he was dead. The rebels were reported to have shelled the hospital after the Union retreat: "The cruelty of the Rebels to our wounded has no parallel in history." Even if the surgeon had escaped death in the burning hospital, the regiment believed that the Confederates had murdered him after his capture. In fact, the surgeon was paroled and returned to his regiment in three weeks.[4]

The same colonel also believed, as "a fact beyond dispute," that the Confederates refused to bury the Union dead at Bull Run and delighted in boiling the meat from corpses and making utensils out of the skulls and bones. "One of these vessels was found with the inscription on it: 'This is the skull of a fine Yankee.' Then followed the motto of Virginia: 'Sic Semper Tyrannis.' " Such atrocities infuriated the Union army; the colonel went so far as to say they "abolitionized" the Army of the Potomac, turning the men against slavery.[5]

A more puzzling Northern belief was that the Confederacy violated the rules of civilized warfare by using black troops against them. Francis Boland wrote that there had been two black regiments involved in the battle of Seven Pines. "They advanced against us. They mutilated our dead and stripped them naked. They bayonetted our wounded and cut their throats in cold blood." He concluded: "It is wrong to bring negroes into battlefields."[6]

It was not just Northerners who detected the lineaments of savages in the faces of their enemy. The Confederates too believed that they fought an uncivilized enemy. Reports reached the South in the spring of 1861 that the Northern army had "soldiers quartered in the Capitol, cooking and eating in these fine halls, hanging their muskets on chandeliars, etc." This "scum" desecrated the capitol, acting the part of barbarians. North Carolinian Dorsey Pender concluded that the North expected to lose possession of Washington to the Confederacy, and therefore did not mind the damage its army did to the public buildings.[7]

Another Confederate dismissed the Northern troops as "a ruthless horde of marauders professing to be Christian." Albert Moses Luria believed that the Union forces had outnumbered the Confederates almost three to one at Bull Run, and that their casualties amounted to ten thousand as compared to a mere one thousand five hundred for the South. The most fantastic rumor Luria accepted was that the Confederates captured thirty thousand sets of Yankee handcuffs, "which they intended to use for their hellish purposes." For Luria, Yankees were not only thieves and savages, but cowards.[8]

A Confederate with Pegram's battalion reported an "outrage" during the Second Bull Run campaign. Northern cavalry had taken potshots at "two estimable ladies" living at Burnet's Ford, hitting one just above the knee and the other in the foot. He thought "Hanging is to good for such miscreants. They ought to be covered with tar and set on fire."[9]

Confederates circulated stories of Yankee outrages when Grant's army destroyed the Richmond and Danville Railroad in the summer of 1864. Besides plundering houses and taking "young ladies Breastpins & finger rings," the Yankees "stole all the negroes they could." Such deeds, Samuel Lockhart argued, placed the Yankees beyond the rules of civilized war; the men who committed them "ought to be hung as soon as caught."[10]

The fact that Confederates called all Northerners Yankees reveals the South's anti–New England feelings. Andrew Devilbliss came with the Eleventh Louisiana to Columbus, Kentucky, in October 1861. There he saw wagon trains of women and children leaving the town in anticipation of the arrival of Union forces. Devilbliss cursed "the cold-hearted Yankees, fit descendants of the

intolerant and murderous race who first landed at Plymouth rock."
New Englanders might have been surprised to hear Devilbliss characterize them as religious bigots, followers of the "heartless and
wicked doctrine of the God forsaken Calvin" and murderers of the
Indians "who fed them, when they would have starved." They no
doubt would have thought Devilbliss well named.[11]

The Yankee was too cold-blooded a figure to be described as a
simple savage. The South added an additional figure to the traditional American repertoire of villains: the fanatic. The fanatic challenged the customary rules of society; he was essentially lawless.
The best example to the Southern soldier was the abolitionist, a
curious kind of savage.

Indeed, the strongest evidence of the sheer savagery of the Yankees was abolitionism—"their Hellish plot of arousing the slaves."
Since the South had gone to war to oppose the abolitionists they
believed to have gained power with Lincoln's election, their accusations of antislavery among the Union forces, while generally
erroneous at the war's start, were predictable. In the white Southern
mind, abolition identified Northerners with the most savage race
of all, the enslaved blacks. And Southerners could not imagine
abolition unaccompanied by slave insurrection—a holocaust that
would murder thousands of whites and destroy the Southern social
order. Nothing could be more savage than that.[12]

Capt. Thomas J. Key, a veteran of the Lecompton Convention,
habitually referred to Union soldiers as "Abolitionists." He hated
"the base and amorous race of Puritans" because of their advocacy
of miscegenation. The Yankees, he believed, wished to amalgamate
the white and black peoples of the South, to encourage the rape
of Southern ladies by the slaves. He was outraged by a story that
during Sherman's occupation of Atlanta, "a big black negro man
went to one of the most respected young ladies in the city and
offered her $10 if she would come to his tent and spend the night
with him." "The disgusting equalization of whites and blacks under
Sherman" led Key to call for raising the black flag. After this Key
referred to the Yankee forces not only as abolitionists, but as "the
misceginators."[13]

Of course, in making war against Northern abolitionists, Southerners sometimes displayed a disturbing savagery of their own.

Osmun Latrobe, a Confederate officer later on Longstreet's staff, delighted in the death of barbarous "abolitionists." After the battle of Fredericksburg, he "rode over the battlefield and enjoyed the sight of hundreds of dead Yankees." The "[severed] limbs, decapitated bodies, and mutilated remains of all kinds" scattered by the fire of a battery he had directed particularly pleased him. "Would that the whole Northern army were as such, and I had had my hand in it." He later greeted the Union corpses at Chancellorsville as "glorious heaps of Yankee dead."[14]

These tales of enemy atrocities did not belong to soldiers alone. They could be found in the newspapers and magazines both North and South. Neither the Union nor the Confederacy lacked the instruments for propaganda that mark most wars. But when soldiers wrote of enemy brutalities, they rarely mentioned any literary sources; they wrote as though such stories were part of the folklore of the army.

Men saw isolated incidents of brutality as symptomatic—the enemy had let his civilized mask slip, revealing his true savage nature. Furthermore, believing that the savagery of their enemies surpassed the brutalities of previous wars, men suspected the worst of their opponents in commonplace situations. Confederate pickets near Seabrook Island, South Carolina, took a wounded man prisoner; later they sent word by a flag of truce that the man had died from his wounds. This explanation did not satisfy the men of his company, who concluded that his captors had murdered him because he would not reveal military information to them.[15]

A Michigan soldier reported that as the Army of the Potomac followed Lee's retreating army after Gettysburg, one morning the Sixth and Seventh Michigan Cavalry surprised a rebel camp and forced them to surrender. Some Confederates grabbed their guns from where they had dropped them after surrendering and killed fifteen or more of their captors. A Confederate retailed an almost identical story about Union prisoners at Chancellorsville.[16]

Other Union soldiers told of how rebel generals used flags of truce to deceive the enemy. A Massachusetts soldier claimed that after Antietam, Lee sent a flag of truce asking to bury his army's dead as a ruse to retreat across the Potomac before the Federals could attack—that was why there was no second day to the battle. Some Confederates, on the other hand, complained of Northern trickery. During the Atlanta campaign, one rebel observed that the Yankees would not "come up like white men to fight." Instead, Sherman persisted in flanking Johnston's army.[17]

John Fleming, a teen-aged Union soldier in Virginia early in the war, reported that the Confederates had snuck up on federal pickets not in silence but wearing cowbells around their necks. The pickets believed that the dark forms approaching them were cows roaming the wood and were not disabused until they were murdered at their posts. Fleming called this "fiendish cruelty," because "the killing of one man in that Sneaking way, was no advantage to the Rebels. . . ." Its sole result was to make the soldiers hate their enemies more. When the men of Fleming's regiment heard of these murders, they "determined that no living thing of human size should come near our posts," and readied themselves to shoot the guileful rebels. Strangely enough, no disguised rebels ever appeared to Fleming's regiment, nor did Fleming ever hear of such an incident during the rest of the war.[18]

Both secessionists and Unionists believed political treachery had brought on the war; both thought treachery governed the military actions of the other side. Treachery was a form of cowardice—it was a refusal to fight openly and fairly. Men felt that their own virtuous courage was in sharp contrast with their enemy's sneaking cowardice. Such beliefs also reinforced men's confidence in the justice of their cause. A just cause was defended by just soldiers. As one Confederate expressed it, "moral force and courage" had to be victorious over "brute force and superior numbers."[19]

The war shattered no preconception of either side more quickly than it did the idea that the enemy was fundamentally cowardly. If the volunteers of 1861 believed that courage was a monopoly of the virtuous, the veterans of 1865 knew that courage was a virtue possessed by even defenders of the wrong.

Men came to such conclusions with reluctance. For Northerners in places where the Union army met little opposition, it was easy to believe that the rebels were cowards. A Connecticut soldier wrote from New Berne, North Carolina, that the enemy always ran. "The Rebels youst to say that it took 5 yankees to whip one of them, but it is the other way," he boasted, "it takes 5 yankees to catch one of them." Even after the battle of Shiloh—which he apparently missed—William N. Barnard of the 13th Michigan Infantry expected the Northern army would soon drive Beauregard and his army into the Gulf. He complained of the Confederates that, "We have to Corner them before they will fight and then they wont fight if they can find any possible Chance to escape."[20]

Union soldiers might repeat hoary old tales to account for the anomaly of rebel bravery. John St. John explained that the Confederates fought so desperately at Shiloh because Beauregard had primed them with drafts of whiskey and gunpowder. An officer at Malvern Hill explained the headlong assault and resulting carnage among the rebels by the fact that prisoners had canteens of whiskey and gunpowder. He thought no cause could succeed whose advocates required artificial stimulants above the consciousness of their rights.[21]

Southerners also consoled themselves with myths of Yankee timidity. One soldier repeated the rumor that in an engagement in northwestern Virginia, two thousand Confederates handily defeated five thousand Yankees without firing a shot: those federals who did not surrender immediately upon their approach "threw down their arms and ran like yankees." No wonder this soldier predicted Southern victory by August 1, 1862. Another soldier, at the time safely guarding prisoners in Macon, Georgia, reported even greater Confederate feats of arms—in one case, one Confederate regiment "killed and took ten thousand Yankeys an killed the General."[22]

Confederates liked to believe that hirelings composed the Union forces. The true Yankee was a coward, who relied upon the Irish and the Germans—and later the blacks—to do his fighting. These hirelings, of course, had not an ounce of patriotic motivation. The Union soldier fought for "good rations and pay," as one Southerner expressed it. This same Southerner advocated bloodbaths as the way to Confederate victory; "the way to sicken them of war is to crowd the dangers." The mercenary Yankee was a theme that Southerners extended beyond the enlisted men of the federal army to the entire North. General Magruder told his troops at Yorktown that the Yankees would not fight after the war had exhausted them financially. "Commerce is their King. Their God is gold." He promised his troops an invasion of the North, a chance to burn its cities and "dictate terms of peace on their own soil."[23]

Oddly enough, in moments of discouragement, some Union soldiers shared this Southern belief. Capt. Jacob W. Haas compared the Union and Confederate armies in December 1862. "Our men do not fight with the same vim and elan they do." He attributed this to the mercenary motives of half of the Union soldiers. The Confederates "fight for Nationality and for (as they term it) freedom." Northerners had underestimated Southern valor.[24]

But even while retaining belief in the Northern soldier's lack of pure motivation, the Confederates soon had to admit his fighting ability. After the battle of Antietam one Confederate said that "the Yankey army is now as good as ours[.]" The Union soldiers had fought as well as the Confederates, a fact he explained by saying, "They have been gradually trained to do it they dont have the same principals to fight for that we have[.]"[25]

In general, as the war progressed, more soldiers were forced to say of their enemies what a Wisconsin soldier said of Johnston's army during the Atlanta campaign: "Braver men never shouldered a musket. . . ." And after he had been in battle, a Texas soldier realized "we are not fighting children but men; & men worthy any foeman's steel."[26]

So men came to see that their enemies did not lack courage. Bravery, of course, was a virtue not denied even to savages.

Men's impression of the nature of the enemy soldier depended in large measure on their understanding of the society from which he came. True American society, it was hoped, had produced true Americans—virtuous, restrained, patriotic. A perverted society, on the other hand, produced those brutes that composed the enemy's army. The very fact that the other side made war against the side of liberty exposed the villainy that lay at the core of their society.[27]

A Michigan soldier in the Peninsula campaign believed that Magruder tortured and murdered Virginia Unionists and that rebel soldiers routinely cut the throats and lopped off the ears of Yankee wounded. Not surprisingly, he advocated death for the leaders of the rebellion. What was more surprising is that he also advocated clemency for the lower classes: they were the ignorant dupes of their rulers. Their leaders systematically lied to them, telling them that Vice-President Hamlin was a runaway slave and that the North would resettle the South with Union soldiers, driving the farmers from their land.[28]

Secession itself revealed the flaws in Southern society. Only a society corrupted by the institution of slavery, that encouraged the blind, selfish ambitions of aristocrats, could desire to leave the greatest and most just political organization in the history of the world. Unionists believed secession to be an act of despotism. The Southern politicians had lied to the plain people of the South, telling them that once in power the Republican Party would free the slaves.[29]

For many Northerners the cause of the Civil War was simple. Southern aristocrats had enslaved not only those blacks who labored in the field, but the white population of the South as well. These aristocrats, having destroyed democracy in their own section of the country, now sought to destroy democracy in the North, by denying an open election, breaking up a Union that guaranteed free institutions, and waging bloody and treacherous war. Union soldiers fought the Confederate army to defeat Southern schemes of tyrannizing over free and independent Northern farmers and mechanics, but willy-nilly this defense of Northern liberties was also a campaign to liberate the Southern victims of aristocratic domination. Bvt. Brig. Paul Oliver wrote from Alabama in 1863 that the poor whites had been deliberately kept ignorant by the rich, that they had been driven from all the best lands, that they had been told how to vote, and that they said they were treated "worse than niggers." He summed it all up by saying, "I feel well satisfied that in waging this war, we are not fighting for the negroes only—no indeed we are fighting for the rights of the poor white trash of the South, men who tho' good enough originally have been so kicked and abused that they themselves now believe themselves inferior beings—indeed they are."[30]

This belief was widespread throughout the Union army. Long before any invasion of the South, Northern soldiers were convinced that the Confederate armies were composed of degraded, intimidated men, who were, as Hinton Helper had suggested, the dupes of a self-styled aristocracy. Col. James Garfield, later a Gilded Age President, described those Confederates who deserted into his lines as "men of no brains who had been scared into the rebel army and whose lives were not worth to the country what the bullet would cost to kill them." One of the things most notable in the comments of Garfield and Oliver is the contempt they display for the planters' supposed victims, the nonslaveholders of the South. Northerners preferred to believe that secession was the result of intimidation and ignorance than to think that the democratic process itself might produce such a result. And the belief that the Southern aristocrats had trampled on the liberties of the nonslaveholders made it easier to justify Northern policies; Gen. W. T. Sherman suggested that after the war the government give the plain folk the mere trappings of democracy while ruling them, just as the planter class had done before the war.[31]

Union Capt. John Pierson described the war as a defense of free government against "an Aristocratic set of Slave Drivers and outlaws." The Southern aristocrats, he believed, had created a "Sham Government" and a large army from the enthusiasm of the mass of Southern whites. Now the government could "use that force to drive its own subjects into the Ranks and fight for a thing that Renders them infantly wors off even if they sucseed." He was sure the bulk of Southerners wanted peace.[32]

A New Jersey officer attributed secession simply to the ambition of the Southern leaders. He had found a letter in the abandoned house of a former Virginia congressman which he thought proved that the South had been preparing for war long before secession took place. He sent the letter to his wife, asking her to take care of it for its historical value; the letter has not been preserved.[33]

When William G. Dickson arrived in Savannah with the rest of Sherman's army, he commented on the acquiescence of the citizens to Union authority. He attributed this to the fact "They had been so well schooled in military despotism before we came in that they take very kindly to our moderate rule." Dickson, who was living in Savannah at the outbreak of the war, was particularly sensitive to Southern "despotism"; his brother had been jailed for his Union sympathies and later drafted into the Confederate army.[34]

Belief in the coercion or deception of the mass of Southern whites encouraged Union soldiers to predict that the Confederacy would be destroyed by a rebellion of its own people. One Northern soldier saw Jefferson Davis's formal inauguration as the Confederacy's President—he had served as provisional President for a year—as the signal for "the uprising of thousands who at heart have been union men, though quelled by force, but who have become emboldened by the success of Federal arms to throw off their forced [allegiance]."[35]

In 1863 Caleb Blanchard, the Connecticut mill hand, predicted the war would end when social crisis destroyed the Confederacy. The newspapers reported that Confederate conscription had failed and that the rebel soldiers were "shooting down their own officers." The Southern rulers, trying to enforce their will on the free states, now had to enslave their own white people in order to continue the war, drafting them "to fight against there country." Their efforts could not succeed, as their cause was too "wicked."[36]

Confederate impressions of the North were no more flattering. The North had declined mightily since 1776. It had become an odd combination of anarchy and despotism—a land of fanatical but subservient citizens, of weak-willed tyrants. Georgian R. M. Campbell worried frequently that his diary might fall into the hands of Northern soldiers. In case it did, he interspersed messages for his enemies among his other entries. Even though he knew that the loss of his diary would most likely be caused by the loss of his life in battle, he assured the individual Northern soldier he would desire no revenge for his death. "*I forgive you.* I know you are deluded." Campbell wrote the imaginary captor of his diary that the North was "a people who are fighting for revenge not for the restoration of 'our glorious Union' as they say." The Northern soldier was the dupe of an "infuriated populace."[37]

Southerners believed that one way that the Lincoln administration kept the Northern citizens deluded was through censorship of the press. In particular, Confederates thought that the Northern papers covered up Union defeats by printing false accounts of battles. One soldier predicted that when the truth about the military aspects of the war became known it would be greeted with "a dolorous howl in Yankeedom."[38]

Confederates, sharing in the traditional American fear of the military, identified the army as the destroyer of civil liberties in the North. Decimus Barziza, Confederate officer and author, proclaimed Northern popular elections in the latter part of the war to be "farces." "Each party strove to prove its candidate to be a better friend to the soldier than his opponent. They feared not only the votes, but the bayonets of their own hirelings." This rise of military power, in Barziza's account, swelled the authority of President Lincoln, who was the commander-in-chief. Lincoln, Barziza claimed, had "changed a free republic to an obsequious despotism." He had obtained "absolute power." Lt. Albert Moses Luria lamented that the United States, once "The land of the free and the home of the brave," had become, under "that drivelling, baubling fool, Abraham Lincoln," a military despotism. At the same time, however, that Luria thought the North under military control, he thought that the incompetent Lincoln "governed by the whims and frivolities of a dissatisfied constituency."[39]

Union soldiers, who felt unappreciated and looked down upon by Northern civilians, would have been surprised to learn just how powerful Barziza thought them. Lincoln, who dealt with quarrelsome generals and unruly politicians, would have regarded Barziza's description just as ridiculous as the soldiers would have, but probably would have been much less surprised by the charges made against him. After all, such charges were made against him in the North as well.

The similarities between the Confederate image of the North and the Northern image of the Confederacy are striking. But there are differences as well. Confederate soldiers rarely if ever spoke of the North as being controlled by aristocrats; they attributed the perceived loss of civil liberties in the North to politicians such as Lincoln and to the military. Since the United States had been a functioning representative democracy when Lincoln was elected, Southern portrayals of Lincoln despotism implicated the political process itself. Something had gone wrong with democracy, and that had allowed the administration to gain unwarranted and unconstitutional power.

Northern analysis of Southern society was based upon the idea that prewar society had been dominated by slavocrats. The Confederacy had been formed by a political process Northerners viewed as patently spurious; the Confederacy was the result of the ambitions of a clique of Southern politicians and the tyranny of the planter class as a whole. Whereas Abraham Lincoln represented the corruption of the American political system, Jefferson Davis was the political embodiment of an entrenched Southern aristocracy. Since Northerners believed that secession had not been supported by the majority of the Southern population, they did not see it as casting doubts on the democratic process.

But both the Confederate perception of the North and the Northern perception of the Confederacy had to account for the acquiescence of large numbers of people in despotic political arrangements. Both Confederates and Unionists spoke routinely of deluded people, dupes of the politicians, and ignorant masses. Both Northerners and Southerners feared that democratic institutions were not adequate to deal with the realities of nineteenth-century America—they relied too heavily on the existence of a virtuous and intelligent citizenry. The war itself, after all, had been produced by a crisis in the American political order.

In 1861 each side believed that the ignorant and vicious proportion of the citizenry was concentrated in a distinct geographical region, the North or the South. Perhaps, however, when the men of each side contemplated their enemy's society, they wondered if the citizens of their own society might begin to share the enemy's unfitness for democracy.

The Enemy Encountered:
Prisoners, Deserters, Fellow Soldiers

After the first battle of Bull Run, an officer of the Washington Artillery rode alone in the wake of the retreating Union forces. The reluctance of his horse to follow the road he picked convinced the officer that some enemy must be near. The Confederate spotted another solitary horseman riding toward him through an open field. The man—a Yankee—rode toward him, fumbling at something behind his back; the Confederate drew his revolver and took aim at the approaching rider. The Yankee halted and produced not a pistol but a white handkerchief. The Confederate demanded his surrender, but the horseman was afraid to come forward until his captor gave his word of honor not to harm him.

The Yankee proved to be a lieutenant of a New York regiment; the Confederate judged him to be twenty years old or younger. He begged the Confederate to free him, promising to resign his commission, return to his parents, and never fight again. After riding ten yards toward the Confederate lines, the officer had a change of heart, and "told him to go back to his friends, saying that one prisoner more or less did not make much difference." When the Confederate reached the scouts of his own army, they asked him what happened and requested his aid in recapturing the Union officer. The Confederate refused.[40]

The annals of the Civil War provide plenty of evidence for the concept of human depravity. The actual contact of men with their enemies during the war did not always dispel their previous beliefs as to their savagery. But there were also acts of kindness exchanged between the foes, and men were sometimes surprised to find that their preconceptions did not always match reality. After the vivid imaginings of the war's early days, contact with the enemy—whether as prisoners, deserters, or captors—had a gritty reality that reduced phantoms to flesh and blood. Encounters with the human enemy did not ensure a favorable evaluation on the part of the soldiers. In general, those soldiers who learned that their enemies were human too did not abandon their conviction that the war they were fighting was necessary to protect American liberties.

While fraternizing between the armies was not as prevalent as postwar myth would have it, it did go on. Truces might be called to allow burial parties to roam the battlefields; under the white flag soldiers would meet their enemies and discuss the war. On one such occasion outside of Vicksburg, soldiers from both armies agreed that "if the settlement of this war was left to the Enlisted men of both sides we would soon go home."[41]

Confederates waded across a creek to chat with Pennsylvania soldiers near Falmouth, Virginia, in December 1862. The soldiers of the opposing armies swapped "knives spoons pipes money and most everything." The officers of the Pennsylvania regiment disapproved of this communication and forbade the men to talk to the rebels. The Union soldiers disregarded their orders, even though about fifty men of the regiment were placed under arrest for the offense. One of the soldiers explained that the reason the communication worried the officers so much was that "they are afraid we will get to think and wont fight." The rebels told the Yankees "they are sick and tired and if we will stack arms and go home they will do the same and hang their Ringleaders." After the fiasco of the battle of Fredericksburg, such an agreement appealed greatly to the war-weary soldiers of the Army of the Potomac. The Pennsylvanian believed that the only thing that kept the war going was the greed of the officers who "wait till they make enough money and then Resign."[42]

The common humanity of the enemy was one reason for fraternization. Another was his common "Americanness." But perhaps most important was the fact that he too was a soldier—that is to say a patriot and a victim. The gulf between the stay-at-home and the soldier sometimes seemed greater than that which separated the Confederate and Union soldiers. As the war went on, a sense of kinship developed between some soldiers of the two armies. The men whom one faced suffered the same hardships as one's fellow soldiers; in a way, they were fellow soldiers. When Charles J. Mills reached the Army of the Potomac in September 1862, he was "very much struck with the deference [difference] of feeling about the rebels here and at home." The Union soldiers showed little bitterness; one officer told Mills: "We don't hate them at All. . . . we're both in the same boat." The Union soldiers wished "to thrash them in order to end the war and get home but they do not seem to hate them in the least."[43]

Soldiers also encountered their enemy face-to-face when they met prisoners and deserters. Most soldiers, of course, did not serve guard duty in the Civil War's military prisons. But prisoners and deserters passed through the front lines on their way to their final destinations. This passage also allowed for individual contact between the soldiers of the Confederacy and those of the Union.

Some soldiers held themselves aloof from captured enemies. Doug Cater of Louisiana wrote his cousins that he would not speak to the wounded Yankees who were treated at the same hospital where his brother died. "My contempt for them is too great." One night another brother, Rufus W. Cater, contemplated the sleeping prisoners in the Jackson, Mississippi, city guardhouse. He concluded they must be dreaming "of burning dwellings and devastated fields, of pillage and rapine." When awake, the Yankee appearance was not prepossessing; "there beams not one ray of generous feeling or virtuous emotion from their soulless eyes!"[44]

Most soldiers were not so haughty. The chance to actually speak to the enemy, those fabulous beasts, was not one that soldiers often passed up. Observation and conversation allowed them to analyze the enemy and his society.

Union soldiers commented most often on the appearance of the Confederate prisoners they met. Confederates were ill-clothed, poorly fed, and hard looking. If a Union soldier was disposed to judge a Confederate by his appearance, he generally judged him to be some kind of scoundrel. Others felt sympathy for fellowmen who so obviously had endured great hardship. Caleb Blanchard thought the Confederate prisoners brought to Fort McHenry after Antietam "the worst looking set I ever saw." "Some were shot throught the head some in the leg I saw one who had one side of his face shot off several with their arms off and a good many on cruches." Despite their misery, the prisoners still said "they are fighting for their rights."[45]

In September 1862, Allen Landis watched twelve or more Confederate prisoners pass through his camp in Fairfax, Virginia. He decided that they were happy to have been captured by the Federal pickets. "They looked tolerably well, though none of them were dressed in military clothing." Other Union soldiers commented as well on the "rag-tag" nature of Confederate clothing. One wrote, "I do think that the most forlorn picture of humanity is a Rebel Soldier taken prisoner on a very wet day."[46]

Even though the Union generally kept its soldiers better supplied than the Confederacy did, rebels also met bedraggled Yankee prisoners. The 23rd Louisiana Infantry encountered four Union prisoners while at Vicksburg in March 1863. One of the Louisianians reported that the Yankees were ragged, dirty, and tired of the war. In the group was a "small boy" he estimated to be about twelve years old. Even though the boy was barefoot, he was in higher spirits than his fellows; "Among a great many other things he expressed his delight at reaching Vicksburg before the fleet." One sympathetic Louisiana soldier removed his own shoes and gave them to the boy to wear. Whatever this regiment's concern for youthful prisoners was in March, they were less taken with the next batch they encountered. One of them recorded that the Yankees had the looks of "professional thieves."[47]

It was not just the unsavory appearance of prisoners that offended the Civil War soldiers. They also complained of their prisoners' demeanor. The soldiers, who believed their enemies fought in a transparently unjust cause, sometimes spoke as if they expected immediate repentance upon capture. In any case, prisoners frequently continued to maintain their side of the sectional conflict to the disgust of their captors.[48]

Pvt. William C. McKinley moved freely among the rebel prisoners taken at Roanoke Island in February 1862. He found them surprisingly illiterate; few of them could even write their names on the list of prisoners being drawn up. "it looks strange to us," the Massachusetts soldier wrote, "as we have not a child at home 12 years of age that cannot write their name." The Southerners were equally surprised to learn that all the Northern men could read and write. McKinley also found an old acquaintance among the prisoners, Dr. Shepardson of Attleboro. When McKinley and his friends discussed the war with the doctor, the latter claimed that the Confederate forces lost only five men in the recent battle, something McKinley knew to be false. "you see he is A good southern man," he wrote his wife, because Shepardson would "not scruple to lie to any extent to favor his side."[49]

A Confederate sergeant who talked with three Union prisoners in 1862 dismissed two of them as liars: "They would lie as fast as a horse could run." The third he thought honest, because he admitted that he had volunteered to fight in an unjust war "to keep his family from starvation." The other two were "strong for the Union." This sergeant believed that most Union soldiers "live better in the army than they do at home"—citing the amount of coffee concentrate and desiccated vegetables the Confederates found when they raided Grant's supply depot in Iuka. As far as he was concerned, Yankees who cited ideological motivations rather than economic necessity to justify their enlisting were simply lying.[50]

Just as the Confederate sergeant encountered a prisoner who

confirmed his preconceptions of the North, Union soldiers sometimes conversed with prisoners whose accounts verified their notions of the South. For example, as Butler's expedition made its way up the Mississippi River to New Orleans, the Confederate troops at Fort Jackson mutinied and demanded that the officers surrender. A prisoner from the fort explained to a Wisconsin soldier that he had enlisted in the Confederate army one night when a recruiting officer got him drunk—"that was the last he recollected for three days when he found himself in the forts." According to him, more than half of the Confederacy's soldiers had been persuaded the same way.[51]

Particularly toward the end of the war when Confederate defeat seemed inevitable, Union soldiers found their prisoners amiable and repentant. During Kilpatrick's raid the Ninth New York Cavalry had to leave behind their prisoners "after double quicking them all day." One trooper reported that "some expressed regret at having to go back to fight again . . . they shook us by the hand and hoped to see us again and wished us success." These prisoners, whose Confederate loyalties had so diminished, were North Carolinians.[52]

In some ways deserters resembled those prisoners who welcomed capture. Their arrival at the front lines often delighted the soldiers of the other side. Enemy desertion made victory seem more likely and the close of the war seem closer. It is not surprising, then, that Union soldiers generally received Confederate deserters hospitably. A Michigan soldier said that when the soldiers saw them coming, "they jump up from behind their works and waving their hats shouting 'Good boy!' 'Come in out of the rain.' 'You're our man,' etc!" If the deserter reached their lines safely, he was greeted with the inevitable request for tobacco and then treated to that Yankee luxury, coffee. Deserters were also welcomed because they seemed to confirm the soldiers' beliefs about the nature of the enemy. Their unwillingness to continue to fight suggested that the enemy's cause was unjust and that the enemy's government, tyrannical and deceitful, had forced or tricked men into their army.[53]

Confederates were particularly pleased when they found evidence that the Lincoln administration's policies on slavery were not supported by the Northern soldiers. For example, near Pine

Bluff, Arkansas, a Texas soldier encountered a great many Union deserters in January 1863. They allowed themselves to be taken by the Confederate pickets so they could be paroled and sent home. The deserters explained to the Confederates that the Emancipation Proclamation had demoralized the Union soldiers. In March 1863 a Confederate at Port Hudson met three Federal deserters from Baton Rouge. They told him that the Union army was divided and demoralized because of "the negro question," and assured him "that the Yankees will not fight. . . ." Yankee desertions encouraged him—he hoped it meant that the North could draft as many men as it liked without necessarily creating a motivated army.⁵⁴

The Confederacy also had trouble keeping its army motivated, a problem that increased as the struggle continued and war-weariness and fatigue became widespread. Union soldiers found evidence of the expected crisis in Southern society when they spoke with Confederate deserters. Soldiers at Port Royal welcomed "a pretty seedy looking youngster, a down-faced clayeater" who "came paddling in a broken old dugout" to the Union position. He had deserted on the advice of his parents who lived twenty-five miles from Port Royal. His desertion was unusual because most Confederates in the area preferred to come into the Union lines at some different point; he surrendered to a black regiment. But Confederate desertion in the area was commonplace, and, when encouraged by parental advice, a probable sign that civilian dissatisfaction was common as well.⁵⁵

Desertion, of course, revealed lack of motivation on the part of the enemy. Moreover, it suggested cowardice. Perhaps that is why some soldiers came to view enemy deserters with disgust. Certainly, the respect, grudging as it was, soldiers paid to the enemy soldiers was based upon the recognition of their courage, and the soldiers in both armies often compared the bravery of the enemy armies with the cowardly self-interest of the stay-at-homes on their own side. Desertion seemed to betray masculine values of loyalty, honor, and courage. Or perhaps the soldiers simply resented the apparent assumption of the deserters: that they could one moment be enemies and in the next put down their guns, cross the lines, and be treated as friends. Whatever the reason, some soldiers, particularly Unionists, developed mixed feelings about deserters.

On May 22, 1864, a large group of Confederate deserters came into Sherman's lines—five companies with nine officers—saying they were "sick of war." By this time, John F. Brobst and his fellow Wisconsin soldiers were not particularly pleased to see deserters come in; he said, "we hate and loathe the sight of any of the poor miserable half-starved brutes. . . . " The Confederates said they desired "peace on any terms." Brobst's response was that the Union soldiers wanted peace as well, but not on any terms, "but one only, and that is nothing more than an unconditional surrender of themselves and all that belongs to them." Without that, they were willing to fight ten more years.[56]

In Tennessee, Sgt. Hamlin Alexander Coe had much the same reaction to the "ragged, dirty, and ashamed" Confederate deserters who came to his office to take the oath of allegiance. "I pity the poor devils and still I cannot help hating them." Their readiness to admit their "guilt" surprised Coe, and made him believe "they mean to do better in the future." "How heartily they shake a Yank's hand and call him brother, after they have taken the oath."[57]

The reactions of soldiers to these deserters and to prisoners suggest how they reacted to the enemies they encountered after being captured. In general, the soldiers found that soldiers of the other side, whom they had maligned as savages and dismissed as cowards, treated them usually without cruelty and frequently with kindness. For example, C. C. Brown, captured in Kentucky, received better treatment from the Union soldiers than he had expected. "They gave me more coffee and ham than Jeff ever gave me." Union surgeons temporarily behind Confederate lines during the battle of Chancellorsville returned with praise for the Confederates' treatment of them. And when Confederates captured James K. Newton, he expected them to take everything he owned. They surprised him by taking only his gun and side arms, items legitimately taken from any prisoner of war. One guard demanded Newton's canteen, but Newton simply refused to give it up. Newton decided that despite his initial fears, "if I stood up for my rights that I would come out *all right*."[58]

Newton and most other soldiers did come out "all right" in their dealings with front-line enemy soldiers immediately after capture. Civil War soldiers were usually willing to take prisoners and not to abuse them, although brutality may have increased toward the end of the war, and Confederates sometimes murdered black soldiers or sent them into slavery. Soldiers at the front were willing to display the respect that had grown up between the fighting men. Most prisoners agreed that their captors became ruder, conditions sometimes became absolutely worse, and mental strain reached its climax in the war's military prisons. In them, men were exposed to despotism and savagery, and, in the worst cases, they had to face the fact that savagery could corrupt the soldiers of their own cause. If battles such as Gettysburg came to represent much of the glory and part of the horror of war, prisons such as Andersonville represented an even greater horror, one that was unredeemed by any glory at all.

The Savage Society:
The Prisoner and the Prison

Encounters with the enemy in battle were violent and deadly. Encountering them as captors or prisoners passing to the rear could be pleasant; it gave the soldier a chance to investigate their side or at least to confirm his old prejudices. The most odious way of coming into contact with the enemy's army and the enemy's society was incarceration as a prisoner of war. The death rate of military prisoners during the Civil War was so high that being in prison was as deadly as being in battle. The enemy authorities controlled one's life far more than they did in battle, far more than one's own military superiors did in camp. The soldier's resistance to their control was rarely bloody and decisive; more likely he resisted much as slaves or industrial workers resisted—day-to-day, in small ways that maintained one's self-respect. In the end, mere survival may have been the greatest resistance of all.

During the war both the Union and Confederate armies took large numbers of prisoners. Some were exchanged; others were incarcerated. Nobody foresaw at the war's beginning that the demand for military prisons would be so great. The North converted military camps, barracks, and forts into prisons. Johnson's Island was perhaps the most well-known Northern prison. The South converted existing buildings into prisons—Libby Prison in Richmond was an old tobacco warehouse—and built makeshift enclosures, such as Andersonville. The demands for supplies and personnel placed upon these prison networks was very great, and while both sides tried to meet them, prisons were hardly the first priority. As the Confederate supply system broke down, its prisoners particularly suffered from lack of food, clothing, and shelter.[59]

Soldiers, finding themselves at the mercy of the enemy, often complained of mistreatment. Food was poor, shelter insufficient, guards brutal. Men who had gone to war convinced of their enemy's barbarism were not surprised to find it exhibited in prison. Confederate Capt. W. P. Harper felt himself abused by the Yankees. When he and his fellow prisoners from the Virginia front passed through Baltimore in November 1863, they were kept overnight in an open yard surrounded by a forty-foot-high wall. Without shelter, the men had to lie out all night on the bricks. Harper could not sleep, and he "caught a dreadful cold." Before the war their jail had been "an old negro traders establishment"—the irony was lost on Captain Harper.[60]

Once confined, prisoners frequently did suffer from abusive treatment, although less as a result of systematic enemy policy than of individual acts of cruelty, overzealousness, or fear. For example, a North Carolina soldier at Point Lookout recorded instances of guards shooting prisoners for "peepin threw the cracks of the plankin" of the fence, for crowding around the gate, and for "jawing" a Yankee sergeant.

This North Carolinian was both amused and disgusted by the black guards placed over them. He claimed a black guard "shot one of our men and kild him for no cause attall"; he also witnessed two black soldiers clowning around until one accidentally shot the other dead. Confederates often regarded the mere existence of black guards as Yankee humiliation and cruelty.[61]

Prisoners commonly claimed that guards who had never actually fought in battle—and were therefore likely cowards and certainly men who could not appreciate the character of the soldiers they guarded—were particularly prone to brutality. One prisoner at Johnson's Island rejoiced when he heard that their guards, who were being sent to the front for the first time, would be relieved by "old soldiers." "From *soldiers* who fight us in the field, better treatment is expected." His expectations were met. In some ways, actually fighting rebels or Yankees was a prerequisite for respecting them.[62]

Ill-treatment also included poor food. At Point Lookout the prisoners sometimes ate rats to supplement their diet. One Confederate, kept in a prison near Charleston, complained of being fed only one-half pint of soup and one-half pint of mush a day, and of being denied salt. It struck him as a particular sign of pettiness for "a great nation" to refuse its dependents salt. Francis Boyle, a prisoner at Point Lookout and Fort Delaware, advanced an explanation for the short rations there that expressed a common Southern opinion about the North. The insufficiency of food was due less to deliberate cruelty, in his opinion, than it was to Yankee greed and corruption. At Point Lookout the authorities denied the prisoners, first, coffee and sugar, then molasses; at the same time they reduced the meat ration and shrank the size of the bread loaves issued. Upon arrival at Fort Delaware, Boyle estimated the daily ration to be about six ounces of meat and four ounces of bread per man—"and the goverment no doubt charged full rations— What a harvest for somebody!"[63]

Boyle's confidence in "Yankee cupidity" persuaded him that when the prison sutler was forbidden to sell food to the inmates the restriction would somehow be gotten around. True to his prediction, while the War Department's order was in effect, the sutler began "selling us eatables and other contraband articles and charging us extra prices for the risk!!!!" When another Confederate prisoner learned that his brother had not received several letters in which he asked for various items, he decided that the prison authorities had intercepted the requests so that he would be forced to buy from the sutler.[64]

Soldiers found cupidity and corruption to be general in the enemy prisons. At Johnson's Island, for example, a prisoner tried to bribe a guard in order to escape. "At the time appointed, the sentinel appeared, assisted him over the fence, received the bribe—a gold watch and some three hundred dollars—and delivered him over to the officer of the guard who put him in a cell." The Confederates concluded that the soldier and the officer split the money; it was a typical Yankee trick. On the other hand, a Union captain in prison near Columbia, South Carolina, was highly offended because the rebel authorities traded Confederate dollars for Yankee greenbacks at an exorbitant rate. "The Reb Government has thus ascended to the dignity of money brokers."[65]

Unfortunately, it was not simply the malice of the guards or the policy of the enemy government that made prison life so horrible. Soldiers suffered from the conduct of their fellow prisoners. The Confederacy's Andersonville prison was the most spectacular example of this, but violence and theft by inmates disgraced many Civil War prisons. Prisoners trying to maintain life and decency might find themselves plagued by thieves. For example, at Belle Island in Virginia some Union prisoners bought a barrel of flour; the next day "a *Mob* rushed about the camp & upset & stole all the flour in camp."[66]

While the prisoner suffered from the crimes of guards and fellow prisoners, he was also tormented by the temptation to betray his cause and make peace with the enemy, thus risking violence from his fellow prisoners for his apostasy. Soldiers who chose to save themselves the miseries of prison by taking the oath of allegiance to the other side exposed themselves to contempt and attack. Soldiers who retained their patriotism encountered men whose unwillingness to make similar sacrifices cast doubt on their own decisions. It was disheartening to discover that not all of one's fellow soldiers gave the cause complete support; it suggested that the other soldiers might not be any more virtuous than the hirelings and dupes one fought.

A Confederate captain at Johnson's Island was caught by his fellow officers making an application to take the oath. He was "punished" and "turned out of his mess." "He went around begging admission but met only contempt, insult, and rougher usage." The contempt the prisoners felt for him was increased by his statement that "he intended to take the oath only for the purpose of 'getting out' and that he did not intend to keep it"; as one prisoner put it, he was "pleading perjury in extenuation of an equal crime." At the same prison another Confederate's application to take the oath was discovered when a drunken Union lieutenant lost the letter. He was "most unmercifully kicked and beaten," and had to be rescued by an armed guard.[67]

The Confederacy in particular seemed to produce large numbers of soldiers willing to desert the cause. Perhaps this was because men who were willing to betray the United States could not be expected to show greater loyalty to a newer nation; more likely, it was because Confederate defeat appeared increasingly inevitable as the war continued.

In October 1863 prisoners at Point Lookout believed an exchange to be imminent. Prisoners flooded the authorities with letters claiming they had been forced into the rebel army. Some men wrote asking to be allowed to take the oath of allegiance and enlist in the Union army—particularly if they could be "plaste whear thar wil be no danger of falling in to the hands of the Confederate rebs [.]" Others wanted to take the oath, be released, and stay in the North. A group of prisoners explained, "it never was our intention that we should fight against the united States to Support a rotten government for Jeff Davis." They had been at work on the Mississippi River when the war broke out and were accused of being abolitionists by the local vigilante committee, which "compeled us to join the army."[68]

One story is typical of the whole. Samuel F. Duvall, a Marylander, begged not to be returned to the Confederate army. Just before the first battle of Bull Run, his older brother, "whom I was very much attached to," enlisted in the Confederate army in Virginia and persuaded Duvall to do the same. "I have a thousand times regretted that I did it and I maid up my mind several times to return to home but he would alwais persuaid me not to do so. . . . " The brother was killed at the battle of Fredericksburg; Duvall deserted on the retreat from Gettysburg, hiding out in the woods until the Union soldiers came and he could surrender. Now he was afraid he would be sent back into the Confederate army and asked the provost to state his case to the commanding general. "The general will oblige me very much if he will intersede for me and get me out of this scrape this time and I will guarantee him that I will never be caught in such another."[69]

Union prisoners rarely wanted to take an oath of allegiance to the Confederacy, and they longed to be exchanged. But in the latter part of the war, the federal government would not participate in prisoner exchanges. One way Union prisoners accounted for the failure of exchange was their sure knowledge that prisoners held by the South were too sick to return to the army, and their belief that prisoners in the North, well-fed and humanely cared for, could take up arms again immediately. But the conditions the Union prisoners endured caused them to curse more than simply the Confederates. Men began to reconsider their attitudes toward their own government. A prisoner at Andersonville wrote that if the government did not do something soon to relieve them, "it's a poor government to tie to." In July 1864 the sergeants at Andersonville sent a petition to the federal government, "*begging* to be released."[70]

White prisoners grew particularly bitter over their government's protection of black prisoners. In 1864 the Union government refused to exchange prisoners unless the Confederates treated black prisoners according to the rules of war. Some soldiers in rebel prisons viewed this as clear evidence that the administration placed black men above white men. At some time, perhaps after the war, one Northern prisoner altered his diary, so that a prison camp entry read, "I always regarded *Slavery* as a great evil; but war as a far greater evil; & since I have seen the effects of [blank] I *hate* the very name of it." He had originally written "Abolitionism" instead of war, and claimed he would teach his children to hate it.[71]

On the other hand, other prisoners favored the North's policy. Capt. James Gaunt Derrickson, imprisoned near Macon, Georgia, wrote, "I would sooner stay here during the war than have our Government acede to their demands in regard to the negro soldier." To be sure, Derrickson was not in an Andersonville, but in a camp where "you can live very comfortably" if you had money. But Derrickson's argument might well have appealed to other prisoners. He favored the protection of black soldiers not because they were black but because they were Union soldiers. "Anyone, whatever may be his color, who wears the blue of Uncle Sam is entitled to protection, even if thousands have to be sacrificed in protecting him."[72]

If Northern soldiers revealed distrust of their government or displayed latent racism while they were in prison, it must be remembered that they were men trapped in almost hopeless conditions. And if Confederates abandoned their Confederate allegiance or used force against those prisoners who did forsake the cause, it must be remembered they were undergoing suffering both physical and psychological. Even while prisons encouraged the belief that the enemy was despicable—who is a less sympathetic figure than a jailer?—it created doubts about the loyalty and virtue of one's own fellow soldiers.

MACDUFF'S SON: Who must hang them?
HIS MOTHER: Why, the honest men.
SON: Then the liars and swearers are fools, for there are liars and swearers enow to beat the honest men and hang up them.
—*Macbeth*, IV, ii.

In July 1864 a Confederate major at Fort Delaware put an advertisement in the New York *News*. He needed money and clothing and hoped to elicit contributions from the Northern population. He offered to have his family send "provisions, clothing, or Confederate money upon such equitable basis as many be agreed upon" to Union soldiers imprisoned in the South, in exchange for being supplied himself by their friends and families in the North. He could supply prisoners easily: he owned a farm near Andersonville, Georgia.

The major did receive some presents from Northerners, but the authorities soon transferred him to a different prison. When he was no longer at Fort Delaware to "nurse" his scheme, the flow of gifts fell off. Probably neither the major, his fellow prisoners, nor the Northerners desperate to do something for their friends at Andersonville fully appreciated the difference in conditions between the prison for officers at Fort Delaware and the squalid outdoor camp at Andersonville.[73]

In a very real sense Andersonville returned men to a state of nature. Confederate authority, when it could be exercised with impunity from the perimeters of the camp, was capricious and tyrannical. Within the prison, however, Confederate authority was almost nonexistent. The prison commandant, Henry Wirz, and the other Confederates did little to maintain order in the camp.

As in society's beginning, primitive trade sprang up in Andersonville. One prisoner bartered a silver pencil to a guard for a quart of cornmeal and one-half plug of Cavendish tobacco; he then traded with new prisoners at the rate of one chew tobacco for one brass button; when he had twelve he traded with the guard, exchanging the buttons for two more quarts of meal and one full plug of tobacco. The guards made Confederate uniform buttons from the Union ones.[74]

Andersonville also represented the rock bottom of Yankee immorality. Men, scattered across a shelterless plain, part of it swamp and all of it soon poisoned by excrement, no particular provision made for any individual, and the very necessities of life in woefully short supply, had to create their own society—without blueprint, without authority. Their initial product favored wolves and jackals more than honest men.

Andersonville became a pit of depravity. Men with almost no belongings spent their days engaged in gambling. Newcomers were robbed, almost routinely. The greatest talent for organization belonged to a group of raiders who ranged through the camp unmolested by the Confederate authorities. The leader of this gang of robbers went by the name of Mosby, calling himself after the famous Confederate guerrilla. One prisoner lamented, "O Liberty; Law & Order! thou canst not be appreciated till thou art once lost." The soldiers at Andersonville, as befitted defenders of the Union and the national government, came to see no contradiction between true liberty and the rule of law.[75]

Eventually the honest men of the camp could not stand the thievery and brutality of the raiders. In a very real sense they created a social compact: they formed an association to discipline the raiders. They obtained the permission of Wirz—in itself an admission of the inability of the Confederates to take responsibility—and policed the camp themselves, their vigilantism culminating in the hanging of six of the most notorious raiders. When prisoner John Ransom wrote his account of Wirz's turning the condemned men over to the prisoners for their execution, he chose to portray the Confederate captain as Pilate: "Capt. Wirz then said a few words about their having been tried by our own men and for us to do as we choose with them, that he washed his hands of the whole matter, or words to that effect." Wirz told the Yankees they were a hard set, to execute their own, but Ransom was glad to see the murderers punished and some sort of order established in the camp.[76]

Joseph Williams, a Confederate guard at the camp, wrote home the day after the hanging to say of the prisoners "thay still keep killing each other [.] thay hung six yesterday [.] thay fight all most every night in the stockade [.]" According to Williams, the Yankee prisoners claimed that the raiders were all foreigners. Whether or not this claim was true, the prisoners were probably sure that the men they hanged were not virtuous American soldiers.[77]

Just a few days after the prisoners at Andersonville attempted to restore their social order by hanging the raiders, Confederate officers at Fort Delaware banded together to form a Christian Association. Open to all who professed "a saving faith in Christ," the association held weekly meetings; through its standing committees it made arrangements for sick and destitute prisoners, for divine worship within the camp, for education, and for "procuring and distributing Religious Reading." The Christian Association functioned from July 1864 to June 1865.

The association spent the bulk of its time soliciting contributions from prisoners and Northern civilians. Robert E. Lee, Mrs. Robert E. Lee, and Mrs. Thomas J. Jackson were *in absentia* made life members of the association, as was Jefferson Davis after an embarrassing delay. Eventually the association tried to organize other Northern prisons as well.

In the association records there is a copy of an open letter to the people of the Confederacy from the Confederate States Christian Association for the Relief of Prisoners, which was printed in the October 1864 *Central Presbyterian*. This organization pleaded for contributions from the South to ease the burdens of Confederate prisoners in the North. But they also advocated, in the name of Christ, charity toward the Union prisoners in the South: "Let us endeavor to discharge our duty to them as well as to our own prisoners, and exemplify the teachings of Him who said, 'love your enemies, bless them that curse you, do good to them that hate you, and pray for them which despitefully use you and persecute you.' " The Christian Association of Fort Delaware fully endorsed these sentiments.[78]

The Christian Association faced no such problem as did the Andersonville police. Fort Delaware was not a scene of anarchy and starvation. What the Christian Association feared was that away from their families, churches, and government, men would sink into sloth and immorality. The Christian Association hoped to minister to the needs of the prisoners and to instill self-discipline in them as well. The need at Fort Delaware was not as great as the need at Andersonville, so the measures taken were not as extreme. But at both places men had to recreate society.

Henry Wirz, the commandant of Andersonville, would become the only Confederate executed for war crimes. The original indictment accused him of conspiring with many high officials—including Robert E. Lee—"to injure the health and destroy the lives" of Union soldiers. The U.S. government held the deaths of those unfortunates at Andersonville to be deliberate on the part of the Confederacy, and Wirz to be a monster.

It does not make the deaths at Andersonville more palatable to point out that incompetence and stupidity caused them, nor can any defense of Henry Wirz make him simply an innocent victim. Men cannot always escape the blame for the horrors they create. But it is noteworthy that Americans felt the need for punishing their defeated enemy most when he was in his guise as prison keeper. Many of the charges against Henry Wirz, "Hellhound of Andersonville," were based on procedures accepted as standard practice.[79]

During the war, prisons became popular images for the very worst aspects of the enemy and his society. And after the war the prison retained its hold on the imagination of the Civil War generation. Photographs of emaciated prisoners conveyed the horrors of Andersonville with the same force that photographs of Dachau and Auschwitz would for a later generation. Northerners and Southerners exchanged recriminations, justified their own policies, and kept bitter memories of wartime prisons alive.

The prison presented the enemy in his most despotic and savage form: in the prison he had defenseless men under his control. What could better explain the reason soldiers had gone to war against such an enemy than the prisons he had built? Conversely, the prison presented the soldier at his most blameless. The prisoner of war could be seen as victim pure and simple—there was no troubling ambiguity about his role as a killer. Finally, the prison was a model for the society that the enemy had fought to establish. Andersonville in particular resembled the fantasies some Unionists had had of an America plunged into anarchy and lawlessness by secession. Confederates could also discern in prison conditions an America where they were not first-class citizens—and an America where blacks were given power over whites.

But an Andersonville, allowing anarchy its fruition, suggested that all men, even one's fellow soldiers, could be drawn to savagery. Implicit in nineteenth-century men's condemnation of savagery is the belief that savages were not a different order of humanity altogether, but simply a less educated, less civilized order. In the Civil War the enemy, after all, at some point had been American— had been civilized men. The fact that other Americans could slip back into savagery was frightening; it suggested that under the stimulus of war even defenders of the right might become savage.

Men could be shocked by actions committed by their own side, whether in prison or out. A Pennsylvania soldier, whose regiment barely escaped an ambush, visited the scene of the fight immediately after its conclusion. The sight of the dead troubled him. What upset him more was seeing one Pennsylvania soldier cut the chin off of a dead Confederate, and another kill a wounded rebel who was begging for water.[80]

Such incidents, if committed by one's own side, could be interpreted as aberrations, the actions of depraved men who unfortunately had joined an army fighting for a pure cause. Unlike the barbarities of the enemy, which revealed their true nature, atrocities of one's own side were accidents of war. A man could keep his hands clean from such conduct.

But as Nathan Bedford Forrest observed, "War means fighting and fighting means killing." Nothing defined the savage more than the fact that he killed and took pleasure in it. And whether or not the soldier took pleasure in killing, he too had to learn to kill. Killing in battle, killing men who were fighting back in turn, was done in a state of excitement. It required a sort of savage enthusiasm. No matter how virtuous the men who fought regarded themselves to be, no matter how holy the cause they fought for, in the end, war demanded that sometimes they turn themselves into savages, just as their enemies had.

This was not entirely undesirable. Men saw benefits in certain elements of savagery. John William DeForest, who before the war had written a history of Connecticut Indians, observed savage virtues in the Army of Northern Virginia. "They aimed better than our men; they covered themselves (in case of need) more carefully and effectively; they could move in a swamp without much care for alignment and touch of elbows. In short, they fought more like redskins or like hunters than we." Fighting like Indians, the Confederates took far fewer casualties in the battle of Opequon than the Northern forces. DeForest said admiringly of a Confederate charge at Cedar Creek, "No daybreak rush of moccasined Shawnees or Wyandots, was ever more dextrous and triumphant than this charge of Kershaw's Georgians, Mississippians, and South Carolinians." DeForest's appreciation of these Indian virtues was more notable in view of his respect for the military virtues of the regular army; he was no opponent of "alignment and touch of elbows." Discipline was necessary to win a war; perhaps some savagery was necessary as well. War sometimes forced men to emulate those actions of their enemy to which they pointed to justify war. Discipline and savagery both fueled the change from volunteer to soldier.[81]

THREE

From Volunteer to Soldier: The Psychology of Service

In 1862 a New York regiment composed primarily of volunteers of German descent was stationed in Virginia. This regiment had elected a surgeon for its chaplain, as they preferred having an additional doctor to having a legitimate man of the cloth. The chaplain, an elderly man, spoke little English. When one of the regiment's privates died, the chaplain found himself compelled to conduct the funeral service. As the coffin was lowered into the ground, the surgeon "with the most solemn air said in broken English, 'This is the first time that this man was buried in Virginia and D—n me (throwing in dirt) if I ever bury him again. V which in former times stood for Voluntear now is made to stand for victim.' "[1]

The Civil War experience changed men; its subjective component matched its physical reality. Most men who were soldiers for any period of time underwent a psychological transformation. Those men who volunteered for an extended period—three years or the war—tended to lose their prewar identities. Citizens who had been volunteers turned into soldiers. And even if they escaped death, the volunteer soldiers could not escape feeling occasionally like helpless victims—more often than they admitted they were also killers. The wartime experience created new identities.

The conditions of military service helped to create these new identities: wartime was radically different from peacetime and demanded changes in men's psyches, simply in order for them to survive. Furthermore, Civil War volunteers were no more immune to disillusionment than soldiers of any other war. But the new identities were also created by the separation men felt from the

American public—Union or Confederate—at large. As they became isolated from their old patterns of life, men had to make themselves new identities from the very military life that threatened to degrade them. In turn, the identity of the soldier might supplant the previous identity of the civilian—men feared the very psychological transformation they had to undergo to continue to live. Only the justice of the cause for which they fought and its meaning for the civil life to which they planned to return could reconcile many volunteers to their new identity as soldiers.

Men had valued their autonomy so much that they went to war when they felt it was threatened. Military life itself, however, proved a powerful threat to men's self-esteem. Military discipline required that their autonomy be curtailed; the conditions of camp life were frequently degrading; and in the process of becoming soldiers men found themselves increasingly cut off from civilian life. In order to retain their self-esteem under these conditions, volunteers came to pride themselves on their ability to endure and to view soldiers as superior in their patriotism to all those who would not enlist. In short, men who congratulated themselves on their autonomy now congratulated themselves on their willingness to part with it. This willingness was the evidence that one truly deserved autonomy.

Americans found military regimentation hard to accept. North or South, the soldier of the 1860s was most likely an independent farmer or a farmer's son. His work had been regulated by the weather, the cycle of the growing year, and the remote but all-important authority of the market. The authority immediately over him was personal—not the "feudal" authority of the planter, but the patriarchal rule of a father or an older brother who bossed him until such time as he could set up his own farm, and whose authority derived from his place in the family. Besides his relative freedom from discipline in the workplace, the volunteer had been brought up in a political culture that celebrated personal autonomy and democracy. In the North, of course, the Republican Party was based largely on the defense of free labor and free men; and in the South the Democratic Party, with its sometimes paranoid denunciations of corruption and with its thoroughly egalitarian rhetoric, outlived the commercially oriented Whig Party. Finally, American political thinkers had always viewed the military with suspicion; a Confederate soldier could still use eighteenth-century terminology and refer to an officer as a member of the old "standing army."[2]

If regimentation was difficult for most Americans of the 1860s to bear, it was particularly onerous for a Southern white man. For him, subordination and regulation were not simply abstractions in a republican demonology. He had seen them during his life—perhaps every day. The rules and restrictions of the army reminded the Confederate of the humiliation of slavery and of the degraded position that blacks held in his society.[3]

Southerners of all classes referred to military discipline as a form of slavery. Edwin Fay, a Louisiana soldier and perpetual grumbler, had not been in the Confederate army long when he decided, "No negro on Red River but has a happy time compared with that of a Confederate soldier." One regulation in particular drew the ire of Fay and other Confederates: when a soldier wanted to leave camp he had to obtain a pass. The spectacle of white men carrying passes drew the amused attention of at least one Southern slave and probably more. Sgt. C. E. Taylor wrote his father in July 1861 what a black in Corinth, Mississippi, said after he witnessed a guard demand to see Taylor's pass. "He said it was mighty hard for white folks now. He said he had quit carrying a pass and his master had just commenced to carry them." J. C. Owens summed up the resemblance between slavery and soldiering when he wrote, "I am tired of being bound up worse than a negro."[4]

Northerners, too, could feel the comparison between the soldier and the slave. A soldier doing common labor might say he "worked like a nigger." Another soldier wrote from Virginia, "We keep very comfortable *for soldiers*. But its nothing like *white* living." Allen Geer became homesick contemplating the difference in his life after enlisting: "yesterday a freeman—today a slave." The true difference between his slavery and that of slaves in the South was that his obedience was, in a sense, not coerced. "A sense of duty and patriotism made me obedient to all the discipline."[5]

Besides the image of the slave, men used that of the machine to explain their position in the army. One war-weary Northern officer wrote his mother, "The interest I once took in Military is almost gone. I do my duty like a machine that has so much in a day to do anyway." One veteran remembered that the doctor in the hospital looked upon his patients as "so many machines in need of repairs." He explained, "In War men are looked upon and considered as so many machines. Each machine is expected to perform a certain amount of service. If the machine becomes weakened or impaired by service, care is taken that it be mended and restored so that it may again do its duty. But if, in the arduous service and dangers to which it is exposed, the life or moving force is destroyed, then a trench and covering of earth hides the remains, and that is all. This, of course, looks very heartless, but War is relentless and cruel, and so long as War lasts, and men will take up arms against one another, this State of things will continue." The machine and the slave were two metaphors for entities without wills of their own. The soldier was a third. But the machine goes beyond the slave and soldier: it is not even human.[6]

What the men of the 1860s feared in war was not simply curtailment of their freedom. They were willing to give up some freedom long enough to defend a larger freedom. The volunteers also feared what might best be called dehumanization. Many experiences common to soldiering during the 1860s and in other times served to increase such fears. For example, after the war one Confederate soldier recalled that the first time one discovered lice on one's person it was "a very mortifying and humiliating experience." Significantly, his company became lice-ridden during what they regarded as their first military humiliation, the retreat from Yorktown in 1862. "Up to this time we had maintained our self-respect and decency." "I well remember the feeling of humiliation with which we made the discovery we were inhabited. . . ." "We were inhabited"—what could violate one's autonomy more than losing control even of one's flesh? In camp lice were inescapable because of the proximity of large numbers of men with varying habits of personal cleanliness. On the march they were inescapable because men could not wash their clothes or their bodies. Inescapable or not, they made men feel degraded. Infestation, associated with sloth and poverty, became a hallmark of the soldier.[7]

Along with lice and filth, of course, went material deprivation in general. Deprivation is comparative; the war experience probably affected enlisted men worse than officers, Confederates worse than Federals, blacks worse than whites. And whether or not a man judged conditions as onerous in part depended on the conditions of his life before the war. Yet for those Americans of middle-class values, military life produced an intense psychological strain.

Soldiers as seemingly different as an Alabama officer and a Connecticut sergeant shared the same reactions to filth and deprivation. The Alabamian wrote his sister about his desire to return home, however briefly: "And then I could put on a white shirt and have my shoes blacked and ride on horseback or perhaps be exalted to a seat in a buggy and then I could sit down in a chair like a white man, and eat at a table like a white man and feel for a little while like a white man once again!!" The sergeant expressed similar longings. The Union siege of Port Hudson during the summer of 1863 was a particularly grueling experience. The heat of a Louisiana summer, the monotony of a siege, and the constant deadly Confederate sniping all combined to drive men close to distraction. The sergeant told his commanding officer "that if I could only go off somewhere and have a good cry, put on some clean clothes, get a letter from home, that I would be ready to come back and die like a Christian." Both of them valued cleanliness and neatness; more importantly, both found their absence defiling.[8]

Sickness, sometimes minor, sometimes fatal, plagued the country dwellers North and South as they crowded into military camps. Measles, mumps, and colds were common diseases. Life in the army proved more difficult than anticipated. One Confederate warned his uncle that "the camp life is a hard life to live" and asked him to tell the other male members of the family not to volunteer, "for I Dont think that they could stand it for it is hard to do [.]" Another Georgia soldier wrote from his first camp, "There some dying every day on either side the death bells ringing in my ears constant[.]"[9]

Death by disease was not what men had volunteered for. Disease was a far more impersonal enemy than the savage foe men had gone to war to fight. What made such camp deaths even worse was the increasingly matter-of-fact attitude toward them: they were common, barely worth noting. A North Carolina soldier wrote from his first camp that "ef a man dies there is not much sed about it[.]" Anonymous death was not glorious.[10]

One irony of the Civil War was that the hospital, a symbol of concern and care, that even now evokes among the literary-minded memories of Walt Whitman, became a symbol of indifference and dread for many soldiers. A Confederate soldier from Marion, Alabama, wrote home from a hospital in Richmond, "If a man Lives he Lives and if he Dies he Dies   A Dog is thought more of Down in Marion than A Solger is hear." And a Union soldier observed, "I had rather risk a battle than the Hospitals." More so than one's company, the hospital represented military bureaucracy and the dehumanization of the American soldier.[11]

Even at its best, medical practice of the 1860s was faulty and barbaric. Particularly after a battle, when surgeons spent a long night in ill-lit hospital tents amputating the arms and legs of wounded men in an assembly-line procedure, medical care impressed the soldiers not only as dubious and painful, but as dehumanizing. One Confederate visited a military hospital after First Bull Run and saw "piles of arms and legs laying about just as you have seen rags and papers laying about a floor where a little child has been playing." The spectacle of men being reduced to their component parts was not a reassuring one.[12]

During the war, however, medical practice was not at its best. Frequently, soldiers came to feel that their doctors were imcompetent and uncaring. Perhaps they judged too harshly the men who worked in such miserable conditions. Nonetheless, the belief that the army or the government could not provide decent medical treatment encouraged the soldier's sense of neglect.

One Mississippi regiment was cursed with a particularly cowardly surgeon. When the regiment was in battle, he cowered in the rear. A skilled surgeon, his absence from his proper place led to the deaths of injured men. One man underwent a series of agonizing and incompetent operations. "A cannonball took his leg off just above the ankle   A green physician amputated his leg which George stood like a noble boy, as he was, but the wound healing it was found that the bone protruded so our young Surgeon cut it off a second time just below the knee and neglected to secure the arteries properlly." As the wound healed, the improperly treated artery burst and the doctor amputated the man's leg once again, this time above the knee. The operation resulted in his death. "Poor George was a good boy and an excellent soldier. He told the boys when shot he was sorry to lose his leg but was grateful his life was spared.

And told the Surgeon after the Second amputation he knew he was bound to die and if his leg had been properly taken off at first he would have lived."[13]

E. H. Hampton of the 58th North Carolina wrote the widow of a comrade that her husband had only been wounded in the hand, and that the real cause of his death was the doctor's neglect; "the doctor was very mean to him and did not treat him right." A federal cavalryman told his wife, "When a person is sick in camp they might as well dig a hole and put him in as to take him to one of thee infernal hells called hospitals." One man in his regiment had died neglected, while nearby hospital attendants played euchre. After the war another soldier vividly remembered a one-eyed man in the ambulance corps who neglected the wounded to rob the dead.[14]

One last thing that horrified soldiers when they considered military hospitals was the treatment of the dead. Indeed, the Civil War soldier thought burial of great—perhaps ultimate—significance. The dead were entitled to their due. They deserved not just recognition of their valor and patriotism, but proper treatment of their corpses—a decent burial. The anonymous wounded suffered from neglect in the hospital; so did the anonymous dead. One Union soldier wrote from the hospital, "The way the teamsters who bury them treat the bodies is shameful. I have seen them if the coffins were a little short get into them with their boots on, and trample them in even stepping on their faces."[15]

Such treatment of the dead was not limited to hospitals. The wholesale nature of death during the war left many a man an anonymous, neglected corpse. One Northern soldier wrote his sister, responding to her letter telling of her sorrow at attending a soldier's funeral, "if you would haf to see so many dead brother Soldiers laying on the field thousands of them and also thousand of wounded and no body to bury them while the engagement lasts and sometimes they are left lay altogether on top of the earth that is a sad affair." His emotion prevented him from finishing his thought clearly. Men wanted their bodies to be respected after death; they wanted proper burials. One Confederate thought after the disastrous Gettysburg campaign, "the worst of all was we did not get to bury our dead."[16]

For the soldiers of the Civil War, the enemy's treatment of the slain was as important an indicator of their moral worth as their treatment of the living. The faces and hands of dead men sticking out of their graves shocked a Union soldier who visited the Bull Run battlefield. He could not understand how "people calling themselves enlightened should take so little pains to bury their foe." He said the Confederate dead had been buried properly, but the Union slain covered with just a little dirt; some were not buried at all. This was another example of enemy savagery.[17]

But savagery was not limited to the enemy. A Confederate visited the Bull Run battlefield in the fall of 1861 and discovered that the Yankee graves had been dug up "and their skeletons & clothing . . . scattered all around." People seeking Union buttons as souvenirs had disinterred the corpses. Visiting the battlefield at Maryland Heights, some Union soldiers discovered a dead Confederate who had not been buried properly—"only some stones thrown on him." A few of the soldiers took some hair from the corpse as a souvenir. Two who desired more exciting relics knocked some teeth from the corpse's mouth. One man in the party wrote, "the way they acted with him was enough to make a dog sick let alone a man."[18]

When the soldier saw the dead of his own side, he might react with horror or with a learned indifference. Viewing the enemy dead might produce rejoicing at their defeat or sympathy for the suffering they and their families underwent. The sight of the dead also often brought out a strong physical disgust. Some soldiers, upon seeing their own or enemy dead, felt sick at their souls, reminded of their own mortality. Others faced with corpses revealed troubled consciences. And still others abused the dead bodies of their enemies, as if to demonstrate finally the inhumanity of their foes.

Soldiers could not escape identifying with the dead. To serve in the army was to live in the midst of death. A Confederate described that in his company's camp at Seven Pines: "We arrived on the battlefield about 10 PM and again slept among the dead and wounded who were so numerous that it was difficult to walk in the dark the scene was horrifying[.]" Sleeping with corpses strewn about them, the soldiers found the distinction between the living and the dead was not as clear as they would have liked it to have been.[19]

Each man knew he might soon become one of the anonymous

corpses that littered battlefields or were buried near a hospital. The only way to endure such a thought was to try to ignore the humanity of the men who died. Men became numb. One Confederate officer cited as an example of the callousness war produced in men that "We cook and eat, talk and laugh with the enemy's dead lying all about us as though they were so many hogs." It was easier, of course, to deny the humanity of the enemy. No one could stand perpetual sensitivity to the ubiquity of death. Denying the humanity of the dead, however, was one more way in which the soldier's own sense of self was degraded, both as one who is aware of the humanity around him, and as one who is likely to join the ranks of dead soldiers.[20]

So-called primitive cultures use ritual to set their warriors apart from the broader society; the warrior may be said to be "dead" to that society until he has returned from war and been ritualistically cleaned. The ways in which the Civil War soldier was set apart and reincorporated into society were not self-conscious rituals, although the uniforms, parades, flag presentations, and the other paraphernalia of service have ritualistic overtones. But the psychological results of wartime conditions—living in filth, subject to unaccustomed discipline, surrounded by the diseased, wounded, and dead—set the soldier apart from civilian society in a manner as profound as any ritual. The soldier learned his difference from the civilian. It is less clear that the broader society acknowledged the distinction.[21]

One thing that helped a soldier bear the hardships of his life was the respect of his fellow citizens. Men who had made considerable sacrifices and who were risking their lives expected a certain amount of adulation from those who had not joined them in service. If army life degraded him, acclaim could exalt the soldier to the status of a hero. The dehumanization of military service could be offset by the gratitude of one's country. Respect provided a salutory context for soldiering—a means to resist degradation.

Early in the war their fellow citizens willingly gave the soldiers the respect they demanded. The passage of volunteers through a town was a cause of celebration. Just as their hometowns had sent the troops to war with lavish public ceremony, other communities welcomed their patriotic defenders. For example, the Oglethorpe Light Infantry received the warmest greetings as they proceeded from Savannah to the Virginia war front. They marched through the streets of Petersburg to the tunes of brass bands, with the eyes of lovely women on them, and banners waving over their heads. The ladies called them the "company of bachelors"—the soldiers were sixteen to twenty-five, without a married man among them. " . . . indeed, we looked like boys," one wrote his mother, "with our handsome blue uniforms & smooth faces." They were great favorites everywhere they went.[22]

Occasionally civilian response was overenthusiastic. When the 5th New Jersey passed through Philadelphia in August 1861, citizens came to the train station to see them off. Young ladies freely distributed cigars, tobacco, handkerchiefs, and flowers to the soldiers. The train left the station "amid the crack of firearms and the cheers from thousands of throats." One soldier of the 5th New Jersey was shot in the arm during this patriotic demonstration, and later discharged from service.[23]

Such accidents aside, these receptions cheered the volunteers— who felt they deserved them. The public placed the value on the soldier that military life threatened to deny them. As the war continued, however, the sight of a soldier became commonplace. Civilians no longer thronged to meet the soldiers. In fact, as civilians went about their daily pursuits, they did not simply take soldiers for granted—they looked down on them. Or so the soldiers came to feel.[24]

Soldiers began to hear stories of civilian disdain; they began to complain of their treatment on their furloughs home. Cpl. Rudolphe Rey of the 102nd New York Volunteers received a discouraging letter from a fellow soldier who had lost a leg. Upon his return home, the crippled soldier reported that all his friends acted as if they could not remember him; he swore he would be able to support himself without their aid. He warned Rey that if he wore his uniform home while on leave, he could travel with a railroad car to himself. Another New York soldier said much the same thing: at home, "Soldiers and dogs go together."[25]

It might be thought that indifference toward soldiers was characteristic of a money-grubbing, unchivalrous North and not the militaristic South. As early as 1862, however, a Virginia Confederate observed that "six months ago a soldier was the greatest thing in the world but now they are worse than the devil not countenanced by nobody at all but the soldiers." Confederate soldiers, campaigning near Jackson, Mississippi, in June 1863, heard rumors that "The City Council in compliance with the solicitations of many citizens attempted some time since to pass an ordinance forbidding *soldiers the use of the pavement* and *sidewalks* and forcing them to walk in the middle of the streets. The motion was defeated by a majority of *only Three* votes." When the soldiers marched through the city, they would cry out, "Boys, don't get on the sidewalk!" and "Corporal of the Guard, here's a soldier on the sidewalk!" and the citizens nervously assured them, "Yes, you *can* walk on the sidewalks." "The Boys would frequently ask them 'where the Yankees walked while they were here'? They would cry out good-humoredly while passing a crowd of Ladies and Gentlemen, 'Here's the boys that cant walk on the pavements.' *We* can fight for you though.' " Whether the proposed civic ordinance existed or not, it is significant that the soldiers so readily believed that it did.[26]

Whatever the indifference or contempt of the civilian population at large, soldiers felt a particularly acute grievance when it seemed that the members of their own local communities did not respect their efforts. It violated the very notion that the soldier who had gone to war was an extension of that community. As the war went on, soldiers found it difficult not to see themselves as distinct from the folks back home. Instead of representing his community he began to feel alienated from it—another way in which the volunteer became a soldier.

One source of discontent was the soldiers' feeling that the people did not understand how difficult their job was. Both sides went to war expecting a quick victory; both sides were quickly, but not thoroughly, disillusioned. Soldiers who were themselves reluctant to admit that the war would not end with the next big battle were likely to be sensitive to accusations that victory could easily be achieved with different strategy, different commanders, and different armies. Even though all soldiers reserved the right to grumble about the mistakes of their superior officers, most resented it when home folks judged the operations of the army in the field unfavorably. In part, of course, such judgments were felt to reflect not only on the commanders but on the men as well. Furthermore, the soldier felt that civilian judgments were made in ignorance. The folks at home had no concept of the difficulties experienced by the soldiers in the field. A Pennsylvania lieutenant wrote home testily, when civilians were complaining that McClellan allowed Lee to escape after Antietam, that if men there "think the Rebble army can be Bagged let them come & bagg them. . . . Bagging an army is easy to talk about." The men who remained at home had forfeited their right to criticize those who had marched away to war.[27]

A Confederate wrote his cousin on the subject of civilian military expertise thus: "I saw a gentleman who left DeSoto Parish about two weeks since. He says the old men at home are all generals now—gather in groups in the little towns over there and talk about the war and discuss the abilities of our Generals—Know more than any of them—Except General Lee only—They admit him to be a great man, but all the others do wrong all the time. Our soldiers have all come to the conclusion that they have no friends out of the army except the ladies." And Lee himself, admitting that "the movements of our armies cannot keep pace with the expectations of the editors of papers," said he would like to see them exercise their abilities in the field.[28]

Another, more onerous grievance was the difference between the economic positions of the soldier and the civilian. Many civilians did well during the war, particularly in the North. Soldiers and their families, conversely, often suffered. With furloughs home and the surprisingly frequent exchange of mail between the front and home, soldiers were perfectly well informed as to the economic success of those they had left behind.[29]

A particular problem arose when the soldier thought that the people at home were not fair to his family or were grasping and picayune in money matters while he risked his life for the cause. John Pierson, a Union officer, reacted angrily when he learned that one of his creditors in Pontiac, Michigan, dunned his wife. "Those left at home in the quiet pursuit of their business," he told his daughter, "can well aford to wait. The business I am engaged in is a game of heads and I may loose mine and his is in no danger unless they chose to get up a war at home. . . . "[30]

When the man continued to hound his wife, Pierson wrote her "any man that is so avaricious as to dun a woman for a small demand he may have against her Husband while he is in the Army helping to Suppress this Montrous Rebelion is mean enough to make a false bill and ought to lose and honest one." He assured her, "If I get home Pontiac will not suffer much on my account if I get killed they may come where I am and collect. . . ."[31]

The issue was not simply one of personal debts. It was also one of forgone opportunities for profit in the wartime economy. Henry Seys, the Union abolitionist, summed up the soldiers' fears and pride well when he wrote his wife from Chattanooga: "True I sometimes think why should *I* care so much of what is my duty to my country? Why not do as others, stay at home and fatten in purse on the blood of the land?" In ten years, he predicted, "the parvenu, made rich by lucky speculation, or some swindling contract" would "elbow from place the soldier broken down or maimed, by long exposure or ghastly wound received on some battle field or lonely picket post. . . ." But he answered his question by saying that he served because his childhood education and his concern for the respect of his own children made him patriotic both "in *deed* as well as word." He asked his wife to teach their children that "their duty to the land of their birth is next to their duty to God."[32]

Those soldiers who believed that their immediate family had become indifferent to them probably felt the most wretched sense of abandonment. In May 1862 an officer in the Army of the Potomac, then located near Richmond, complained, "I am tired of soldiering and were it not for us being just where we are, I would not stay a day longer not careing whether you wanted me home or not I cannot understand why you deserve [desire?] me to stay I see other letters to young men from their parents, begging and imploring of them to come home this makes me feel sad and sometimes I think I am not wanted at home by my parents[.]" He was killed not long after, at the battle of Seven Pines.[33]

Civilian disdain was as potent a source of degradation as military life. Still, the soldiers' resentment of civilian contempt and indifference was not always unambiguous. Sometimes they feared it was deserved. Soldiers knew that military life might indeed transform men into beasts and this could inform a soldier's reactions to civilians. For example, in the fall of 1862 a Union soldier in Illinois suffered from the usual camp diseases and decided to treat himself with "some fresh air and a good bed to sleep in. . . ." He went to a farm near camp to request a place to stay for the night; the "old lady" was obviously suspicious and reluctant to shelter him but the soldier persuaded her to relent. When he wrote his parents, he explained, "The people here are suspicious of soldiers just as Ma is of pedlars and dont like to put them into their beds and I cannot blame them either some of the soldiers have not pride enough to keep themselves halfway decent. Some of them seem to think that being a soldier is a license for a man to make a brute of himself."[34]

In 1863 a Mississippi Confederate heard that a military hospital was planned for his hometown. The idea depressed him. "It seems to me that wherever soldiery predominate decay and scarcity follow, and a certain appearance of cheerlessness (as far as the inhabitants are concerned) seems to exist in proportion as the number of soldiers (locusts) increase." Charity compelled him to add, "Anyway, as they are stationed upon you, you do the best you can for poor fellows! they have a hard time even when not sick."[35]

So while men sometimes prided themselves on their patriotism and soldierly qualities, they also worried about the changes military service had made in their fellows when they compared the men around them to their families back home. The psychological transformation caused by war sometimes upset men more than anything else. Lyman C. Holford, a Wisconsin soldier, wrote in his diary entry, "a little after dark I saw something which was a little the worst of any thing I have yet seen in the army. Some of the boys of the 24th Mich (a new Regt lately attached to our Brigade) found a cow which had been dead for several days and being a little meat hungry they went to work and cut meat from the cow and carried it to camp and ate it." It was not just the spectacle of dead animals and rotten meat that disgusted Holford; as a veteran of battle he had seen far worse. What disgusted Holford was seeing men reduce themselves to hyenas. Somehow the dehumanization implicit in that selfish and sickening act was greater than that of killing and wounding in battle, for it showed men turned into beasts.[36]

Dehumanizing treatment was inflicted from outside; it might be resisted. Psychological transformation was more insidious. The

changes that soldiering made in men might be impossible to erad-
icate. The Assistant Surgeon of the 12th Michigan observed, "Soldiering is certainly not beneficial to the mind, and the large lists
of sick do not look as if it improved the bodily health much. I think
it certainly engenders laziness." He attributed this laziness to "the
alternation of very hard work, which is compulsory, and nothing
at all to do, with very few resources for amusement." Laziness,
unfortunately, might become a permanent part of the volunteer's
personality. The Surgeon feared, "When the war is over if that
happy time ever comes, I believe the greater part of them will join
the regular service, from sheer unfittness for anything else."[37]

The Union surgeon was echoed by Confederate soldiers. Henry
Greer wrote his mother from the lines near Petersburg, "If I stay
much longer in service I fear that I will never be fit for anything
but the army." Richard Webb, a regimental chaplain, may have
been more worried about the changes he detected in himself. "This
is a very demoralized kind of life. So hardening to human feelings.
I can now walk over a battlefield and see the ground strewed with
dead bodies, or see a man's lim amputated without any of that
tendency of fainting that the sight of blood used to cause." The
irony was that serving as chaplain hardened Webb's feelings at a
time when a chaplain was particularly valued by other frightened
men for his sensitivity.[38]

In some cases, men were surprised by the direction of the moral
transformation engendered by war. One Confederate soon learned
that "War is a strange scale for measuring men." He described a
fellow soldier, from whom nobody expected very much, who "made
as good a soldier as there was in the Regiment. Cool and brave in
battle and always on hand and never shirking duty in camp." This
man proved a far better soldier than "others who occupied honorable positions in society." A New York regiment enlisted one of
its soldiers after finding him sleeping drunkenly in a lumberyard.
"He was dirty filthy and covered with vermin." They exchanged
his rags for a new uniform. John Fleming remembered that "Strange
as it may appear, that man became very steady, and one of the
cleanest men and best soldiers we had." While such improvements
in character were no doubt welcome, they also served to reinforce

the distance felt between civilian life and the life of the soldier. These reformations were only extreme examples of how little one's peacetime identity seemed to relate to one's soldiering.[39]

The families back home shared the fears that the Civil War experience would change men beyond recognition. Soldiers frequently reassured wives and parents in their letters that they would not change or that their love was constant, apparently responding to the distressed queries of their loved one. Such fears found their expression whether those they possessed wanted to admit them or not. A dream about her husband terrified one Georgia woman. She dreamed he had gone mad and had to be brought home. "I thought you would not speak to me. I thought all you wanted to do was to fill up the roads with logs and brush so that Lincoln's Army could not pass through the country. it pestered me worse than any dream I ever dreamed before but I hope there is nothing of it." Such a dream revealed the fear on the woman's part that the war, which ironically was often cast as a defense of the home, would alienate husbands and fathers from their families.[40]

In most cases the transformation experienced by Civil War soldiers was not as dramatic or as clear-cut as that from drunkard to model soldier, devoted husband to madman, or man to beast. Men found that the war called forth a broad array of emotional responses. One of the most perceptive analysts of the psychology of soldiering was a Union soldier, James T. Miller. While Miller's letters home reveal him to be a man particularly concerned with the ways war was influencing his character, his observations probably applied to men less articulate and introspective.

The battle of Chancellorsville sparked Miller's self-scrutiny. In May 1863 he wrote home, "i can hardly make it seem possible that three short weeks ago that i was rite in the thickest of a terrible battle but such is a soldiers life. . . ." Miller confessed that such a life had its appeal "for a brave reckless man who has no family even in war times it has a good many charms and i think i can begin to understand something of the love an old sailor has for his ship and dangers of the Ocean." The appeal, in part, may have been aesthetic. A month after Chancellorsville, Miller explained to his parents, "steadyness under fire is the great beauty of a soldier[.]"

One is reminded that Robert E. Lee, watching the advance of Burnside's troops at Fredericksburg, said, "It is well that war is so terrible; we should grow too fond of it."[41]

Miller analyzed at length the emotions experienced by the soldier. He admitted the danger inherent in war, but explained "in regard to the danger I have passed through that part is very pleasent[.]" Soldiers amused themselves after battle by sitting around campfires and laughing over stories of "hairbreadth escapes" told in a "gay reckless carless way." An observer "would be very apt to think that we were the happiest set of men" he had ever seen.

"But if you should go with us to the battle filed and see those that are so gay thier faces pale and thier nervs tremblings and see an ankziety on every countenance almost bordering on fear," Miller said, "you would be very apt to think we were all a set of cowardly poltrouns[.]" The soldiers should be imagined this way "just before the fight begins and the enemy is in sight and the dul ominous silence that generaly takes places before the battle begins[.]" The soldier does not fear the dangers he has been through already, but he fears those that are to come.

Once skirmishers had been deployed, and the firing of cannons and small arms had begun, Miller observed that the soldiers' expressions changed remarkably. They could now "see the solid columns of the foe advance in plain sight every man seeming to step as proudly and steadily as if on parad and even while the artilery tears large gaps in thier line still on they come hardly faltiring for a moment[.]" This spectacle of war left the men still pale, "but see the firm compressed lips the eye fixed and [persevering?] and blood shot and the muscels rigid and the veins corugated and knoted and looking more like fiends than men[.]" When the order to charge came, "away we in to the very jaws of death and never for one moment faltering but yeling like devils up to the mouths of the Canon and then to hear the wild triumphant cheer[.]" Yet in a few hours these men who had resembled devils would be ministering to the wounded left on the field, both friends and enemies, "with the kindness and tenderness of a woman[.]" Miller concluded that, "by the time you have seen this you will begin to think that a soldier has as many carackters as a cat is said to have lives[.]"[42]

Miller's description points to the fact that a soldier could not be well-defined in simple terms—either as patriotic hero or as savage beast. The war demanded a full range of responses from men. Miller understood that "a soldiers life is a sucession of extreems, first a long period of inactivity folowed by a time when all his energies both mental and phsical are taxed to the utmost[.]" The rapid and extreme changes that men underwent increased the anxiety created by the war. No one "character" would serve for a man in such an environment.[43]

This was true in other ways. The Massachusetts college student, Samuel Storrow, wrote home about the various physical tasks in which military life required proficiency. "When I get home I shall be qualified for any position, either that of a boot black, a cleaner of brasses, a washer–(wo)man, cook, chambermaid, hewer of wood & drawer of water, or, failing in all these I can turn beggar & go from door to door asking for 'broken vittles'. In all these I should feel prefectly at home by long practise therein." Storrow was middle class and was perhaps more amused—or chagrined—by his new roles than most soldiers were. But the occupations he lists were all notable for their lack of dignity. Most of them were associated with servants and other dependents; beggars commanded even less respect; and "hewer of wood & drawer of water" was a Biblical phrase that usually denoted a slave. These demeaning roles were unwelcome additions to one's image as a soldier and hero; they were ways in which military life broke down civilian ideas of status and identity.[44]

Another contradiction experienced by the soldier was that between his image of the volunteer as the preeminently virtuous patriot and the reality of the men with whom he shared army life. Where he had expected to find paragons, he found mortal men. Both the Union and Confederate armies had their share of petty thieves, drunkards, slackers, and other lowlife.

The camp was simultaneously immoral and virtuous, full of temptation and full of piety. Christopher Keller of the 124th Illinois was shocked by the temptations to vice open to men when they first went into camp after his regiment was raised in the fall of 1862. Apparently the other men of his company were shocked as well, for they soon voted to have their captain teach a regular Bible class. Shortly after their arrival Keller wrote a description of his camp that caught the two contrary impulses displayed there. "My bunkmate is reading his bible and in the bunk below they are having a prayer meeting on a small scale while others are cutting up, some swearing, some laughing, some writing, and others reading." He concluded that camp was "the place to see human nature in all its different varieties."[45]

Luther C. Furst, who volunteered early in the war, noted that "The history of the four kings" was the most popular book in camp. His discouragement with the immorality of the camp was deepened by his belief that the war was brought on by national wickedness. And a soldier in the 140th New York observed that the only reason many men in camp knew when it was Sunday was that stores were closed that day and they could buy no liquor.[46]

One Confederate pronounced camp "the last place for me or any other sivil man." The noise and misconduct of his fellow volunteers appalled him. And another deplored the absence of religion in camp. "I haven't heard a sermon in I can't tell when. You hear no more talk about religion here than if there was no such thing. The army is more demoralizing than I ever dreamed of. Three-fourths I recon, of the officers and men in this Regiment are profane swearers and card players."[47]

The contradiction between image and reality, the excitement and fear of combat, the psychological exhaustion caused by the extremes in a soldier's life, the dehumanization of the army, even the risk of bestialization—the volunteer had to suffer all these to fight for his cause. It is not surprising that he sometimes felt resentful of those who had remained at home and that he acquired a new identity as a soldier. It is not even surprising that some soldiers did act like the beasts that most soldiers feared they might become.

After the surrender of Confederate Gen. Joseph E. Johnston's army, Union Gen. W. T. Sherman marched his victorious soldiers north from Bennett Place, North Carolina, to Washington, D.C. Along the way they stopped to visit the battlefields of the east, where the Army of the Potomac had long struggled with Robert E. Lee's forces. Robert Strong's company passed through the Wilderness, where one of the greatest battles of the war had been fought. "Right in the line of breastworks stood a lone house," Strong remembered. "When we passed the house it was occupied only by women, not a single living man. They were surrounded by the bones of thousands of dead men."

The women in the house came to the door to watch the Union soldiers march by. One of Strong's fellow soldiers had picked up a skull from the battlefield. He greeted the women and asked them, "Did you have any friends in this fight?"

One of them replied her brother had been killed in the battle.

"Here is his head," the soldier said, and "tossed the skull in among them."[48]

The soldiers of the Civil War did not escape the psychological terror most associated with war: the full shock of the horrors of combat. A surgeon with the Army of the Ohio expressed both the romanticism that led some men willingly to war and the reality ultimately encountered. Joshua Taylor Bradford felt "the attraction of war and *fascination* of its *pomp* and *glitter*" as the army marched in February 1862, "with banners flying and music filling the air with melody." The army passed crowds of spectators, cheering it on. Nine days later, as Buell's columns left behind sick men who had fallen out, the surgeon commented on the pathos of war. And in March, when he visited military hospitals in Nashville and saw "hundreds, yea, thousands, in their narrow *bunks,* some dead Some dying, and many tossing the 'wild and fevered limbs in delerious forebodings,' " he found the sight "a sermon preached to the understanding, more potent than words." He called it "a humiliating evidence of war." A month later he participated in the battle of Shiloh.[49]

Eric Leed, in *No Man's Land,* a study of World War I soldiers, suggests that the changes produced in soldiers by exposure to the realities of war are more than psychological. He argues that they are also cultural stereotypes—that the disillusioned soldier is just as much a cultural artifact as the innocent volunteer. The classic point at which disillusionment occurs, whether in fiction or in the experience of the Civil War soldier, is battle—the soldier's initiation into large-scale horror.[50]

Many soldiers awaited their first battle impatiently; they felt eager to prove their courage and to defeat the enemy. One Confederate wrote a friend, "I want to be in one Battle, just for the curiosity of the thing." An Illinois soldier fretted that the war might be over before he had a chance to fight in battle. "I sometimes feel as if the war was to end now I would never dare to say I had been a soldier. I do not feel as if I had earned it." He explained his desire to participate in a battle by saying, "I hope we will have something to do not because I *want* to get into a fight but if there is fighting to do I am willing to bear my share so as to have this war over as soon as possible so I if alive can return home. . . ."[51]

The disillusionment that followed such eagerness is predictable. One Union soldier had complained when he was promoted to Ordnance Sergeant as it diminished his chance of fighting; "when I think of you & the babies I am almost glad for what would you do if I should be kiled but that is not what I came for I came to fight & kill and come back[.]" A year and a half later he wrote his wife, "it makes me laugh to see the papers talk about this regiment and that and that the men ar eager for a chanc to get at the enemy   all   in   your eyes, thare is none that wants to fight or will if they can keep clear of it."[52]

The actual experience of battle horrified some men. One Confederate wrote home after his first battle, "I have bin in one battle and that satisfied me with war and I would beg to be excused next time for I tell you that there cannons and the shot and shell flying as thick as hail and the grape and cannister flying between the shot and shells." The battle had been furious; "there was a [patch] of woods behind the gun that we was at work at and to look back through the woods and it looked like the trees were falling faster than a hundred men could cut them down with axes and the ground was torn all to peaces holes large enough to bury a horse and so thick that I did not see how a man escaped for it looked like there was not room any where for a man to stand up nor lay down without being hit by a shot or shell[.]" A Union soldier who survived the inferno at Cold Harbor simply noted, "God has spared me this time   I pray he will spare me to return to you alive & well. I shan't reinlist."[53]

Shiloh was the first great battle in which many western soldiers participated. One Confederate, who told of seeing the branches of springs all colored with blood, wrote a correspondent, "you could never form an idea of the horrors of actual war unless you saw the battlefields while the conflict is progressing." He explained that "Death in every awful form, if it really be death, is a pleasant sight in comparision to the fearfully and mortally wounded. Some crying, oh, my wife, my children, others, my Mother, my sisters, my brother, etc. any and all of these you will hear while some pray to God to have mercy and others die cursing the 'Yankee sons of b——s.' "[54]

One Union soldier wrote after Shiloh, "I have seen since I have been here what I never saw before and what I never want to witness again." George W. Crosley, an Iowan, admitted he could not describe the battle, but tried to evoke the quality of the corpse-strewn field after the fighting had ceased by telling his correspondent to "call to mind all the horrible scenes of which you ever saw or heard. then put them all together and you can form some faint conception of the scene I witnessed in passing over this bloody Battlefield of Pittsburgh Landing."[55]

Yet horror did not entirely overwhelm men during their first battle; they responded in other ways as well. Crosley recalled that during the battle of Shiloh he did not fear death because he knew "I was in the performance of the noblest duty—except the worship of God that a man is ever permitted to perform here upon earth." And one thing that kept him from fear was the image of the woman he loved: "My dear Edna I have thought of you a hundred times while engaged in Battle. Your image would rise before me in the heat of conflict. . . ."[56]

Many men felt bolstered by such images. Shepherd Pryor, a Confederate, admitted to his wife that he thought of her and their children all through his first battle. A devout man, he thanked God he "had the nerve to stand it," but confessed, "I felt bad thinking I might be shot dead every moment[.]" The association of family with the bloodshed of battle might seem incongruous. But the men of the Civil War era quite sincerely regarded their participation in the war as an extension of their duty to protect their family. It was appropriate then that when that defense reached its moment of greatest stress, in battle, men should remember their sweethearts, wives, and children. Of course the duty for which these remembrances steadied men was that of killing.[57]

Both Crosley and Pryor also received consolation from their religious faith while they were in battle. This was not uncommon among Civil War soldiers. American Christians were particularly prone to attribute escape from death in battle to providential intervention, the result of prayer and devotion. "I have not Received as much as a sratch," R. F. Eppes wrote after the Seven Days Battles. "Surely God has been with mee hee has kept me in the hollow of his hand Surely he has heard theese heart pleadings of those near and dear ones at home for the Fervent Effectual Prairs of the Writious availeth much." Just as men might think of their loved ones to strengthen them in battle, they might also think of God.[58]

Other men found themselves caught up in the compulsions of battle from the first. One Confederate ran across a field with his company under Union fire in his first engagement; he positioned himself behind a tree where the soldier next to him was wounded. While they crossed the field, he "expected to get shot every step." But once he had gotten into a place he could return fire in relative safety, he "did not think of any thing but shooting yankees." Joseph Cotten was grateful for having been at Bull Run, even though Providence had prevented him from actually firing his gun. He described the battle as "sublime." Looking forward to at least "one more great struggle," he thought that it would suffice to win Confederate independence.[59]

Adjusting to battle meant more than facing and overcoming fear. As long as the soldier concentrated on the possibility—often probability, occasionally near-inevitability—of death, he could think of himself as a suffering patriot or a victim of war. Soldiers could not, however, free themselves from the moral burden of killing other men, for that was the nature of war. Despite the cruelty of the foe, some soldiers had trouble reconciling themselves to the idea that going to war for liberty meant killing their fellowmen. One expected savages, dupes, and mercenaries to murder without thought—the enemy was far more bloodthirsty than the legitimate ends of war demanded. But to embrace killing personally was to give way to impulses that society had long demanded be kept under strict self-restraint. Needless to say, different men felt very differently about the bloodshed of the Civil War.

When his company was first issued ammunition, Confederate Edmund DeWitt Patterson meditated, "These are the first 'Cartridges' that I have ever seen, and is it possible that we are actually to *kill men? Human beings?* . . . Yes, this is war and how hardened men must become." Richard M. Campbell made a diary entry as he hid in the bush watching for Union soldiers while on picket near Williamsburg: "My gun lies near at hand & my orders are to shoot whoever of my fellow man shows himself in front of the line. Such are the ways of war. It is a terrible scourge to any nation." The tension of the wait and of holding still wearied Campbell as if he "had been taking active exercise all day."[60]

In May 1863 Hugh Roden confessed that his fellow Union soldiers admired the late Stonewall Jackson a great deal. He explained, "there was something so daring a[nd] Noble in his way of fighting that made his enemys love him." Nonetheless, he said, "those men that praise him and his daring would not hesitate a moment if they had the Chance to send a Ball through his *heart*." The soldiers welcomed Jackson's death as they would the death of any rebel. "A soldier praised Bravery no mater where found a soldier will shake hands with the enemy one moment and shoot him the next— Such is war."

Roden recognized this mixture of respect and cold-blooded killing as only one of the psychological strains combat placed upon the soldier. War's "sickening sights" saddened men, yet its excitement made them "unconscious of danger." In battle "everything *home life* everything that is dear" was forgotten and a man changed into "a Blood thirsty Being." "all his Better feelings forsake him" He reached the condition where he not only could kill his fellowmen, men whose bravery he respected, but where he rejoiced in their deaths.[61]

Other soldiers showed more hesitation in embracing their role of killers. Numa Barned, who had fraternized with rebels against orders, said, "I don't know that I ever shot any one or dont want to know." He had shot at many Confederates but in battle his policy was "as long as I can see a man head in front of me I will shoot and never look at the consequences." If he knew he had shot a man he would not admit it; "I do not want any man's blood on my hands." Having volunteered to be a soldier, Barned seemed to think he could kill and not be a killer if he only remained ignorant of the deaths he caused. During the battle of Arkansas Post, Henry C. Bear thought of his wife's Dunkard convictions against war, but shot at the Confederates as much as anyone else did. But when the battle was over, and he and the rebel prisoners had shaken hands and shared a meal of bread and meat, he wrote his wife, "I hope I did not hit any person if they are Rebles."[62]

Hatred was one way soldiers reconciled themselves to killing. A Southern soldier wrote in 1863 that he hoped they could drive the Yankees from Virginia "without having to kill them, but if it is impossible to move them, I hope that we may slay them like wheat before the sythe in harvest time." He had some Christian scruples about his animosity toward the Northerners, but confessed, "if it is a sin to hate them, then I am guilty of the unpardonable one." After his first battle, Michael Donlon was no longer "afraid of the Rebel guns, for i have had one trial of them and I shot 4 men." He told his brother that he must not judge him a murderer for these killings, "for it wer my duty to Shoot as many of the Devils as I could and so i did."[63]

Sometimes the eagerness with which men approached battle surprised even themselves; it could represent a strange reversal of emotion. A Union soldier remembered a counterattack he participated in during the battle of Gettysburg: "Charge we did drove the foe like chaff before the wind. Strange it does seem to be these men that a few moments before was driving our Men Now threw Down their arms & begged for mercy at our hands   they said they could not stand our fire   Strange too, our men that A Short time before seemed to be almost Dead was now as full of life and vigor as men could be   As for myself, I never felt better then I did when making that grand charge"[64]

Other men felt no such excitement while in battle. William Nugent, a Confederate, wrote, "You have frequently heard of the wild excitement of battle. I experience no such feelings. There is a sense of depression continually working away at my heart, caused by a knowledge of the great suffering in store for large numbers of my fellow men, that is entirely antagonistic to any other emotions. It is doubtless true that I feel exhilarated when the enemy is driven back and our troops are cheering and advancing. Still I cannot be happy as some men are in a fight. I believe the whole machinery of war is indefensible on moral grounds, as a general proposition, and nothing but a sense of duty and the sacredness of our cause, could at all buoy me."[65]

Nonetheless, a soldier's lack of enthusiasm for battle made little difference so long as his loyalty remained constant. Duty and patriotism were as successful as hatred and bloodlust in motivating men to fight. The soldier who did not relish combat continued to fight—out of "a sense of duty"; because of "the sacredness of our cause." John Frederic Holahan, a Union soldier, explained that he belonged "to Uncle Sam, mentally, morally, and physically." Part of his obedience lay in fighting. He belonged to Uncle Sam "*Morally*—for my virtues and vices must correspond to that of my fellows; I must *lie* to rebels, *steal* from rebels and *kill* rebels;— Uncle Sam making vicarious atonement for these sins." Both the Confederate Nugent and the Federal Holahan resigned their moral sense to the greater cause, trusting that that would absolve them of any moral blame. And they continued to fight. Thus they reconciled their Christian morality with their patriotism and tried to soldier without becoming a soldier. Thus they resisted the final transformation from citizen to killer. Perhaps those men who embraced the warrior's role had an easier time of it.[66]

Before the battle of Agincourt, in Shakespeare's *Henry V*, John Bates, a common English soldier, explains to the disguised Henry that if the cause for which they fight is wrong, "our obedience to the king wipes the crime out of us." But Michael Williams, another soldier, adds, "But if the cause be not good, the king himself hath a heavy reckoning to make when all those legs and arms and heads, chopped off in a battle, shall join themselves in the latter day and cry all, 'We died at such a place,' some swearing, some crying for a surgeon, some upon their wives left poor behind them, some upon the debts they owe, some upon their children rawly left."

Perhaps there is less difference than is immediately apparent between the attitude of Bates and Williams and that of Union veteran Oliver Wendell Holmes when he praised the faith of the soldier. "But in the midst of doubt, in the collapse of creeds, there is one thing I do not doubt, that no man who lives in the same world with most of us can doubt, and that is the faith is true and adorable which leads a soldier to throw away his life in obedience to a blindly accepted duty, in a cause he little understands, in a plan of campaign of which he has no notion, under tactics of which he does not see the use." But where the Shakespearian soldiers at least hope that the cause they fight for blindly is just, the modern man is reduced, in relativist fashion, to justifying the cause because of the soldier's faith.

The Civil War volunteer, however, was certain that his cause was just. It was not simply the cause of the king—or of Uncle Sam. In a democratic society the volunteer had helped make the decision to go to war. The cause of the Union or of the South was bound up with one's community, one's home and family, and one's God. That is what allowed men like Nugent and Holahan to fight when they feared fighting was immoral, and that was why the Civil War volunteer not only submitted to his transformation into a soldier, but took pride in it. Ultimately, the worth of the cause was the worth of the soldier.

In 1864 a soldier reflected on the death of his comrades. He believed the people back home said of those who died for their country, "He was nobody but a soldier. We will enjoy the rights that he died for. We care not who suffers death for the good of the country. We will undo all that they can do." The men who said such things must shut up or be silenced. The soldier threatened, "The day is fast coming when such men will have to curtail the cowardly and unruly tongues that hang in their heads or they will fill a grave more degrading than that of a soldier."[67]

In order to make war, men had transformed themselves—from citizen to soldier. Men who had changed themselves, who felt increasing resentment toward civilian society, predictably demanded that society at large be changed. Part of the soldiers' transformation was learning to endure—and value—discipline. That was not the only discipline they thought war required. The soldiers began to ask that those who stayed at home be disciplined as well.

The soldiers feared that the enemy, so much less scrupulous than they, had a significant—perhaps overwhelming—advantage making war. Their society was free and open, the enemy's tyrannically efficient. Their society let dissent, even treason, have its voice; the enemy's was united—perhaps by deceit and force, but nonetheless united. The soldiers' belief in the repressiveness of enemy society not only informed his attitudes toward the enemy: it was a justification of the war he fought. Indeed, this belief protected his faith in representative institutions—no democracy would wage the unjust war that the enemy waged. But democracy had two flanks, and this defense left one uncovered. What if democracy was not compatible with making war successfully? Men wanted to fight the other's tyrannical society, but they worried that a successful war would require them to emulate their enemy's tyranny. And as they made their own sacrifices, they became less reluctant to advocate discipline for those who stayed behind.

One of the most important mechanisms for enforcing support for the war was conscription. First the Confederacy, then the Union had to draft men into the army. This was a radical departure from earlier American practice—and it was one that soldiers in the field generally welcomed. After all, they had already volunteered and they were not too concerned if the stay-at-homes were forced to come into the field. Besides, whatever the constitutional scruples offended by the act, the soldiers knew that the larger their army, the better the chances for victory. Few resolved the issue as straightforwardly as Confederate Edwin H. Fay did, but many would have shared his sentiments: "I think the act tyrannical but am satisfied it is the speediest way to put an end to the war." Fay was particularly pleased that the act would bring in "strong young speculators under 35."[68]

Since Northern soldiers fought not only for liberty but for a strong national government to defend it, they had fewer qualms about conscription. Some of them welcomed it as confirmation of the government's power. One officer believed that "the enforcement of this Draft is of more vital importance than the most brilliant victories in the Field." He did not want the war to end without "the Governments rights to the Services of all her Citizens" confirmed. "The *Individual* power of the Government to *Command* her Subject must go hand in hand with that other fact that all the just Powers of the Government are derived from the governed."[69]

Some soldiers tried to hide the "tyranny" of conscription by disparaging those who raised the charge. A Texas soldier wrote that "Some here whose 12 months is nearly out effect to be afraid a dangerous power has been used—that conscription is made only by tyrants, but I rather think that the men who talk thus have other fears beside those for Constitutional liberty." The Confederate army that was fighting for true Constitutional liberty needed men—volunteers or conscripts—to win; without victory there would be no liberty. "Afraid our liberties are suffering violence forsooth— they had better *help* achieve it first, then they may become its defenders." James Miller could not understand why "the loyal North cannot make as large sacrifices to suporte the constitution and the laws as the rebles can to destroy them." "Rather than see this acursed rebelion succede i hope that they will draft every man in the northern states from fifteen to sixty and bring them all into the field." Sgt. George Jewett, who feared that most draftees from his hometown would buy their way out, had no sympathy whatsoever for conscripts—if they had volunteered at the beginning of the war their enlistments would be nearly expired, and the North, having had sufficient men in its armies, would have won the war already. Soldiers believed that men who were not willing to fight for their rights had thereby renounced them: they had no right to resist conscription.[70]

Men in the battle lines very easily wrote of bringing the stay-at-homes into the army: men who would not fight for their rights must be made to do so. But while most soldiers were eager that shirkers be drafted, they were also reluctant that their brothers, sons, or fathers be exposed to the hardships of military life. Sergeant Jewett, who advocated drafting those who would not enlist, told his brother, "I am glad that father is too old to be drafted, and that you are too young, and I hope Bill won't be taken, as I think one is enough from *our* family, and don't want any more to go out of it." His attitude was far from unique. A soldier could advocate conscription—"No *man* can stay at home *now*"—at the same moment he rejoiced that his own brother was exempt. He might advise his brothers, "Do as I tell you, do not do as I did," and tell them to stay home. E. J. Lee was disappointed when the young men in Union Parish did not join the army, but he wrote his friends advising them not to volunteer and hoped they would avoid conscription—"you could not stand the fairs and hardships of a soldier." A Virginia soldier wrote his sister in 1864 that "Pa had Better stay at home." Another soldier told his father to lie about his age and stay out of the army: "there are a plenty of men who do it." James T. Binion of the 10th Georgia begged his brother to stay out of the army.[71]

These men were not simply being hypocritical. They saw themselves as representing their families. After their family had provided one son for the cause, it should not be called upon to provide another, until less patriotic families had done their part. Soldiers saw conscription as an instrument that would enforce equity. All would benefit from victory; all should share the burdens of war equally. As far as the volunteer was concerned, the draft was not unfair to those whom it affected; rather, their absence from the army was unfair to those who had volunteered. The refusal of those at home to enlist made the draft necessary.

In soldiers' eyes, this refusal reflected a larger problem: a lack of total commitment to the war on the part of those outside of the army. Enforcing the draft was one way to demonstrate the nation's power to prosecute the war. Another way would be to silence those who spoke against the war. Soldiers began to demand that those who did not fight would not speak; "it is real mean to stay at Home and discuss war affairs." Political dissent could destroy the people's will to fight. Soldiers were never sure of anyone's patriotism apart from the army; in fact, fellow soldiers often shocked them by indifference or war-weariness. Civilians back home, particularly men who did not emulate the soldier's sacrifice, could not be relied upon. Furthermore, civilians might go so far as to infect the army itself with their fecklessness, destroying its will to fight. Samuel Storrow felt "perfectly sick at heart" when his fellow soldiers expressed defeatism. "To hear *men* avow openly and boldly their conviction that the restoration of the Union by force of arms is hopeless, that the war is worse than useless, that all this outpouring of noble blood is a fruitless sacrifice and will meet with no fit recompense, this and more of the same kind of talk have I been listening to." He called this mental cowardice. Soldiers sought its origins in civilian society, in politics and newspapers.[72]

Henry Pippitt indignantly wrote his mother upon the receipt of two newspapers, asking that she never send them to him again. Instead, she should send him loyal papers. He gave her a rule of thumb for recognizing a secesh newspaper: if the paper said "the Confederates have crossed the Potomac," instead of "the rebels have crossed the Potomac," it was a secession paper. If Pippitt's identification of disloyal newspapers lacked sophistication, it still represented the profound distrust soldiers had for newspapers. Men feared dissent in civilian society; newspaper editors spread that poison. Both Confederate and Union soldiers lamented the ways newspapers undermined morale within and without the army. Soldiers faulted newspapers for lying, for criticizing the war effort, and for demoralizing both the army and the general public. One Confederate complained that when the newspapers attacked the government, "they do it in such a way as, if believed, to undermine all confidence in them." After all, "confidence is indispensible to success. How can our people be expected to make the heavy sacrifices now required of them if they believe that imbecility presides at Richmond and madness governs at our Army Headquarters?" When newspapers threatened the will to make war, they became dangerous. Suppression was required. Samuel Eells, an anti-Copperhead soldier, welcomed the order forbidding circulation of the Chicago *Times* in his department of the army; the paper was nothing but "a great source of consolation" to rebels. Soldiers forgot that previously they claimed the enemy's denial of freedom of the press had been prime evidence of despotism. Now they saw an unbridled press as an aid to the destruction of the liberties for which they fought.[73]

In the North, Peace Democrats became known as Copperheads. Many soldiers did not view them as a legitimate opposition. For them, those who wanted to end the war with anything less than total victory were traitors, and their dissent dangerous. One soldier warned that "the Coperheads of the North had better crawl down on there neese and hide themselves"—the Union army had enough men to take care of the rebels and whip all the traitors at home. Others called for the government silencing "rebels at home" or sending the soldiers to do so: "we would make short work of it if we only had the chance."[74]

Sgt. Caleb Blanchard complained of the way the Democrats in his regiment grumbled about the war. When he heard soldiers criticizing the administration or predicting Southern victory, he "told them to shut their head and stop talking treason or they would be handled as traitors." He explained that "to hear them talk so" was "against my liberty and rights." Blanchard could not silence the Democrats at home as well. In March 1863 he wished that "a portion of our army could be a home and shoot the traitors there." "it will not be safe from them to show their faces when the union patriots get back." He blamed the Copperheads for the lack of volunteers in 1863 and wished that the Northern Copperheads would reveal their true allegiance by joining the Confederate army. Three months later, during Lee's invasion, Blanchard longed for "an army of a million men in the North" to "march through and make peace there annihilite the copperheads."[75]

Blanchard's distrust of Democrats extended beyond common soldiers and civilians. He believed that General McClellan, who botched the Peninsula campaign and permitted Lee's army to escape after the battle of Antietam, had been motivated by treason. He thought that politicians deliberately prolonged the war because they feared successful generals would prove rivals for the voters' affections.[76]

Northern volunteers were more prone to detect disloyalty in their commanding officers than Southern soldiers were in theirs. This was particularly true of the period before emancipation became a policy and the need to break the Southern will became commonly accepted. Joseph Lester believed "our Generals are tinctured with the same leaven the Rebels are." They wished to replace "Republican Institutions" with monarchy, destroy "Free Thought and Speech," and extend slavery.[77]

"Disloyalty"—if that is the right word to use—in the Confederacy went to further extremes than it did in the North and was met with more stringent repression. A Confederate in north Georgia reported the hanging of a local parson who had helped organize an anti-war meeting. "his olest daughter was up hear when he was hung & I supoze taken him home[.]" The Confederate government had arrested other local men for the same offense of disloyalty. The Confederate government was remarkably careful about freedom of speech in many ways—its record was considerably better than that of the Union—but when faced with strong Unionist insurgency, it retaliated viciously.[78]

Soldiers tried to justify the denial of rights to dissenters by arguing that they had lost them by their unpatriotic behavior. Douglas Cater said of Confederates at large, "There are those who deserve liberty and peace. There are those who do not." Another Confederate said of the people at home, "if it was not for the women & children they ought to be under Lincoln." A Northern general wrote that "The man who doesn't give hearty support to our bleeding country in this day of our country's trial is not worthy to be a descendant of our forefathers, and he ought to be denied the protection of our laws and shipped at once to South America, where they will have a government that suits them." Dissenters, whether or not they cherished their own rights, did not have the right to give up the rights of soldiers and their families. Soldiers wanted them punished.[79]

The vengeance soldiers took against the people at home was rhetorical: it served to relieve feelings of bitterness, but was not acted on. While their governments did repress dissent—the Confederacy far less so than the Union—soldiers themselves almost never engaged in violence against their own citizens, no matter what their threats. Still, as the war went on, they habituated themselves to the notion of repression. Power joined liberty as a fundamental American value.

How much this habit of thought, even though it was rarely acted on, influenced postwar political behavior is a matter of speculation. In the South both Republicans and Populists, white and black, would be suppressed violently by a society intent on forcing unity. In the North the years following the war would witness state-sponsored violence against the labor movement and "foreign" anarchists and socialists. The men who wielded repressive power would see themselves as tough-minded realists free from sentimentality. Perhaps tough-mindedness was a legacy of the Civil War.

But the appeal of power during the Civil War was not unalloyed. Power was to be a tool of the righteous, for the righteous had to discipline the wicked. The erring section must be punished; the traitors at home must be forced to obey; even the patriot volunteer must be subject to military discipline. The war itself could be seen as God's chastisement of His disobedient American children. "It is Gods inexorable Law," a Northern volunteer explained, "that wrong 'doing' must receive Punishment, whether it is Nations or Individuals, and our Sin has found us out, and the Penalty is being meted out to us." A Confederate private believed that when a nation became too proud, "War has been the means which the Great Creator has resorted to, to humble that Nation." Northern and Southern soldiers alike could agree the ultimate cause of the Civil War was American sin.[80]

FOUR

The Landscape of War:
The Union Soldier
Views the South

Soldiers wrote their letters on anything handy—backs of military forms, old brown paper, letters from home. But they preferred proper stationery, and many varieties of letter paper for soldiers and other patriots were marketed during the war years. Most of them had the conventional symbols one might well expect—flags, cannon, sentries in blue (or gray), swords, eagles.

One Northern stationery—a not very popular one, judging from the infrequency of its appearance in preserved collections—offered a much less warlike motif, one that was pastoral and patriotic. A young man, with foppish curls, a flowing tie, and a broad-brimmed hat, is pictured seated on a bale of wheat; he is surrounded by agricultural implements and has clearly, despite his elegant appearance, harvested the grain himself. The words that accompany the picture make the ideological point; the scene presents "The way our Union Boys are raised."[1]

Northern soldiers went to war convinced of the industry and virtue of "Union Boys." They also had a corresponding belief in the superiority of Northern civilization. They thought that Southerners and the culture that had produced them were inferior. The Union soldier who campaigned in the South found evidence of this inferior culture all about him. He interpreted the various elements of the landscape in order to understand that culture. He wrote home lengthy descriptions of Southern climate, agriculture, housing, and cities; he was fascinated by the Southern civilian population, white and black, hostile and friendly. And he drew conclusions about the nature of Southern society and what needed to be done to it in order to defeat rebellion and establish loyalty.[2]

The observations made by Northern soldiers were not new. Pre-war travelers had come to many of the same conclusions about the South; Frederick Law Olmsted is only the most famous of a group of Northern critics. The earlier travelers, however, could not act on their observations—if a plantation displeased them, they could not put it to the torch. Soldiers could. Their preconceptions of the South and their perceptions of it when they came through it contributed significantly to their understanding of the war's meaning.

Even though the soldier had gone to war with the belief that the South was an integral part of the United States, he often talked about it as if it were a foreign country. In the South the soldier found signs of sloth—decaying houses, ill-tended fields, poverty. He also found evidence indicating to him that there was indeed a Slave Power conspiracy and that most Southern whites were kept in subjugation by the slaveholding aristocrats. And finally, he found Southern blacks to be exotic beings whom he judged to be dirty, ignorant, superstitious, and lazy, and he was perplexed about what role they would play in postwar America. When the Union soldier returned home in 1865, he became a voter whose wartime experience would help determine what policies he thought should be applied to the defeated section.

The Union soldiers' reactions to Southern culture influenced their behavior while they occupied Southern soil. Union soldiers were, comparatively speaking, well-behaved while they were in the South. But many of them acted in ways that most Southern whites, many Southern blacks, and not a few of their fellow soldiers regarded as cruel and immoral. Theft and vandalism were perhaps the most common vices. Rape and murder, while rare, were not unknown. Cultural contempt—the sense that one was in a foreign and backward country—made such actions easier. Furthermore, some Northern soldiers came to think of the war itself as a war against the Southern way of life. Burning plantations were only the concrete manifestation of the desire to remake the South in the North's image. That desire too could be justified only by a belief in the South's cultural and moral inferiority.

Of course, Union soldiers saw many new sights before they reached the South. Northern culture itself was hardly monolithic. For example, one New Yorker happily reported to his parents that the people in York, Pennsylvania, and the surrounding countryside acted far friendlier and much less haughty than those of New York, although he found their "Dutch" difficult to understand. A Massachusetts soldier passed through Jersey City on his way to the front. He liked the city, but thought it secessionist. "The only demonstration made was by a little girl about 8 years old who said three cheers for the Union." Soldiers in the West wrote home descriptions of the farming areas they passed through. In particular, southern Indiana and Illinois came in for comment. The South, it seemed, did not necessarily begin at the Mason-Dixon line. One soldier from northern Illinois admitted that the people of the southern part of the state did not look very much different from those back home, but he pointed out a few differences which many Union soldiers associated with Rebeldom. Their teams were poor; they wore "butternut-colored"—i.e., home-dyed—clothes; and they used a "Southern" vocabulary.[3]

The South indeed did possess a material folk culture different from that of the North in terms of food, housing, farming techniques and implements, and furniture. In fact, folklorists have distinguished between two general Southern folk regions: the Upland South, with a heavier Scotch-Irish and German influence, and the Lowland South, with a predominantly English folk culture. African influences were greater in the Lowland South.

But folk culture is a term applicable to regions north of the Mason-Dixon line as well. Federal soldiers were not simply representatives of a "modernizing society" with a "popular" culture encountering pockets of resistance to change and an old-fashioned Southern folk culture. Folk culture persisted in the North; a Northern soldier commenting on Southern customs and manners was likely to be comparing them to his own folk culture.

Furthermore, there was not a unified Northern folk culture. Scholars have identified three primary Northern cultural groups: a Northern culture based on English culture—significantly, however, a culture derived from different parts of England than Lowland Southern culture—and centered in New England; a Mid-Atlantic folk culture, which added Germanic and Scotch-Irish elements to the English mixture and which contributed to the Southern Upland culture; and a Midwestern region where various cultures tended to form pockets rather than blend. But while the Union soldier noted Northern regional differences, they did not seem to him as large as the differences he encountered in Dixie, the enemy's territory. Nor did he spend as much time during the war in the North as he did in the South.[4]

One place barely within the North's boundaries that the soldiers did frequently visit and that they explored with great curiosity was Washington, D.C.—a city that many then and now would have been reluctant to call Northern. Their attitudes toward the nation's capital, which most saw for the first time during the Civil War, in some ways foreshadowed the attitudes they would have toward landscape farther south.

A soldier might go to the Capitol, the Smithsonian Institution, the Treasury Building, and the War Department—"these places are worthwhile to visit." Later, he could cross the Potomac to Alexandria, where he might worship at George Washington's old church—perhaps even sit in the general's pew and use the Washington family hymnbook. At the Patent Office one might admire a dress suit of Washington's and the coat Jackson had worn at the Battle of New Orleans. Wilbur Fisk particularly enjoyed visiting the Patent Office, where he examined "the marvellous displays of Yankee ingenuity exhibited there." Fisk was a Vermonter.[5]

Despite the many attractions of Washington, many soldiers found the city disappointing. George Bates thought Washington the ugliest city that his regiment passed through en route from Connecticut to Alexandria. "The Capitol is a splendid building but for that Washington would hardly pass for a great City." John Faller was also disappointed in Washington, "the most miserable, contemptible place I ever met with in my life." He claimed that the courthouse in his hometown, Carlisle, Pennsylvania, was more attractive than the Capitol itself—since the Capitol was still under construction in 1861, he may well have been right. Lucien Waters complained of "the worthlessness of the place." He admired the public buildings but thought "The stores & private buildings with a few noble exceptions almost unworthy of the name as compared with those at the North and the quality of buildings which should characterize a place like *Washington*." And the artistic soldier Charles

W. Reed, after lamenting the "shanties and mean looking brick houses inhabited by Irish Dutch and Negroes," and the pigs, ducks, and geese that filled the streets, proclaimed Washington too old-fashioned. "There appears to have been no advancement at all in architecture everything having an old and revolutionary appearance[.]"[6]

The soldiers' dissatisfaction with the national capital reveals much of the nineteenth century's attitudes toward landscape. The capital of a great and virtuous nation must look great and virtuous itself. The fact that Washington did not meet the expectations of the Union soldiers meant that it could not adequately represent all that they believed America to be. In the abstract, it might not matter whether Congress, the Cabinet, the Supreme Court—all the federal institutions that made up the American political system—conducted their business in marble palaces or in cheap, ugly buildings. But it did matter to the Union volunteers, because they believed that the visual aspects of a society should have an immediate relation to its true nature.

Therefore, we must not be surprised that these soldiers judged the South according to its appearance. When they reached the Confederate states, they would determine the nature of Southern society by what that society presented to the visitor's eye. The South would be judged—and found wanting—not simply by its institutions but by its landscape.

The final grisly act of sight-seeing in the capital was left for soldiers near Washington in April 1865. They could go into the city to view President Lincoln's body, which lay in state under the Rotunda of the Capitol. Pvt. Jeremiah T. Lockwood made the trip; he thought the President looked "very well."[7]

The South disappointed Capt. Howard Smith. He "had dreamed of the South as a land of orange groves, of bright winged birds, and sunny skies"—a land of romance. Serving in Suffolk, Virginia, he found the countryside "desolate and dreary," and the roads muddy. Suffolk boasted few birds and fewer orange trees. Captain Smith could only hope it was not "a fair specimen of the South," and that romantic beauty waited for him somewhere farther in Dixie.[8]

Smith and Northerners like him expected to find the legendary South that figured so prominently in minstrel songs and plantation myths. Even before the Civil War, the notion that the South was exotic and foreign, a region far removed from Yankee norms, was widespread among Northerners; the golden vision of the South served as a counterpoint to the savage vision of the South—both were embodied in books like *Uncle Tom's Cabin*. The romantic South was an integral part of American popular culture.[9]

The South did not always disappoint Northern soldiers who hoped for a tropical Elysium. A Connecticut man who remembered the farmers back home were busy "getting up a large wood pile to keep them warm," thought it strange to see Florida planting begin in February. "it dont seem as if their could be so much difference in the climate of the two states." Christopher Keller sent home a description of one Deep South curiosity: Spanish moss. John Augustine Johnson found the Mississippi River lined with orange trees and poor houses. The greatest curiosity he saw was an alligator; the soldiers fired at him without effect. And another soldier described "alligators as large as cows and twice as ugly."[10]

Of course, finding the South exotic only confirmed the Northerner's belief that it was in some ways a different culture. But far more soldiers were disappointed in what they found. It proved to be not a land of romance but a land of poverty, sloth, and slavery. Even romantic spots could be marked by Southern laziness—indeed, the results of laziness could add charm to the scene. A soldier admiring the falls of Sypsy Creek, Alabama, found there "a queer old mill, and a quaint little miller." The existence of a mill might smack of Northern enterprise, but the water trough had broken down, "and the little old fellow waits contentedly for high water to run his mill, instead of repairing his water trough."[11]

But, for the most part, the Union soldier found the South ugly and dreary. For example, John Crosby, a Connecticut sergeant, complained of the country along the Mississippi south of New Orleans. "The few houses we've seen are a kind of hut filled with nigger or poor dirty-looking white folks." And he thought "this Mississippi mud is the nastiest slipperiest stuff you ever saw."[12]

If Southern mud was bad, Southern insects were worse. Soldiers at Beaufort complained about the abundance of mosquitoes the place afforded. Orra B. Bailey suggested that their presence might even be an explanation of slavery: he himself would want at least three hundred slaves to keep the insects away from him. At Ship Island, "this most god forsaken spot," a spot as hot as hell in August, there were "mosquitoes, sand fleas, and the thousand and one bugs that infest us that Lt. Col. Allison says God Almighty could not find time to give a name to."[13]

Beyond mud and mosquitoes, the Northern soldier confronted Southern swamps. John Crosby wrote, "I thought I'd seen some swamps in trout fishing but these Louisiana swamp took all the conceit out of me, for the rail road runs the whole way through a swamp where the trees are all huge misshapened monsters, crowding each other into all sorts of fantastical shapes by the very luxuriance of their growth. their limbs all covered with long masses waving grey moss, their trunks embraced by every variety of climbing vine, while up out of the nasty stagnent black water grow huge rushes and all kinds of water plants climbing over and over each other till in their struggle they out topple themselves and tumble down in heaps, to become resting places for innumerable snakes and Alligators, as we came along we could get a glance at a heap of snakes so thick they were all done up in knots, next would be a devilish looking Alligator lying close to the top of water, with his head and tail out and paying no more attention to us than if he was a log, but Tom Marshall says that is no swamp at all, to some here, I don't want to get into them."[14]

Swamps, insects, and mud—all different than the North's but all naturally occurring features of the Southern landscape. Man-made things had a greater impact on Northern perceptions of the South. In a sense, an entire society can be judged by its houses, farms, towns, and cities. The Union soldier judged the South on its physical characteristics and found it wanting.

The map reveals one reason that Northerners found the South strange. Those Union soldiers who had grown up in the old Northwest or had come from the newly pioneered areas of the plains had lived in a landscape which had had the national grid system superimposed on it. This Jeffersonian ordering of the countryside ran straight lines and drew right angles over thousands of square miles of America. Roads followed the surveyor's ruler; towns, with courthouse squares, symbols of authority and republican institutions, appeared precisely at the intersections of these roads. Jefferson had designed a national pattern of replicable, equal units, to suit his dream of an egalitarian republic. One result of this was to give the Midwest a landscape characterized by monotony.[15]

Compared to this, what disorder, confusion, and illogic lodged in the Southern landscape. Towns were smaller, roads poor and irregular, much of the land still in frontier condition. Vast areas of the South, primarily in the uplands, were devoted to subsistence agriculture, and vast areas of the Lowland South were carved into those most unfamiliar organizations, plantations.

The Union armies entered the South from a variety of approaches: the Burnside Expedition to coastal North Carolina, for example, and the Butler Expedition to Louisiana. But the majority of Union soldiers served in armies that came to the South from the North. In the west, armies followed the Mississippi and other rivers as an invasion route, fighting first in Tennessee and Mississippi and ultimately marching under Sherman through Georgia to the Carolinas. In the east, where rivers lay athwart the road to Richmond, the Union armies fought primarily in northern and Tidewater Virginia.

Virginia did not generally make a favorable impression on the Northern soldier. Lewis Martin complained of the lack of towns in Virginia and found signs of Southern sloth in the state's plantations. Many of them were beautifully located and somewhat attractive; they could have been made "magnificently beautiful" if the owners kept the buildings, fences, and fields in good order. But the planters had neither industry nor ambition. Samuel S. Ely was struck by the contrast between people and countryside in West Virginia. The people lived in "miserable huts made of mud logs and sticks," erected in swamps, "so as to have the water convenient for family use and the mud for the amusement of the children and pigs, which from appearance herd together." The countryside was a series of magnificent mountains and charming valleys.[16]

Poor housing was a common theme in Northern letters. One soldier commented that the houses in northern Virginia were so old that they remained standing "from force of habit." Another complained there were only old-fashioned houses in the "great

Wilderness of VA." And a third noted that when his company came to Virginia, "The first house we came across was built of logs it being plastered between them. It was inhabited by negroes and judging from the little picaninnies it was quite a prosperous family."[17]

Just as Union soldiers in the East crossed the Potomac to find themselves in "the Wilderness," Union soldiers in the West experienced the ominous sensation of leaving civilization behind and referred to the Southern terrain in much the same terms. Michael Bright thought the area around Corinth "one of the most forsaken places" he had been in; the area south of the Tennessee River was "almost a Wilderness," with only a few widely scattered houses that hardly deserved the name.[18]

A Michigan captain was frankly contemptuous of the pretensions of Clifton, Tennessee, a town on the Tennessee River. By local standards, Clifton was a major city, but compared to "Yankee Towns of the same importance" it was "a miserable place." Captain Pierson thought this illustrated the difference between slave and free society—"since leaving Paducah, there is not a place that deserves the name of a village."

Still, Pierson marveled at the blooming roses and the fast-growing wheat along the Tennessee River and admitted that as they followed it southward into cotton country, the plantations became larger and better cultivated. When his regiment reached Corinth, Mississippi, they were pleased to find that not all the inhabitants had fled before them. In this area they saw attractive houses and some ladies living in them. A few of the latter even waved their handkerchiefs as the Yankees marched past.[19]

The plantations of Tennessee and Mississippi were in marked contrast to the hill country of the South. One Northern soldier described the area around Gallatin Tunnel, Tennessee, as "rough, hilly and barren." "The country all around us is wild, poor and uncultivated"; he observed, "the inhabitants look starved and poverty-stricken—but nothing else could be looked for considering the soil, and the broken and desolate condition of the land."[20]

Yankees thought few things more ludicrous than the pretensions of Southern hamlets that styled themselves towns or cities. Viewing Charles City, Virginia, John Fleming concluded that it got its name because "it was probably as easy to say city as anything else." A Michigan soldier wrote of another Southern town, "Cottonville is no place at all; if you abolish the name, there is nothing left." And Samuel Storrow observed, "The rule in North Carolina seems to be that it takes two houses to make a town & that three and a barn constitute a city."[21]

The South's lack of towns occasioned considerable comment from the Northern soldiers. This is hardly surprising. The town was a central institution in Northern society. It was the locus for politics, education, business, and the law. It symbolized the community; the companies that the soldiers belonged to were raised in the small towns of the North.[22]

In fact, the even smaller towns of the South served many of the same purposes. The South could no more have functioned without towns than the North could have. But because many parts of the South had barely emerged from the frontier, and because the plantations of the very largest slaveholders—miniature towns themselves—could provide some of the services offered by towns, many Southern towns remained small and unimpressive.[23]

To Northern eyes, it seemed that the Southern landscape lacked one of the most necessary institutions for a civilized society. They did not accept the ramshackle collection of buildings that constituted a Southern county seat as a real town at all. If the South did not possess these centers of law, politics, schooling, and business, the reason was clear: the South did not have any law, politics, education, or business that a civilized man would recognize. The absence of towns suggested that Southern society was as savage and undemocratic as the Union soldiers already believed.

Southern cities did not appear much better than the towns, when compared to those of the North. Lavalette Griffin wrote from Pensacola that Southerners were twenty-five years behind New York in the arts and sciences. He admitted that the city had some fine houses, but in the old-fashioned style and poor condition of the majority he saw the typical Southern "lack of energy and 'good-headedness' that there is in the North." If Northern men had the management of Pensacola harbor, it would become a thriving commercial city. Only the cemetery met with Griffin's approval: it was up-to-date. This cemetery, covered with flowers and shade trees "left to grow promiscuously as nature intended," satisfied Griffin's sentiments far more than Northern graveyards whose straight lines and punctual intervals did nothing to make death romantic.[24]

Thomas S. Howland, a Massachusetts soldier, wrote home from Atlanta. "At last I am here in the Gate City of the South. It is quite a place. There are more large buildings than in N[ew] B[edford] but they look rather shabby, many of them being built of poor brick. The streets are wide and generally very good though of course out of repair. The sidewalks are not paved except on the principal streets." The one thing he could find to praise was the abundance of trees growing alongside the streets. From Horace Snow's viewpoint, Petersburg, like most other Southern cities, revealed "lack of energy & enterprise in the inhabitants," with its "old-fashioned houses, narrow streets." Richmond impressed him rather more. Its streets were broad, well-paved and clean, and Main Street reminded him greatly of Pennsylvania Avenue, Washington. Richmond's buildings were more like Northern buildings. "There are very few of the old fashioned sloping roof, gable windowed, moss covered houses that one sees in Alexandria, Norfolk, Petersburg, and Lynchburg."[25]

Christopher Keller admired the beauty of houses in Lagrange, Tennessee, but thought it marred by the fact they were generally surrounded by "miserable negro huts." Furthermore, the white owners had fled the area and left the houses deserted; Union soldiers had little respect for abandoned property; the beautiful houses had been "left to ruin." Newton Wallace also commented unfavorably on the Southern practice of mingling white opulence and black misery. He said the effect of Alexandria, with its well-laid-out streets and squares and fine houses and gardens, was spoiled "to the eyes of Northern people" by the "Negro houses stuck in between the better ones."[26]

Wallace also gave a fair specimen of Yankee aesthetics when he praised Kingston as the most attractive town in North Carolina. Unlike other Southern cities, Kingston looked brand-new instead of "old-fashioned"—its houses had been built more recently and a railroad ran through the middle of town. Despite Kingston's charm, the soldiers "ransacked the place & got something to eat & burnt part of it." An Ohio soldier could refer to a Southern town as "beautifully situated on a branch of the Mursfreesboro & Chatanooga railroad."[27]

When a Northern soldier wished to speak disparagingly of Southern cities, "old-fashioned" was the pejorative term he used. Presumably the Northerners of the 1860s would have been amazed to see how many Southern cities created a thriving tourism industry from the old-fashioned houses and narrow streets that Progress passed by. And the railroad was beautiful to those who believed in Progress; it was Progress's most concrete symbol. There was nothing more absurd about finding beauty in the railroad train, even if it did spew out smoke and cinders, cut through the peaceful countryside, and trouble the world with noise, than there was in finding it in the broad lawns and stately houses of the Southern cotton plantations, with their miserable shacks and constant brutality.

Christopher Keller, who had been struck by the contrast between fine plantation houses and squalid slave quarters, discovered the same phenomenon in Southern ladies and their maidservants. A well-dressed and respectable lady might promenade down the street, yet be attended by a black woman clothed in filth and rags. Keller found the spectacle both disgusting and amusing. As the planter could build lovely homes and then live surrounded by poverty and wretched conditions, the lady would give herself airs and show no signs of realizing that the appearance of her slave could be in any way a commentary on her own elegance. What Keller observed was symptomatic of the psychology of the Old South. Southern whites simply closed certain sights from their vision. The misery of blacks was invisible and thus could not spoil the beauty they thought they had created in a slave society.[28]

The Northerners looked at the Southern landscape, however, and saw natural beauty disfigured by an inefficient and savage society. They could also admire the plantations of the wealthy, but they judged the South by a standard in which utility was part of the beauty of man-made things. In the 1860s the United States was still a predominantly rural nation; rural men predominated in the Union army. Not surprisingly, they examined Southern agriculture carefully. It too was found wanting.

It should not be forgotten that Europeans used the "poor" farming methods of the Indians as a justification for conquering their land. By not making the best use of his land, the savage lost all claim to it; without proper farming he did not "possess" the land. Furthermore, the charges made against Southern farming were the same as those made against colonial husbandry on the eve of the American Revolution. Bad ploughing, poor fences, and inefficient implements were characteristic of American farms according to the author of *American Husbandry*. Even in New England, where Puritan duty and Yankee thrift might be expected to demand neat farms, unpainted, weather-beaten houses were the norm.[29]

The years since the Revolution had seen the spread of commercial agriculture throughout the United States; the plantation economy was an example of this. But many segments of the South remained outside of the market economy; subsistence farming persisted the longest in the South. The Union soldier, who often talked as if he accepted classical notions of "economic man," rarely saw any virtue in subsistence farming or the desire for leisure. And he assumed, much as abolitionists did when talking of slaves, that if men did not embrace the work ethic, some social dislocation was at fault. The existence of "lazy" Southern whites was due to slavery. Ironically, since plantation slavery was geared to efficient production, the Northern soldier occasionally found the acres tended by slave labor more attractive than the fields worked—or neglected—by free labor. But in general, Southern agriculture did not please the Yankee.

Tidewater Virginia, where land exhausted by tobacco had been reclaimed by the forest after the planters had moved west, presented a particularly dreary spectacle to Northern soldiers. They could see cleared land and old plantations grown over with twenty-year-old pine; the countryside was full of wasteland, "rendered useless by poor cultivation." Lyman Foster, a Pennsylvanian, did not agree that Tidewater Virginia was farmed-out by the Civil War. Stationed at Gloucester Point, he could only marvel at the Virginia farmland and lament that the inhabitants did not know how to farm it. With the same land up north, he said, people "could live like kings." The spectacle of inefficient farming persuaded some soldiers of the immorality of slavery. "Old tobacco fields with the last ridges of the plow still visible grown up with pine fifty feet high were good representations of the wastefulness and wickedness of slavery," according to one Union soldier.[30]

Soldiers in the west reached similar conclusions. Michael Bright doubted that there was "a better State in the Union for wheat than Tennessee." The state's natural advantages, however, were lost, because of poor cultivation: "they don't know anything about farming down here." The reason for this ignorance he thought to be slavery, and he told his parents, "You can't form the remotest idea of what a curse Slavery is to our country, unless you travel in a State where it exists." Bright also observed that whatever their deficiencies in growing wheat and most other crops, the residents of Tennessee could raise cotton and tobacco "well enough." Cotton and tobacco were preeminently the crops raised by those farmers who had begun to embrace market values. Indeed, it had been a long-standing rebuke to the planters that they concentrated on cash crops to the exclusion of food crops, preferring to buy supplies from their profits. Market-oriented farmers were much more likely to own slaves. They were also much more likely to create the orderly, well-managed farms so dear to the hearts of Northern soldiers. Bright's harshest judgment of Tennesseans was directed at those who did not raise cotton; they were "the most forsaken looking creatures I have seen yet."

In the Huntsville area, however, Bright found another flaw in the slave system. The orchards were full of good fruit, but the slaves did not care for it very well. Bright attributed this to the fact that most of the planters were absentees, residing in Huntsville and only rarely visiting their plantations. Yet he also mentioned that the planters relied on overseers who intimidated the slaves thoroughly. It is unclear whether or not Bright thought the principal defect of slavery was that unfree labor was inefficient or that blacks were inefficient by nature. Bright's objection to slavery was founded on its economic inefficiency rather than its immorality—or, rather, its economic inefficiency was its immorality.[31]

A Michigan soldier contrasted the two shores of the Ohio. Since Ohio and Kentucky shared the same terrain at the river, the differences in appearance between the two states had its origins in their distinct labor systems. The vineyards and houses of Ohio were "the product of free labor"; the shore was "a continual garden."

The Kentucky shore was "in a state of nature with now and then a cabin and truck patch to mar the scenery." Free labor added to the beauty of the landscape; the slipshod products of slavery detracted from the natural beauty.[32]

The First Philadelphia City Troop was stationed in Williamsport, Maryland, in June 1861 and made several forays into Virginia from that point. Riding "miles through a miserable poor farm and pasturing district," they had the opportunity to examine the effects of slavery firsthand. Horace Evans soon decided, after viewing the countryside, that the impression Northerners had of slavery was correct. "It curses man, the land, & its produce."[33]

Some soldiers came to hate slavery because of its brutalities and sinfulness. James T. Miller wrote home from Virginia that his experiences in the South had made him an abolitionist. They had convinced him that slavery was "the most abominble insitution the world ever saw"; he wanted no end to the war until every slave was free. In the neighborhood of Miller's camp was a man who owned two slave women, each of whom had borne him children, four of whom he had sold. This traffic in the master's own flesh and blood would have shocked Miller enough if it had been but an aberration; what shocked him more was that "public sentiment is so corrupt that no one seemes to think that thier is anything wrong in such actons"—the man was a member in good standing of the local Baptist church. Miller said such instances of slavery had caused him and many others in the army to embrace abolitionism; in his opinion "these two years of war have made more Abolitionists than the lectures of Wendle Phillips and Gerit Smith and Wm Lyod Garison would have made in one hundred years." Miller was right.[34]

Another soldier who saw convincing evidence of the depravity of the slave system was Elbert Corbin. He came across "an old Batchelor" who had children by a slave—and who then begat his grandchildren on his own children. And Luther C. Furst found that slaves on the Peninsula lived poorly; their houses would be considered unfit for animals in the North. He also discovered that the slaves wanted freedom, and the more he saw of slavery, the more he agreed with them.[35]

Other Union soldiers saw nothing in the Southern countryside to turn them against slavery. "Slavery has been pictured to us in the North in its worst form," John D. St. John wrote his parents from Tennessee, and he judged from talking to slaves that "their treatment is nowhere as bad as we have been made to believe." The contrabands in their camp told him that their masters treated them far better than the Union officers did; a master would at least doctor them when they were sick while the officers would leave them to die. When one's first taste of freedom came in a military camp, apparently it was not as sweet as dreamed of. The only complaint they made of their old masters was the selling of slaves.[36]

An Iowan cavalryman stopped in Montgomery, Alabama, during Wilson's Raid in the spring of 1865, and observed with pleasure the "fine mansion" where headquarters was made. He admired the gardens and groves, the rich, cultivated land, and "the happy, jolly darkies." At first the slaves approached the soldiers with trepidation. But in the evening the regimental band played and they crowded eagerly around to hear the music. Later that night there was a "jubilee" in their cabins. As the soldier listened to "their dancing, fiddling, singing, and laughing," he concluded that "the negro is in his element and his condition cannot be bettered." Thus, even as the slaves celebrated the arrival of the freedom that was held to accompany Union soldiers, a Union soldier found in their celebration reason to believe they did not need to be free.[37]

Whether they saw slavery as an injustice that oppressed their fellow humans or as an institution that fostered bad economics, many Northern soldiers learned to hate slavery. It was the South's distinctive feature, its "peculiar institution." The soldiers also despised the Southern character that seemed intertwined with the vicious institution. Indolence, whether the cause or result of slavery, was the Southern sin. From Virginia one soldier wrote, "In every place that we have been, I was struck with the entire absence of those evidences of enterprise and civilization that we find common even in the most remote parts of New York State. The whole country and even the people that are scattered through it have a strange wild appearance that is very noticeable to a stranger." He added, in a line that revealed the frequent confusion Northerners shared as to the economics of slavery, "The common people are as ignorant as the slaves they own, and appear to care but little

about any advance in civilization or art." Francis E. Wheaton thought
the country around Falmouth, Virginia, attractive, and the farms
lacking only Northern caretaking to be "the most pleasant homes
in the country." Unfortunately, they were "tenanted by Ignorance
and Indolence." Edward H. Sentell described the area around Ope-
lousas, Louisiana, as "some of the finest country I ever saw but it
needed the Industry of the north to make it appear right[.]" Of the
city itself Sentell said, "Opolousas is a very pleasant place & very
healthy & would make a splendid City if it had northern enterprise
to put it through in good style."[38]

The resources and beauties of the South, marred as they were
by white indolence and black ignorance, inevitably created dreams
of a transfigured South, one that could be best achieved by Northern immigration. If the enterprising sons of the North settled this
bountiful land of the South, they would enrich the land and set an
example for white and black Southerners alike. Capt. George Anthony advised his brother to sell his home in Orleans County, New
York, and emigrate to Virginia where the weather was mild and
business opportunities were growing. "I tell you the difference
between a winter here and in Orleans is no small item when mul-
tiplied by the years of a man's life." The South was "the place for
men that wish to pursue a quiet even business life desiring nothing
but certainty of legitimate returns for investments of labor and
capitol"—unless by some chance the end of the war brought undesirable policies or made Northern men unwelcome.[39]

Samuel S. Ely of Philadelphia envisioned Northern settlement of
the South as the solution to the Negro question. Northern settlers
could take care of the black population at the same time they
educated it for responsible citizenship. They would provide support
for the national government and earn benefit for themselves as
well. The presence of Northern whites in the South would ease the
transition from slavery to freedom and help the freedman enter the
political world. "The old system from which they have been lib-
erated has degraded them; but something of the same system with
freedom I think will be the surest and best."[40]

Southern planters were hardly likely to welcome a stream of
enterprising Northerners or the liberation of the slave. But if they
believed the proslavery arguments of the antebellum South, they

would understand why Ely wished to put the freedman on probation and the need for educating an inferior race. In Ely's case, racism undermined free labor ideology to the point he advocated peonage—the same solution, historically, that America arrived at for the "problem" of black freedom.[41]

The vision of loyal immigration to the South appealed to more than Northern self-interest. While the immigrants would presumably benefit from their residence in the South, they would serve the national interest as well. They would "Northernize"—civilize—the South, establishing the institutions and attitudes necessary to create a loyal and patriotic part of the Union.

Until that time, Southern society would remain unredeemed, the Southern landscape strange and un-American. The Northern soldier in the South felt himself in a bizarre and hostile environment. One soldier in Virginia wrote, "This is a queer country and queer people to. I often take my wife (musket) and go to see the sights." And another, contemplating the Confederacy and its people, said, "I sometimes wonder if I am not in a foreign country."[42]

The Peopled Landscape

Surgeon Henry Seys came to the Union army from an unusual background. His father had been born into a wealthy West Indian family and had scandalized his relations by becoming a Methodist missionary. Henry Seys was born at his father's mission to the Mohawks and spent three years of his early life in Africa. In 1850 Seys's father became director of the Maryland Colonization Society. Seys attended medical school in Baltimore and set up practice in Ohio. He joined the Union army in the spring of 1861.

Understandably, Seys was more bitter toward the South than most. When Union troops took Bowling Green in February 1862, Seys claimed that rebel vandalism in that city had been immense and that the people had been forced to live under a "reign of terror." From northern Alabama, in the summer of 1862, he reported with disgust General Buell's too-kind treatment of the local civilians. The Southerners therefore snarled at the Union soldiers and insulted them, only to be thrashed in return, "for few of these 'chivalry' with pipe stem legs can match our athletae from the North." Seys predicted that eventually one of the locals would be shot by some soldier "who will not wish to soil his fists—Amen."[43]

Seys witnessed the blacks leave the parts of Tennessee the Union army passed through and welcomed the exodus. If the blacks departed, he reasoned, nobody would be left to farm, and the Confederates must come home or let their families starve. "At last," he rejoiced, "we are striking at the root of the rebellion—for every negro that we take leaves an acre of ground sterile—and adds one to our fighting strength."[44]

While stationed in Triune, Tennessee, Seys fell into the habit of visiting local families who were friendly if not loyal. Most of the men in the neighborhood he dismissed as "poor trash," while the women showed some "evidence of considerable cultivation"—even though nine out of ten of the women used tobacco. Seys thought the women invited officers to their homes because they wanted better company than the resident male population could provide. He made his visits, however, in order to tell the Southern women "some very wholesome truths"; in fact, he delighted in telling them what he called "rough things."

One attractive woman of about twenty made the mistake of defending the Confederacy in his presence, making statements Seys "knew" to be false. His reply was "That if Miss Adams would take the trouble to study a little—she would probably betray much less ignorance than she was now doing." When the woman shifted the conversation to interpret a federal order a certain way that Seys disagreed with, Seys told her she must have lost the ability to understand good English because of her long association with blacks, "and with the power to understand it—to speak it."

Seys's bullying obviously afforded him great pleasure, even though his own examples of wit are little above blunt insult. Yet he could indeed speak "wholesome truths" to Southerners whom rhetoric and myths had led astray. When one woman defended slavery by speaking of "the happy relationship existing between master & slave," the doctor was only too ready to agree. He told the woman that not only was she right, but that she had neglected her strongest argument—"The *color* of your niggers madam—That proves beyond a doubt the *very* kindly relationship that exists betwixt the master and the slave."[45]

The war provided the men of the Union army more than the chance to observe the Southern landscape. Men like Seys encountered the men and women, black and white, rich and poor, of the South. Conversation supplemented observation in creating the Yankee vision of the South. The South was judged not just by its barns and fields, houses and towns, but by its people. The people were not prepossessing. Soldiers' letters home were a litany of complaint about the Southern people. To the Northern eye, they were as foreign as the landscape.

Popular imagination divided the white South into planters and poor whites. Northern soldiers sought evidence of the degradation and ignorance of the nonslaveholding proportion of the white population. The Northern interpretation of the war's causes required that the masses of Southern whites be pitiable slaves to aristocratic domination. In the wartime South the soldiers frequently found the evidence they needed. Their letters home portrayed people who lived in houses full of flea-infested "measly hounds"; whose "long light hair and sallow complexion" made them all look alike; whose children rolled "about the bare floor the flies thickly studding their mud beplastered molasses-smeared scabby faces"; people who were "ignorant, habitually filthy and lazy," many too ignorant to know the name of the towns they lived in and who could not write their own names; who were "little if any above the negros." One Northern soldier wrote of the nonslaveholders of the Peninsula, "They are very ignorant, scarcely above the slave & have no idea of the cause of the war or what they are fighting for."[46]

One of the more graphic descriptions of the South's impoverished whites was written by a Northern lieutenant. Joseph F. Culver had heard much about the poor whites of the South before the war, but he had to confess that the reality exceeded his imagination. On a trip into northern Alabama he saw "many families who scarcely seemed to possess intelligence above the brutes & scarcely were their equals in instinct & self-preservation." That he saw misery is certain, but one may hope that the example he gave his wife was not common: a hovel inhabited by an unmarried and pregnant mother with her several children, a diseased woman, and "a raving maniac" who "lay upon the floor amid all kinds of filth, tossing about and making a very hideous noise."[47]

One characteristic of some Southern whites surprised Northern soldiers. These miserable, shiftless, and oppressed people did not always realize just how badly off they were. For example, near the Rappahannock, Union soldiers found "poor white trash" inhabiting the countryside, renting small farms from absentee owners who lived in Fredericksburg. One said that if he did not know better, he would find it hard to believe such degraded beings were residents of the United States—yet the poor people he talked with prided themselves as F.F.V.'s. Such snobbery, independent of material possessions, made no sense to this Union soldier.[48]

Far more pleasing were those Southern nonslaveholders whose stories confirmed Northern beliefs—those who complained of planter oppression. One soldier explained that "the common class of people or in other words the poor whites" owned no land and had "to go into the army or starve." He predicted that once the Union army had defeated the Confederates, class war would break out between the common people and the planters. "I think that the people south will yet take Jeff and all of his cabenet and hang them."[49]

George Ward Nichols, an aide-de-camp to Sherman, encountered a South Carolina poor white—"a weak creature, with pale face, light eyes, and bleached beard"—and his family. Even this ignoramus recognized "that the success of the Rebels would certainly establish the bondage of his own class to the aristocrats of the South." The poor white told Nichols, "The poor whites aren't allowed to live here in South Carolina; the rich folks allus charges us with sellin' things to the niggers; so they won't let us own land but drives us about from place to place. . . . They hate the sight of us poor whites." Nichols's reply was "And yet you are the class that are now furnishing the rank and file of their armies."[50]

One poor white, possibly the same man who spoke to Nichols, told Maj. Henry Hitchcock that "he had known more than one instance in the neighborhood of the rich planters taking 'poor whites' on accusation of trading with their negroes—which is a heinous offence, for it encourages the negroes to steal, etc, etc—tarring and feathering them and riding them on a rail across the

Savannah River." One of the so-called poor whites for whom Hitchcock felt sorry owned a four-hundred-acre farm but few or no slaves.[51]

Hitchcock's reference to landowning poor whites reveals the difficulty Northerners had in gauging the social status of Southern whites. Convinced that the South was divided into planters, poor whites, and slaves, they thought all whites who did not meet their preconceptions of leisured, slaveholding wealth were poor and oppressed. In fact, the owner of a four-hundred-acre farm could not have been "a poor white"; and if he indeed owned even only a "few" slaves he would have been wealthier than the average Northerner.

Assistant Surgeon S. H. Eells was perceptive enough to see past the ramshackle appearances of the Southern landscape that convinced most Northerners that they were surrounded by "poor white trash" living in abject poverty, the victims of shiftlessness, slavery, or both. As a doctor, he had frequent occasion to visit the homes of citizens around Middleburg, Tennessee. The farms he visited looked "as poor as our backwoods settlements and are not nearly as comfortable." Nonetheless, his patients were not very poor. The citizens judged a man's wealth and position by the quantity of slaves he owned. "The richest man in this region lives in a tumble down old log house that we should not consider fit for a barn, but he has a good many negroes or had before the war."[52]

In many parts of the South, men and women still concentrated all their energies on acquiring wealth. The purchase of land and slaves and the raising of cotton counted for more than the comforts that Northerners desired in their lives. Money that might have been spent on furnishings, clothing, delicacies, and other amenities was invested in the means of production instead.

Such behavior, of course, was capitalistic; indeed, some Southerners could be said to be in the "heroic" phase of capitalism, the stage in which no sacrifice is too great to make in order to increase one's capital. Before a Southerner could exploit slave labor, he sometimes had to exploit himself and his family, by denying them the comforts their labor could produce. Such behavior could lead to accumulation of money necessary for the purchase of slaves whose labor was essential in the Southern version of agrarian capitalism. And it might continue after the initial investment in slaves. But Northern soldiers did not always calculate a white family's "means of production," although they frequently evaluated the fertility of their land. Instead, they judged a family's wealth by the condition of their houses, their clothing, their persons. Shabbiness proclaimed poverty.

The issue of white status was further complicated by the fact that many Southerners, who were independent landowners, were nonetheless slaveless and poor in terms of other material possessions. Not all Southerners were incipient planters. Some of those who avoided capitalistic agriculture may have been preserving their independence from the constraints of a market economy—they may have preferred independence over wealth.

Some Northern soldiers regarded such behavior as sloth. Others, more firmly imbued with free labor principles, assumed that such behavior had to be the product of an oppressive social system— one in which the planters denied the poor whites the right to own land. Since men were economically motivated, they would, if free, work for material gain and social advancement. This free-labor ideology underlay much of Northern policy during Reconstruction; it influenced soldiers' perceptions of the South.

Some men felt sorry for the poor white trash who suffered from the war. An Iowa soldier in Alabama, who had seen families with no more than a meal's worth of food left in their houses, said, "I tell you the poor class of people here are to be pittied." However, he had no sympathy for the planters and their families even though he had "seen them aweeping over their lamentable condition," because the leaders were responsible for the suffering that everyone in the South was undergoing. "I think if there is a place of torment they will certainly get their just dues."[53]

Northern soldiers, viewing those plantations of the South that did meet their expectations of opulent luxury, concluded that the South was indeed ruled by the aristocracy they believed had fomented rebellion. One soldier wrote from Georgia that "There are some nice plantations around here, but it is not like the North. One rich planter will own 5 or 6 thousand acres of land while North 30 farmers would [live] comfortably on the same; nothing but a Monarchical government suits th[em.]" Such concentration of wealth, they thought, must produce concentration of political power.[54]

Ohio politician and future President James A. Garfield confessed to his wife that in Kentucky "nearly all the cultivated & enlightened people . . . are on the side of the rebellion"—even his fellow Disciples of Christ. He called this "one of the painful facts of the Rebellion," and attributed it to the leadership of the Southern Aristocracy in secession.[55]

When he later reached Athens, Alabama, Garfield stayed with one of the aristocrats, at his fine townhouse. The Southern way of life, he found, had its charms, at least for the wealthy. "When once a man is rich, wealth flows into his coffers easily and bountifully. Their homes are luxurious with magnificence & wealth." Garfield believed that slavery was based on "self-deception." "They pursue such a course with their slaves and [as] to render it manifestly true that the mass of their blacks are wholly incompetent to direct the business of their own lives. Then they point to their slaves & say with an air of triumph, 'These people are infinitely better off here than in freedom. We are religiously bound to take care of them.' " Perhaps these sentiments had been expressed to him by the wealthy slave owner of Athens.[56]

The tug of attraction toward the planter class that Garfield felt underneath his revulsion affected other Northerners as well. Capt. John Pierson initially felt sympathetic toward the planters of north Alabama. "They are . . . placed between two fires and it is a hard matter for them to know whether they had best cry good Lord or good Debel. They have allways treated me well where ever I have had the pleasure of meeting them." He described the planters as "the Blood and Rank among the aristocracy," as people who prided themselves on their gentility. He said they hated contact with the common Union soldiers but were happy to oblige officers. Pierson, an officer himself, did not seem to resent this snobbery; instead, he appreciated the good manners of the Alabama planters.[57]

Whatever the planters' manners, Pierson soon came to hate and fear them. A local planter, with the aid of an overseer and a slave, murdered the servant of a Northern officer while he was searching for his employer's horse. They shot the servant and, weighting the body with stones, tried to hide it in a creek. The planter fled, but the overseer and slave were arrested after the servant's disappearance. A party of soldiers found the body. "On the returning of the Party and their report of the body of White our men ware verry much enraged and would have killed Stanly the overseer that had a hand in the Murder on the spot if the officers had not restrained them from it I do not blame them much but Law and order is our motto and we try hard to observe it." But Pierson and the soldiers had learned that there were planters ready to murder Northerners. "We live a life of care and watchfullness," he wrote.

After the owner's sudden departure, his plantation was confiscated. His wife decided to go south to the part of Alabama still held by the Confederacy. She wanted to bring some of her slaves with her—this was before the Emancipation Proclamation—particularly a twenty-one-year-old woman slave whom Pierson described as "white." Pierson's regiment prevented her. Instead of being sent south with her mistress, the woman went north on funds raised by the officers of the regiment. She was to work for the colonel's family in Michigan while her husband, "a bright Mulato," served as a cook in the Union army. The plantation mistress had "wanted this woman that we sent off and her husband to go with her verry much but we could not permit her to hold them as Slaves any longer I think we would have permitted her to take on or 2 Servants if Negroes which she has plenty of that are not mixt would have answered her purpos and may do so yet."[58]

Ironically, after acquiring his contempt for the Alabama planters, Pierson became one in a way. He managed the confiscated plantation. "I left Michigan an uncompromising Democrat I am now a Negroe driver and Proprietor for Uncle Sam." And the Michigan captain enjoyed his work. "I have really fell in love with a cotton crop I visited the cotton growing on the Plantation yesterday and it looks beautifull Some of the buds have bussted and the buds are parted so to look like a white Rose others are just cracked opene on one Side while others are green and unbroken." He also learned to deal with blacks; in fact, he found himself wishing his men were half as obedient as blacks.[59]

After the murder, however, managing a plantation could not make Pierson feel kindly toward planters. No longer did he sympathize with those caught between two fires. Instead, he advocated clearing the country as the army proceeded southward. "Every man in the South is either for or against us and if he is not for us he must be treated as an enemy in armes and his property confiscated and he taken prisoner or Shot on the Spot as they will cut throates if they get a chance at a Single man." The blacks would reveal where the rebels were hiding.[60]

The experience did increase Pierson's concern for blacks. After he left north Alabama, he considered sending his servant Isaac, a slave from the plantation, home to safety in Michigan. "I do not intend to see him go back into slavery." Pierson later became an officer in the United States Colored Infantry.[61]

Other Union soldiers also encountered planters who were blood-thirsty and treacherous. Alva Griest reported that one wealthy civilian, the owner of an eight-hundred-and-thirty-acre plantation, murdered a sick soldier who had been left at his home. "He took him out and tied him up by the neck, shot two revolvers empty in him, then threw him in a cart, took him to a pond, and threw him in." One conclusion many Union soldiers reached while down South is that the planter class of the South simply could not be trusted.[62]

While most planters were not murderers, soldiers thought many of them guilty of arrogance and selfishness. For example, when a poor Tennessee Unionist's mother died suddenly, the daughter went to her nearest neighbor, a secessionist planter, to ask that he let her bury her mother in the plantation graveyard. The planter refused her the burial place and even boards for a coffin; the planter's female kin refused to help with the laying out. The poor woman turned to the commander of a camp of Union troops in the neighborhood. The general "informed the Old man that he owned the land around here at this time." The planter supplied the wood for the coffin, a grave was dug in the planter's burial ground, and a squad of soldiers, bayonets fixed, marched the planter's family to the woman's house for the laying-out.[63]

In general, what Northern soldiers complained about the most in their dealings with Southern whites, whether they were planters or not, was their attitude. They did not seem to realize that North-ern ways were superior to Southern mores, or that the Union cause was just and secession immoral. They forgot that they were both powerless and traitorous. The women in particular seemed intent on maintaining Southern dignity and property rights.

A group of soldiers camped on property belonging to a Confederate officer. The teamsters drove their wagons through the yard before the house and did not always keep them strictly in the driveway. When the provost marshal visited the owner's wife, a member of the "true highminded Southern Aristocracy," "she told him she wished he would stop the men from walking over her grass and flower beds & the wagons too." His response was "she need not trouble herself any more for that property belongs to Uncle Sam now." Another Southern woman was highly offended when General Osterhaus took shelter from a rainstorm in her house; his soldiers with their muddy boots crowded her porch. She demanded that he order the soldiers off the porch as they were treading mud on it. Agreeing, the general went to the door and said, "Boys, come right in the house, don't stand there, you are getting the porch muddy."[64]

On the other hand, Union soldiers had little respect for those Southern whites who did humble themselves before Northern might. Not only did there seem to be something unmanly about too ready submission—it was hypocritical and self-serving. A soldier in Plymouth, North Carolina, saw dozens of civilians every day taking the oath of allegiance to the Union, not because they were loyal but because they wanted the army to issue them much-needed salt, "eagerly inquiring in the same breath with which they take the solemn oath, when they can get the *Salt*." Another soldier, this one in Alabama, noted that "Every man and woman down here is loyal as soon as a soldier comes around the house."[65]

Soldiers were disgusted by the cowardly hypocrisy of some Southerners, such as the Mississippi planter who had three sons in the Confederate army, but flew the U.S. flag over his property when the Union forces arrived. Some slaveholders fled their plantations when the Yankees approached, sometimes only hours in advance, but left their overseers behind; the overseers would claim to be good Union men. Soldiers who stopped for lunch—"corn Bread Boiled Ham and Cool Milk"—at one plantation were told by the slaves that the master was a *"Union Secessionist."* At least one of them thought the phrase summed up quite nicely most of the Southerners he had met.[66]

In short, Southern whites, no matter what their class and no matter what their attitudes, did not please the Northern soldier. Their way of life seemed too different, too bizarre. The poor ones looked too poor and the wealthy were too rich. He could not understand them.

Sometimes he felt sorry for them; he warmed to them as fellow human beings. At other times he felt they were not worthy of his concern. Perhaps most often the Union soldier was torn between contempt and grudging sympathy. One of them, a New York officer serving in war-ravaged Virginia, made a diary entry in December 1864, when the Confederacy was on its last legs.

> All I pity are the little children. They look up so sad with so much astonishment wondering, I presume, why we are all armed, filling their little hearts with terror, & why they are all so destitute & why Papa is not at home attending to their wants in this bleak cold winter weather. Poor children! They know not they are suffering the curse of treason.[67]

The Northern soldier regarded blacks as the most exotic people he found in the South. Almost anywhere they went in the South, Northern soldiers encountered black men, women, and children. Blacks flocked to the army, seeking freedom from their white masters. Most men had gone to war to preserve the Union, not to free the slaves, but the Union soldier found himself willy-nilly the agent of emancipation. The black people of the South welcomed the soldiers. Despite the fact that blacks offered the soldier the friendliest reception he would receive in the South, he did not always, or even usually, find the people who thought he had come to free them attractive. It is impossible to say that there was one single Northern attitude toward blacks; if there was one attitude, it was an ambivalence compounded of pity, affection, disgust, and hatred.

The foreign quality of blacks impressed some soldiers the most. Some Northern soldiers came from communities where blacks were infrequently seen. William H. Bradbury, in writing home to his little children, thought it necessary to explain to them what Negroes were. "I have seen lots of Negroes—which are black people—and little negroe children. . . . Their skin is dark brown and their hair short and black and curly." Bradbury regarded a simple description of blacks as sufficiently novel to be worth writing to his children.[68]

The men of the 24th Connecticut who served in Louisiana thought the black population ignorant and incredulous; the slaves had been told by their masters that the Yankees, "creatures that had horns," would murder them all. Nonetheless, the soldier who reported the blacks' fears of Yankees also wrote that wherever the Union army went, the slaves lined the side of the road, eager to watch it pass, which suggests curiosity overcame terror, or that the slaves believed their masters' lies rather less than the soldiers believed.[69]

Calvin Mehaffey shared the amusement of many federal soldiers at the behavior of the slaves. As soldiers marched down the roads of the Peninsula, blacks lined the road, dressed in what finery they had, and regarded the Yankee approach as "a grand holiday." Yet Mehaffey quickly realized something else. When the Confederates surprised many of his fellow officers by evacuating Yorktown, he had already predicted their retreat, because a black man had told him of it earlier. Mehaffey had learned that the slaves made good spies; they were devoted to the Union army. He put confidence in what information the local blacks brought him.[70]

Mehaffey also recorded a more violent act of assertion than either welcoming the Union army or spying for them. After the arrival of McClellan's army, a black named Lightfoot went to the house of a Peninsula family before daylight. He convinced them that McClellan wished to see all of them, then tied them to trees and raped the women. He was tried by military court-martial and found guilty, but escaped. The army wanted his execution to be an example to all who might be tempted by their presence to commit depredations; Mahaffey said that McClellan "intended to have him suffer death on the roadside so that the Army in its Advance from Ropers Church might read as was painted in readiness—'Lightfoot hung by the US Military Authorities for the Crime of Rape.' "[71]

Soldiers believed that "darkies would rather dance than eat." One of the most common spectacles observed by Union soldiers stationed at one place for any length of time was a "Negro breakdown." Dances were particularly memorable when they took place the first day a regiment arrived in the area, and even more so if the regiment was accompanied by a band. When the 45th Pennsylvania arrived at Otter Island, South Carolina, the band struck up a tune, and the blacks left their huts and began dancing—an obvious celebration of the arrival of Union soldiers and freedom. The soldiers enjoyed the dancing, but thought the blacks ludicrous. "I think if you could see them dancing you would almost die laughing," one of the musicians wrote home. "the idea of some of the negresses—black as pitch—holding out their dresses and aprins after the manner of some of the Southern belles was entirely too much for me and I laughed until my throat was sore." His amusement at the blacks apparently did not prevent him from observing some other aspects of their life, for he concluded by saying, "I have seen enough of slavery to satisfy me and if men wish to call me an abolitionish they can do so"—he now embraced a doctrine previously thought too radical.[72]

Another form of contact that Union soldiers had with Southern blacks was through commerce. Just as whites in the areas surrounding Union camps did, local blacks came to the Northern soldiers to sell them food—apples, oranges, pies, and the like. The soldiers were happy to buy; it was a trade conducted with profit to both sides. But on occasion it also reenforced certain white stereotypes about blacks, for the assumption made by the purchasers was often that the food they bought had been stolen by the blacks.

Since the food often came from a plantation owned by a white master, in strict legal sense the food was stolen. In any case, Union soldiers, who proved ready to steal such items and more from Southern plantations, were hardly ones to blame the blacks for taking a few oranges or the flour, sugar, and berries necessary to bake blackberry pies. What damage was done lay in the fact that when the soldiers returned home, they would remember the blacks of the South as thieves—thieves who had engaged in theft that was understandable and forgivable, but thieves.[73]

Soldiers also sought out blacks. Just as they diligently took in the sights of Washington or the historic places of northern Virginia, they investigated black life. For example, soldier after soldier stationed down South took advantage of the opportunity to visit black prayer meetings. Their responses varied.

Men such as Jabez Alvord of Connecticut dismissed the prayer meetings as "howlings." A German-born soldier who attended a black Methodist meeting dismissed it as simply shouting and noise, such as one would expect from "a lot of niggers." A soldier stationed in Louisiana described a "negro babtizing" by saying, "Sum of them fell Down an hollard as loud as they cold ball[.]"[74]

Others approved of black religion. Silas W. Browning, a Massachusetts private, was offended when their regimental chaplain reported the blacks ignorant after attending a meeting near New Orleans. The chaplain himself admitted that the worshipers were "honest and in earnest in thier devotions." Browning insisted that such piety was more important than any learning and that it was unfair for the chaplain to expect the same level of erudition from slave preachers as might be expected from a college-educated white minister. Indeed, in Browning's opinion, some better-educated ministers showed less fervor than the black ministers, and if slaves were ignorant, that should call forth sympathy, not condemnation. Another Union soldier, Alva Griest, reported listening to "an able sermon by a negro, which although in crude language was deeply felt by all and I firmly believe he was more sincere in his preaching than our Chaplain often is, for his words seemed to go right to the heart." This sermon was delivered to a mixed congregation—contrabands and soldiers—that listened respectfully.[75]

In general, those soldiers whose abolitionist sympathies were the greatest, admired black religion the most. Besides their pre-existing concern for blacks, they were the most impressed by an affective preaching style in which, as Griest put it, the preacher's "words" "go right to the heart." This suggests what many have argued: that Northern abolitionism had its roots in Northern evangelical culture. It is also worth noting, however, that soldiers such as Griest and Browning use the effectiveness—and affectiveness—of black preaching as a rebuke to white ministers, specifically chaplains. In that sense, black religion offered a truer Christianity, one that had not been corrupted by sinful pride in one's learning and cold insincerity. Perhaps Northern abolitionism, in some ways a logical outcome of the free-labor principles of an emerging capitalist order, in other ways embodied a cultural revolt against the emerging order. In any case, the religion of the powerless had considerable appeal to abolitionist soldiers.

The average Northern soldier, however, had not gone south with any great sympathy for its slaves. Furthermore, it was simply not the case that meeting the blacks of the South firsthand necessarily diminished the racism of the Union soldier. In fact, at times it seems to have increased it. Charles Dunham said that "any man that will go in to a negro regiment aint fit to be cald a man. I have seen enough of the baboons since I have been down here." Clearly he had not seen many blacks back home in Illinois. Whether or not Dunham had prejudice against the blacks before his years in Kentucky and Tennessee, he did after.[76]

Gleeful Southerners had always predicted as much. "Let the Yankees just live with the blacks long enough," they said, "and they will learn that slavery is the only place for them." This Southern notion was based, of course, on popular notions of black inferiority—but Southerners were certainly correct that such notions were shared by Northern whites even if they remained dormant. A trip down South, the first exposure to large numbers of blacks, could indeed bring white prejudice to life.

On the other hand, many of the things that prejudiced Northerners against blacks when they encountered them were products of slavery. Northerners found the slaves to be ignorant and uneducated, dirty and ragged. Those who did not realize that the condition of blacks was because of slavery could condemn them straightaway for these failures to meet Northern standards of judgment—and those who did realize the relationship between slavery and misery might still irrationally but all too humanly hold the slave's own misery against him.

A Connecticut soldier constructed a brutal syllogism that his tentmates found hilarious. He asked another soldier, *"Don't kissing create love?"* The second soldier replied that it did. The wit pointed to a passing black and said, "Well, go kiss that nigger." In some soldiers racism curiously combined revulsion at black skins with a belief in black licentiousness that attracted the white man's lust. This white attitude was occasionally revealed by soldiers' correspondence, although its cultural inadmissability rendered it subject to self-censorship. One profane Northerner wrote from Beaufort, South Carolina, that his primary objection to the war's continuance was that he was stationed where he could not have sexual congress with a white woman; there was "nothing but these damn negro wenches." His racism was sufficient to cause sexual revulsion: "I can't get it hard to go to them." A few more months of being stationed in Beaufort overcame his objections; soldiers on detached picket duty used their freedom from supervision to engage in illicit sex. Still, he found himself in a quandary. He did not want to turn to black women, but the white prostitutes who were now coming to Beaufort carried veneral disease.[77]

One Union company used black children to haul wood to a storage room near the kitchen of the plantation where they were stationed. The children, carrying the wood on their heads, dropped it off at the command "Fire!" The Union sergeant observed, "The little coons were delighted. They thought they were *real* soldiers!" After the wood had all been carried in, the sergeant amused himself by locking the children in the dark storage room. "Such a yell of terror as they set up, Pandemonium never heard! They shrieked, groaned, yelled, prayed, and pulled their wool!" The sergeant cracked open the door and allowed the children to escape. Then, "to atone for our fun, I ordered Ben Mercer, the cook, to give them a pot of beans that he had burned too much for us to eat." Even this permitted the soldiers one further source of amusement: the children plunged their hands into the narrow-mouthed pot and, unable to pull them out because of the crowding, burned their hands on "smoking-hot beans." The sergeant found the shrieks caused by the infliction of physical pain as impressive as those caused by fear of the dark.[78]

The brutality inflicted on blacks by the Union soldiers could be quite casual. A group of soldiers in Nashville entertained themselves by taking a black child and tossing him in a blanket until an officer, noticing the large crowd the amusement drew, freed the boy. Some Indiana soldiers tipped a child into a hogshead of molasses: "He nearly drowned before he could get it out of his nose and mouth." Union soldiers in Bowling Green amused themselves by attending black dances and "sprinkling a little Cayenne pepper over the floor which rises up under their clothes! and becomes *obnoxious*." Drunken soldiers shot blacks in the streets of Alexandria.[79]

Simple racism is an insufficient explanation for this kind of cruelty. These acts of violence occurred during wartime, when men became more hardened—many soldiers did not see in them anything but a source of amusement. Furthermore, they allowed soldiers to release some of the frustrated rage they felt toward the enemy, toward the army, and toward civil society. This displaced anger, directing it against targets that were both safer and more accessible. Underneath it all lay the soldiers' sense that blacks were responsible for the war: they were the slaves whose presence helped disrupt American institutions. When the war for the Union became a war for emancipation, soldiers felt they were risking their lives for undeserving blacks. James W. Hildreth, who believed slaves would be better off with their masters, complained that blacks had become so independent since the Emancipation Proclamation that there was nothing to do but kill them. If a black came into the camp of the 4th New York Heavy Artillery, the soldiers would cry out, "Kill him," and club the unfortunate. His reaction to the sentencing of a white teamster to hanging for shooting a black was that now "a nigger is better than a white man."[80]

The 99th New York Infantry may have displayed the most cynical attitude toward blacks. According to the major of the First New York Dragoons, members of that regiment—"about as hard a class of customers as you will often find"—used to kidnap blacks around Deep Creek, Virginia, and "sell them to the Rebels."[81]

Some Union soldiers, however, did find that actually meeting blacks mitigated their hostility. It may have been easier for a soldier to respond sympathetically to an individual black man or woman than to blacks en masse. The specific human being might overcome inherited prejudices. Furthermore, many blacks, in their struggles for freedom, displayed characteristics of bravery and loyalty that soldiers admired.

In September 1862 a garrison stationed at Jackson, Tennessee, expected to be attacked momentarily by the forces of Sterling Price. The Union soldiers had built a makeshift fort of cotton bales, and that night they left their tents and took refuge in it. Among those in the fort was a large, strong freedman who served as a cook. This cook took a gun and seated himself on a barrel. No attack coming, the soldiers went to sleep, and one of them later wrote of Adam, the cook, "the last I saw of him at midnight he was still there and his eyes shone like silver dollars on a burnt blanket. . . . He intended to fight for his liberty." That intention kept the black man awake as the white soldiers fell asleep in an improvised fort built of cotton, a product of the black man's enslavement.[82]

Early in 1862 a slave ran away from his master and crossed the Potomac River to the protection of a Union post. After his escape he immediately began laying plans to rescue his wife and children. One night he recrossed the river in a small boat and brought his family back, one at a time, as the boat was too small to hold them all at once. Each trip he made he had to pass by the Confederate pickets, but he succeeded in freeing his family. A Union officer had warned him of the dangers of such an endeavor, but the contraband replied that "he was bound to get them or die in the attempt."[83]

That summer a slave followed a New York cavalry regiment across the Potomac. When he reached their camp, he was fortunate enough to encounter Sgt. Lucien P. Waters, a man nicknamed by his fellows "The Abolition Sergeant." Waters sent him to the colonel, who was sympathetic to the man's desire for freedom. The next day the owner of the slave, "the rankest kind of a Secessionist," arrived at the camp. The sergeant and a black servant hid the runaway in the woods. The owner demanded the return of his property. "The boys swore by all they held sacred that he should never take the darkey out of camp. He quailed & said he was a loyal citizen. It was too late to play that game." The runaway later told Waters had he been returned, his master would have surely killed him; the man had already killed several slaves. The regiment's colonel had him smuggled away to Washington, hidden in the bottom of a boat. But as one runaway left, another arrived. This one, who had informed the colonel of his master's Confederate sympathies during their expedition across the Potomac, was "a noble looking fellow, having more natural wit & intelligence than any of the dutch & irish soldiers among us." "His master we expect here today in search of him. If the rebels continue to visit us they will surely get dragged through the river."[84]

In 1863 a Kentucky slave—one of those not legally affected by the Emancipation Proclamation—ran away to a camp of Illinois soldiers. After he had served as a cook for a while, a white man came to claim him. Unfortunately for the white man's purpose, he found the runaway near a company that had a reputation for abolition sentiments. Charles Calvin Enslow observed the fracas. "The White Man caught the negro by the coat collar after which he made a few plunges and got out of his coat. Then began a race for liberty or death. The negro struck Company "C" and the White Man after him. I never saw such running in all my life. Just as said negro got in the Abolition Company there was an immense crowd gathered and told Mr. Negro Catcher to flee for dear life." He did so, and the black man went free "just what God Almighty and the Declaration of Independence intended he should be," as Enslow said. Enslow explained, "we never came here to catch niggers for anybody."[85]

If slavery was thought of as the aggregate of these individual cases, the soldiers' positive response to heroic black men and women whom they saw struggling for freedom might have been enough to build support for black civil rights within the ranks of the army. Witnessing exceptional cases of bravery and determination, however, did not necessarily mean that soldiers would regard the mass of the enslaved as equally brave and determined.

The army did not always protect those slaves who came into Union lines. January 1, 1863, proved a sad day for abolitionists stationed in Louisiana. The Emancipation Proclamation did not extend to large areas of that state that were judged to be no longer in rebellion. Louisiana planters took advantage of this to reclaim slaves who had run away to the Union army. Near the camp of the 75th New York Infantry one slave whose master attempted to bring him back to the plantation succeeded in drowning himself in the bayou, but others were carried off by ropes tied around their necks; "a soldier who interfered was taken to jail and confined." Planters took away blacks who had volunteered for Union regiments but who had not been mustered.[86]

Contraband labor was frequently leased to civilians who came south to operate cotton plantations. Soldiers were used to enforce these contracts and to discipline unwilling workers in ways that seemed no different from the ways of slavery. A Union soldier stationed near a government-leased plantation might spend much of his time capturing runaway blacks and returning them to their new masters. Lucien P. Waters, the Abolition Sergeant who had helped rescue runaway slaves in Maryland, had to witness contrabands beaten by soldiers in Louisiana. In 1864 he wrote home, "To see the corruption which is gradually creeping into this Dept. under the management of Banks is painful in the extreme to one who is anxious to see the *spirit* of the Freedom Proclamation carried out to its fullest extent. There is hardly any chance for a slave (?) to gain redress for wrongs committed by the lessees of the government plantations." He believed the local provost marshal and the lessees conspired to cheat the blacks out of their proper wages. Even worse, his fellow soldiers willingly abused the black laborers. "Disgrace of disgraces, when a union & northern soldier will help to tie up & gag a helpless negro-woman & after doing this whip & kick her naked body!!!"[87]

In the summer of 1862, a Michigan soldier said, "When we cease to fight for the Union and begin to fight for Negro equality I am ready to lay down arms and will." He did not desert after the Emancipation Proclamation, but in 1864, when he was asked to reenlist, he went home. The war created sympathy for the enslaved among some Northern soldiers; others, including those who whipped black women or murdered black men, found their racism in no way diminished by their wartime experience. Those many whose views fell somewhere in between were uncertain what to think of blacks and their future in American society. When the Emancipation Proclamation made the war an antislavery war, some soldiers were jubilant, others horrified, and still more accepted the war's transformation with troubled minds.[88]

In January 1863 Jacob Seibert believed that the soldiers of the Army of the Potomac desired a speedy end to the war, by recognition of the South's independence if necessary, and opposed the Emancipation Proclamation. The primary reason for his opposition to the proclamation was his fear that the freed people would settle in the North, where they were not wanted; it was better to leave them as they were. Another soldier wrote, "we dont care much witch wa it gose sense we found ourt we are fitine for nigers."[89]

The Emancipation Proclamation satisfied most Northern soldiers that the war for the Union must be a war against slavery. Even those who did not welcome the new policy were inclined to accept it. Most soldiers, whether or not they opposed servitude for blacks, recognized what later historians sometimes had trouble believing: that emancipation was not only a legitimate war measure, it was a necessary one. As Capt. John Pierson, whose experience with Southern gentlemen had soured him, put it, "I have been among Slavery for over 10 months and most of the time among the large Slave [owners] and I am satisfied that if you want to strike the Rebelion in a tender place, hit the Negro on the Shins. There is no Species of Property that they seem to lament over looseing Except the Negro." Slavery he said, would end "as a natural result of the war not as one of the war measures." And James T. Miller, who wrote so perceptively on combat, welcomed "old Abes emancipation proclimation" because "as far as i can see there is no other cause for this war but Slavery and the sooner it is done the better for us."[90]

The war provided an opportunity for pragmatic abolitionists like Lincoln to forgo argument directly concerned with the merits and morality of slavery. Soldiers who loved the Union and hated rebels would support emancipation as a means of attacking Southern whites, even if they were indifferent to the rights of Southern blacks. They were like the Puritans in the joke, who opposed bearbaiting not because of the pain it gave the bear but the pleasure it gave the spectators.

Abolitionists could hardly be faulted for seizing the opportunity for emancipation that the war offered, any more than the slaves who fled Southern plantations could be faulted. The struggle against slavery had lasted, for many of them, a lifetime—it must have seemed an entrenched institution that only a miracle could destroy. Southern secession and the war that followed was that miracle.

The emergence of the Republican Party and the election of one of its members to the Presidency suggested that it was possible that

abolitionists might have won the political argument over slavery—
that they might have persuaded a majority of Americans not only
that slavery was immoral but that it was the government's business
to set the slaves free. If the attitudes of Union soldiers accurately
reflected those of Americans at large—and they probably did—
most Americans of 1861 had not yet been convinced by the abolitionist argument.

Political abolitionists like James Garfield recognized this. Early
in 1862 Garfield wrote that emancipation should not yet be proposed by Lincoln's administration; it "would be a most fatal mistake." "The logic of the argument wielded with the varied power
of all the minds that have labored upon this theme has not brought
the people of the North even, up to the necessity. Nothing but the
terrible logic of events will do it."

Indeed, underneath Garfield's moral rhetoric one hears the cynicism of the professional politician. "Let the war," he proposed,
"be conducted *for the Union* till the whole nation shall be enthused,
transfigured with the glory of that high purpose." The emotions
that war created would aid the cause of freedom. "Let all the deeds
of valor add their glory to that purpose, all the love [of] the people
for the fallen's ones sanctify & exalt it, till the integrity, indivisi-
bility, & glory of that Union shall gather round itself all the hero-
worship, pride & power of the nation, & then, perhaps not till
then, they will love the Union more than slavery & slay the python
because it[s] slimy folds roll toward the cradle of our infant Her-
cules."[91]

Unfortunately, the very accuracy of the argument for emancipation as military necessity, and the readiness with which the soldiers accepted it, the very efficacy of Union sentiment and wartime
fervor as an inducement may have obscured other reasons for emancipation. Presenting the issue in pragmatic terms made emancipation possible; in view of the resistance of the Northern soldier
and the Northern public at large to emancipation, the appeal to
victory was necessary. But by avoiding the issue of black rights,
the proclamation did little to change the minds of the soldiers, and
it did less to prepare them to meet future demands for black civil
liberties.

Of course, there were many Union soldiers who went to war as abolitionists and others who learned to hate slavery in the South. But it is easy to exaggerate their number. One Union soldier said, "Our regiment that has I believe been called an anti-slavery regiment, is as a body decidedly pro-slavery." Yet even these soldiers, he said, favored emancipation "but only because they are heartily sick of the war, and willing to approve any measures that will tend to end it." They supported emancipation; they would support a compromise with the South just as strongly. "I have heard many say that they would like to see every colored man shot, and every night around the camp fire you will hear any amount of cursing and blackguarding niggers and abolitionists, and if any one ventures to waste his breath in talking with them, they damn him with them." Still, he assured his mother that "the anti-slavery sentiment is much stronger than anyone would suppose from hearing the camp talk, as the abolitionists are generally the better-educated, who are not given to blustering and swearing."[92]

Even some soldiers who supported abolition found themselves nervous at the prospect of emancipation. One confessed he could not see what was to be done with the freed people. Some of the blacks he encountered in the South seemed willing to work, but most of them, he said, "would rather steal their living any time than work for it." He gave up on the generation of blacks raised in slavery and could only hope that education might improve their children. At present they were a burden to the government and suffered terribly; "they are neglected by those whose business it is to take care of them, and die off rapidly in consequence, and everybody seems to feel as if that was about the best way to get rid of them."[93]

Charles Calvin Enslow, the Illinois soldier, was more sanguine, but his optimism was alloyed with racism. "I advocate the entire abolition of slavery and I believe in equalizing the negro with the white man so far as life, liberty, and the pursuit of happiness is concerned, and no farther." Intellectually, blacks were inferior to Anglo-Saxons, and no amount of education could remedy that. But Enslow denied that blacks were innately lazy; in fact, their labor had built the South. "They above all others have been hard laborers earning a home in the South, they have always been here, they are acclimated to this one climate and the white people have never learned to work and could not live without the negro therefore, I say keep them in this part of the country, let the white people pay them reasonable wages, let the negro have schools all over the country so he may educate his children." After the next generation had been educated, they would desire a nation of their own "and then let the United States buy them some country and they would gladly go there by their own choice and they would make room for almost five million white laborers who are now born down and trod upon in Europe." Black emigration was necessary for white immigration: "You cannot have the white man come to the south and labor as long as the negro is here laboring." Enslow clearly believed that this program was the best for black and white alike. But one belief limited his charity toward the freed people: "I do not believe in having them in the North." And while he wanted the government of the United States to do justice by the blacks, he looked forward to the day when the South as well as the North was white only.[94]

Another soldier, William H. Dunham, believed that the war could not end until the slaves were free, and that the North was "guilty with the South" in the sin of slavery and had so earned its suffering in the war. He hoped that "the darkies will make their mark in this fight yet, and show themselves worthy to be free." "May God give the nation grace enough to deal justly by the downtrodden" was his prayer. Yet when it came to the place of the black in America after emancipation, he could only say, "It is a matter of great concern to many what disposition will be made with the Colored race when freed, but "sufficient" unto the day is the evil thereof I shall not be troubled much with about that question." Slavery was immoral and had to cease—Dunham saw that far but confessed himself unable to see further. And the immediate task—emancipation—was so great that it is hard to blame him for directing his thoughts primarily on it.[95]

Finally, at least one Union cavalryman found a purely practical use for the Emancipation Proclamation. George Starbird thought "a negro was made for a slave." "You no any other body could not learn them enough to earn their salt an you let them fall to their own resources and they will starve without lifting a hand to save themselves." Nonetheless, he benefited from the proclamation.

While out on picket near Suffolk, Virginia, in October 1862, he would present himself at the house of a black family, demand a meal—breakfast, lunch, or dinner—and then tell them of the proclamation "to pay for it."[96]

If one aim of the war was to protect and extend Northern civilization—not simply to preserve the Union or emancipate the slaves—then the destiny of the South could not be left to either its native whites or blacks. Both were "Southern"; both lacked the industry, thrift, and intelligence intrinsic in Northern civilization. Most Union soldiers found little to love in either of the South's races.

There were exceptions. Some abolitionists fought in the Union army, giving us heroes such as Col. Robert Gould Shaw, killed leading black soldiers into battle. Men such as Lucien Waters, the Abolition Sergeant, entered the federal army and rejoiced when the war for the Union became the war for freedom.

But if the Union army had recruited only abolitionists, it would have been pitiably small. The Confederacy would soon have achieved its independence. And it is unhistoric for us to claim that the Civil War, the War for the Union, really was a war for freedom, when most who fought cared so little about the rights of black people.

Furthermore, these flawed men, as racist as they were, won the war. Without them there would have been no Union victory; without them black freedom would have been delayed indefinitely. Charles Sumner and Wendell Phillips made many speeches, but the Union soldier freed more slaves. One abolitionist whose fellow soldiers complained of his advocacy of black rights nonetheless saw them as instruments of Providence: "I tell them that God sees fit to make them do his will."[97]

In John William DeForest's fine war novel *Miss Ravenel's Conversion from Secession to Loyalty,* Capt. Edward Colburne, a brave Union officer who was wounded in the service of his country, is shocked when self-righteous civilians tell him he has Copperhead sympathies; he had expressed the opinion that the rebels were not cowards. His protest at the charge could be the defense of a generation of Northern soldiers. "I was the only practical Abolitionist in the company—the only man who had freed a negro, or caused the death of a slaveholder."[98]

The Threatening Landscape

Rufus Mead and a small party of men spent a sleepless night near Wartrace, Tennessee. Their brigade had gone after guerrillas, but Mead, a commissary sergeant, and all but one of the others had been left behind as "noncombatants." The exception was a drunk soldier suffering from delirium tremens. That night a woman warned them guerrillas were in their neighborhood; the group loaded up all the available guns and sat up in a log house until two black companies arrived, whereupon the small band retired for the night, expecting to sleep. The drunken man, crying out and struggling, prevented that. In desperation the doctor dosed the man first with laudanum, then morphine, and finally chloroform, and the other soldiers tied him down. "yet he would writhe in agony and shriek for us to save him." The man fantasized death in three forms: he was to be executed for desertion, he was to be executed for murdering a black, or the rebels were coming to kill everyone. When he would scream out the last fear, the other soldiers started, almost believing that the Confederates were there.[99]

Contempt was not the only emotion the South aroused in the Union soldier. He also felt fear and the rage to which fear gives rise. A man who is in an unfamiliar landscape is literally a man who has lost his bearings. The Union soldier, trapped in such a landscape, surrounded by a civilian population half of it hostile and all of it bizarre, felt tremendous anxiety. The drunken soldier near Wartrace simply expressed some of his fears more vividly. He feared desertion and its penalty—the fear that he could not stand continuing the life of a soldier and its psychological strains. He feared he would murder a black man—a fear, in part, of his inability to control his own racism at a time when authority did not sanction it. And he feared death by the enemy. The enemy that threatened him the most at the time was not the regular Confederate soldier, whom one might encounter on the battlefield, but the irregular, the partisan, the guerrilla—the man who did not abide by the rules of war, the man who pretended to be a civilian—perhaps a Unionist—the figure most indistinguishable from the Southern landscape.[100]

One Union soldier referred to such men as "the much dispised and outlawed Guerilla—the man who is to mean to enter the Southern army—but goes forth with murder in his heart and a gun in his hand [his] wait to trap a Union Soldier and Shoot him down from ambush—Coward—Assassin." He was entitled to none of the respect one might have for the soldier of the other side. But the guerrilla did inspire a kind of awe. His ability to deceive the innocent, to ambush the unwary, and to murder the brave and strong made him the South's most mysterious inhabitant. The odds of being killed in battle were far greater than the odds of being killed by bushwhackers, but those exposed to the latter fear found it harder to live with. The guerrilla transformed the rural country-side of the South and its ignorant people into something threatening.[101]

One soldier in Virginia felt "The guerrillas have a regular guard established around our camp." They preyed on those who went beyond the Union lines; the soldiers caught individual guerrillas frequently, but the threat was not diminished. An officer explained how guerrillas would "creep up and shoot our pickets in cold blood." "Such men deserve no mercy; hanging is too good for them." In Kentucky guerrillas would imitate hogs and sneak up to the lines grunting until they could shoot the men on picket.[102]

New soldiers had particularly vivid imaginations. Henry Pippitt, who was only sixteen when he enlisted, wrote his poor mother from Virginia, requesting that she buy him a revolver, a piece of equipment denied to privates that he regarded as nonetheless essential. "expect some Dark rainey night 5 or 6 guralers come and surrounded me then the pistol would come handy." Without the revolver to defend himself against so many sleathy raiders, he would be forced to surrender and then hung; Pippitt understandably concluded "i need it bad."[103]

Charles Dunham went scouting for guerrillas in the area around South Tunnel, Tennessee. He associated these expeditions with a great sense of uncertainty: "A person never knows when they will run on to the enemy." The enemy was one for whom he had no respect. "Thare aint any fite in the devils that are prowling a round hear. Fight is not thare mottow, rob, steal, & tare up the rail road track. If they see half thare equal a comeing every last buger will run for sweet life." His contempt for these men and perhaps the anxiety that scouting produced in him made him resolve to adjust his conduct to the realities of guerrilla warfare. "I have maid up my mind when they throw up thare arms and holer dont shot I will never pull my gun down again." After forming this resolution, he wrote home about the "tall slautering done heare with the rebels," and said, "everyone we cach without killing some how dont get into camp."[104]

Guerrillas were savage and cruel. In Kentucky a group of them captured two Union soldiers, William B. Montgomery and John Vance. The prisoners were "tied to trees like dogs, and shot." The three bullets that hit Montgomery killed him. "Vance was shot three times through the head (one ball going in his right eye) after which they started away and left them as they supposed, both dead." One of the guerrillas returned to shoot Vance once again through the head. Incredibly, Vance survived, "and as soon as he was satisfied they were no longer in the vicinity he crawled away after taking a last look at poor Montgomery." Vance reached the pike and lay there several hours until found by Union soldiers and brought by ambulance to camp where his company returned later that afternoon. It is no wonder that the news of this atrocity "almost set the boys wild with rage and thoughts of revenge."[105]

Such rage, however, led to lapses in judgment and decency on the part of the soldiers. The 36th Ohio Infantry served in the area around Summersville, in what would later become West Virginia. Much of their time was spent tracking guerrillas, whom they sometimes preferred to kill rather than take prisoner. William Dunham, an officer in the regiment, hated such work and longed to engage in more honorable service, presumably on the front, where one fought uniformed enemies in proper lines of battle, rather than chasing bushwhackers and living in the midst of a hostile population. Since front-line service was vastly more dangerous than patrolling backwoods areas, what Dunham really was saying is that he would rather dramatically increase the risk of death than to live subject to the contradictions inherent in guerrilla warfare. Dunham was horrified when the 36th Ohio executed a young man suspected of bushwhacking.

He had been found casting bullets—"*evidence incontestable that he was a bushwhacker* (especially in this country of game where nearly all men are hunters)"—by a group of soldiers searching for guerrillas. He told them all he knew of the local guerrillas but denied that he was one of them, a denial Dunham credited. "They kept him until they got within a few miles of home and then in *cold blood, barbariously shot him.*" As the soldiers marched back to camp, the corporal commanding the prisoner and the Price brothers, who had been selected as executioners, fell to the rear of the column. "The corporal told the fellow now was his time to escape and for him to run for his life, he did so, not seeming to know the object, when a few paces off—the Prices fired upon him and brought him to the ground, A. Price then ran up and shot him again with the pistol he took from the man he killed in the fight— and thus put an end to his life—the boys described his *screams* after he was shot first as *heaert-rendering*—they left him unburied." Dunham could only add, "My God: has it come to this?"[106]

Ordinarily, however, the soldiers could not deal so immediately with guerrillas or suspected guerrillas. Instead, they had to operate through the communities the guerrillas came from, coercing those civilians who were their friends and families and whose support was necessary for the guerrillas to continue fighting. And of course, one could not always be certain that the innocent civilian was not in reality a guerrilla himself.

When partisans destroyed the railroad in that part of Virginia known as "Mosby's Confederacy," the Union army arrested "two or three of the most prominent FFVs." These prisoners were tied to the cowcatchers of the trains. "They were fed upon this *Luxury* for a *few days* and then given to understand it would be made a *regular diet* should the least occasion arise for it again. Their devastated Virginia homes were so much more promising than their chances in the next world that they showed no desire to Exchange and we think the road is [tolarbly] safe now." The theory was that citizens could stop the guerrillas' activities if they chose.[107]

Intimidating leading citizens to influence unreachable guerrillas may have been politic. The usual form of retaliation against guerrillas—the destruction of property—wore a guise of reasonableness too but was more clearly a product of rage and the desire for revenge. A Missouri Unionist regretted the violent expression of such emotions during the Sherman-Porter Expedition down the

Mississippi River in December 1862. At points the expedition "was considerably annoyed by Guerrilla parties, stationed on the bends and narrow places of the river, and firing into our transports with cannon." Periodically troops were landed to fight these guerrillas but their enemies disappeared before they could be caught. "All the revenge we could take was to burn the houses, plantations and villages near which such depredations had been committed. Thus the rebels gave us considerable to do and the consequence was, that soon the whole river was lined by burning dwellings and plantations. Nevertheless the rebels persisted in their useless and to themselves so destructive mode of fighting, and the natural consequence was, a general burning of nearly all the plantations between Helena and Napoleon." When the rebels did not fire, towns went unmolested.

The expedition halted for the night twenty miles below Napoleon. The Unionist sergeant recorded that "The night was a splendid one, and to the splendor of a clear bright sky, was added the horrible grandeur of hundreds of burning buildings, fired by our troops for resistance they found in landing. It was a grand, and 'horribly' beautiful sight but deplorable and disgusting to me, at the same time." What disgusted him was that this "wanton destruction of houses and splendid farms" was not "a 'military necessity,' " but simply an expression of "thirst for vengeance, and licentious desire to sack and burn." The military rationale of retaliation was insufficient to persuade this soldier that such behavior was justified.[108]

Stripping the countryside of food that might feed guerrillas could serve as both a threat to civilians and a direct blow at the bushwhackers dependent on that source of supply. One officer, on one of the many fruitless expeditions after Mosby, confessed, "No honor to be expected in following him for you can not reasonably expect a fight with him on any fair ground." His soldiers, "citizens in the day and Bushwhackers at Night," were "all around you watching your movements." On this expedition "We captured 13 of Mosby's men a number of Horses & Mules & large drove of cattle and returned without loss." This was not random looting or even an attempt to supply the Union army; rather it was part of the policy by which Mosby was to be fought. "We told the people that we intended in the future to live upon them while among them and take all the horses & cattle that would be of use to us that if they would harbor Mosby they might expect us among them also."

"One woman demanded to see my authority to search her house (her husband was present) she holding the Keyes. I pointed her to a line of soldiers standing in front of the house and told her there was my authority and the power to enforce it." He justified taking food from civilian families by saying, "We know their Sons & Brothers are in the army fighting us." There were no men left in the area who could serve in the Confederate army; "if we find one no matter what may be his excuse you would be safe in arresting him." Even though this officer supported the policy, he admitted it was hard to enforce "where women Plead & children cry."[109]

But as some sentimental soldiers were surprised to learn, women aided the guerrillas. One woman came to brigade headquarters at Warrenton, Virginia, and requested that soldiers be assigned to guard her property. Three men, with an aide to post them, went to the woman's house, only to be ambushed by guerrillas; one soldier escaped. Maurus Oestreich, who recorded the incident in his diary, thought the woman would be hanged.[110]

There was one irony about the struggle between guerrillas and Union troops. Private Smith of the 51st Illinois, who helped capture guerrillas in the vicinity of Murfreesboro, pointed out the fact that some guerrillas were, in one sense, frauds. Even though they were nominally Confederate, they were hardly partisans of the Southern cause. They belonged to no army and plundered all the citizens without regard for their political sympathies. When the Union forces broke up guerrilla parties they protected "the families of confederate soldiers, whom these guerrillas rob," as much as they protected themselves.[111]

In general, however, making war on guerrillas required making war on civilians. Indeed, after 1863, when the Union realized it had to break the Southern people's will to fight, making war on the Confederacy required making war on civilians. The war could no longer be restricted to engagements between two opposing armies. Hurting civilians violated some soldiers' ideas about protecting the innocent and about the high and virtuous role of the Union volunteer. Other soldiers were more prepared to accept this new mode of warfare, partly because the guerrillas themselves had made distinctions between foes and civilians impossible to maintain. But the landscape also played its role—it was so foreign it seemed to demand destruction, and many soldiers embraced the work of destruction with zest.

Furthermore, the landscape had convinced soldiers of the cultural inferiority of the South. The so-called new mode of warfare was not new. Burning crops, destroying homes, and inflicting suffering on women and children had been standard practice in wars with Indians. What horrified many at the time and earned W. T. Sherman the dubious credit of originating "total war," was that this war was being made on whites—fellow Americans. The perceived inferiority of the Indians reduced them to less than human status and so justified extreme methods of warfare. The same feelings of superiority influenced the Union soldiers as they fought Southerners.

Those who attribute "total war" primarily to General Sherman ignore the fact that unleashing soldiers against the civilian population would not have been successful if the soldiers were not willing to forage and burn. They were. If the March to the Sea represented a new mode of warfare, it was not simply forced on automatons by an omnipotent commander. Many Union soldiers had advocated destruction of rebel property long before the autumn of 1864. If the Civil War was the world's first total war, the decision to fight it that way was the soldiers' as much as it was the generals'.

In May 1862 a cavalryman on the Peninsula complained that the rebels were treated too leniently. He had "captured a beautiful mare" but was uncertain that his officers would let him keep it. Perhaps "some bloody Rebel will come and claim him and if that is the case he will have to be given up as the Rebels are treated as if they had never done anything wrong in their lives." One incident he thought represented the whole. A Union cavalryman died and "one of the bloody cutthroats refused enough Boards and nails to make him a box to be buried in," until forced by the provost marshal. Yet this "cutthroat" "had a man of our Regiment put in the guard house for taking a few rails to cook his grub." Rather than returning property to such men, the cavalryman thought it would be better to hang them to the nearest tree.[112]

Connecticut soldier John E. Morris also accused the Union authorities of undue leniency toward rebels. He wrote from Suffolk, Virginia, in April 1863 that "There is one old man near here who signals with the Rebs, and it is known that he does so, and doubtless gives them much information regarding our movements in this vicinity, yet the government, so far from having him arrested or put where he can do no harm, keeps a guard around his house to *protect his property.*" Consequently he was delighted to hear a month later that in the future they were "to *burn* every home we come across and not waste our time in *guarding* secesh property," and reported that in accordance with this order "every house about here has been laid in ashes with the exception of those which we use for hospitals." At the same time, since the local inhabitants refused to sell anything for U. S. dollars, the soldiers confiscated anything they wanted, "so their refusal to take 'greenbacks' dont trouble us much."[113]

In July 1862 James T. Miller welcomed Gen. John Pope's orders permitting foraging and ending the guarding of rebel property. "that guarding of the property of the rebles has been the greatest Curse to us in this army that could have been thought of for the men had got so mad about it that a good many of them did not care whether they did anything or not." Miller claimed that the protection of rebel property had convinced many soldiers that the war was not being prosecuted with the necessary vigor. But with Pope's new policy, "the soldiers begin to think that we are going to have war in earnest and that we are to be supported by the Government and that no false notions of mercy are to save the scoundrels that have caused this war."[114]

Alva Griest also complained about guarding rebel property. He argued that the only way the war could be ended was by making the civilian population "feel the horrors of war by confiscation." If the army stripped the South of its property, its inhabitants would eagerly return to their allegiance, "a better and wiser people." Griest was a soldier in the same regiment as Montgomery and Vance, the men shot by Kentucky guerrillas. A few weeks after the shooting, he was engaged in rounding up horses and mules that had been hidden by their owners. "As an old negro said, 'Dem Yankees, dey'l find anything.' Well that is at present our business and those men ought to have lived north of the Ohio or else not trampled the glorious stars and stripes in the dust."[115]

Yet the destruction of property sometimes had an antic quality, even when described by men who advocated it as a serious tool of victory. Joseph Lester, a soldier writing from the area around Vicksburg, reproduced the carnival flavor that accompanied the looting of a plantation house. According to Lester, pillaging came first. "Like bees going to a Hive, the Boys one after another would crowd on to the Porch, into the Hall. Parlor, Kitchen or Bedroom, appropriating every thing useful or ornamental which they thought they could take care of." After that, the work—or play—of destruction began. "Beautiful Pianos estimated as having cost 1000 dollars, would be sat down to by some of 'Uncle Sams' privates and melodious strains of music drawn therefrom, enchanting those in hearing of it, reminding them of Home or its associations, or firing up their Martial ardor by the liveliness of its strains, until broken in upon another bevy of Boys, who would accost it as though it had Life and Intelligence, makes requests of it and receiving no response, would in a set speech, declare it to be Sesech, when down would come a clubbed musket, and what was a few minutes before, a thing yielding Pleasure and [altering] all persons in hearing of it, is in a few minutes a shapeless wreck.

"But the most amusing of all would be to see a crowd before a large dressing mirror, dusty and travelstained, when seeing themselves full length, clothes in rags, faces dirty and not shaven, they would involuntarily begin to pull up Shirt collars or arrange some article of clothing, readjust their hair, step back, put themselves in attitude and admire themselves to their fill after which a conversation would take place of a similar nature to the above, to the parties seen in the mirror. when sufficient response would be given by standerbys to condemn them as Rebels, and 'Charge Bayonets' would shiver the glass into peices."

Lester thought destruction of rebel property necessary to win the war, and he defended his fellow soldiers' actions—and probably joined in. "If any of your readers should think that there was too much Vandalism in any of these acts, let them think of the necessity which requires our army to be down here, of the danger to Life and Limb, each one is subject to, besides doing as our brave fellows did, march and fight under a hot sun upon seven or eight hard crackers for two weeks, and do as some of our men actually did, rifle the havresacks of the *Dead* for food, and give from half a dollar to a dollar for a single cracker!" The defense was not simply against the charge of vandalism. Lester also was defending the soldiers against the charge of silliness, which he implicitly justified by reference to the hardship and tension that made men prone to occasional giddy behavior. What Lester is describing could simply be schoolboy pranks. In fact, the Union army, like most armies, was composed primarily of young men not much older than school-boys. If rage and violence against civilians represent one extreme of soldiers' behavior, youthful high spirits represent the other.[116]

Soldiers on an expedition against guerrillas might instead capture geese. One soldier looted a Southerner's library, stealing sermons "which were preached by his Grandfather in 1771 to 1812"; he mailed them home to be preserved "as relics of war." Soldiers passing through Summersville, Virginia, found a comfortable farm-house whose owner had fled. They killed and ate the livestock— kicking a hole in the floor over the fireplace so they could suspend a turkey over the flames with a length of bedcord. Union soldiers in Hampton, Virginia, knocked away the wall of a church to ex-amine the cornerstone. The 42nd Illinois encamped on the site of the University of the South in Sewanee, Tennessee. The university at this time was little more than a scattering of outbuildings. Before the war the cornerstone of the main building had been laid. While the 42nd Illinois was there, the soldiers tipped over the cornerstone and stole all the papers deposited in it. As one of them asked, "What wont a Soldier do?"[117]

During Sherman's campaign in north Georgia, a Michigan lieu-tenant made a revealing comment. His regiment marched through Cassville, a town he admired. Soldiers went into the beautiful houses that had been abandoned by their owners and wantonly destroyed what had been left behind. Lieutenant Miller blushed to admit their vandalism but insisted that the soldiers would have behaved them-selves if the Cassville residents had not fled their homes. A similar observation was made by Joseph Lester in his account of the looting of the plantations near Vicksburg. He insisted that the property of families who remained was not bothered. Most of the property owners, however, had not stayed long enough to find this out. "Such a scene of desolation which our advance left behind has been seldom witnessed, the absense of owners making it legitimate to plunder."[118]

Soldiers regarded an empty house as an invitation to loot and burn. Loyal citizens, after all, had nothing to fear; the very flight of the owners revealed their treason. Despite occasional mistreatment of civilians and the myths furthered by *Gone With the Wind*, Northern soldiers in general were not heartless barbarians or mere thieves who took advantage of the confusion of the times and the license warfare gave to plunder. During the war Southern citizens were known to talk the Yankee vandals into respecting their homes. When citizens abandoned their property at the Yankee approach, they not only admitted their own guilt, but they implicitly accused the Northern men of being no better than barbarians. The soldiers tended to live up to expectations—expect the worst, and you get it.

Northern behavior exposed contrary impulses. John Wesley Marshall's regiment, the 97th Ohio Volunteers, foraged indiscriminately in Tennessee, taking sheep, hogs, potatoes, fruit, and other edibles. Marshall thought it "hard to thus deprive families of their hard earned living," but justified doing so as an inevitable consequence of a war for which Southern civilians, not Northern soldiers, bore the guilt. The Union soldiers in the area had been on short rations for several weeks, and foraging was the only way they had to supplement their meager diet. Loyal citizens were paid for their involuntary contributions, but as Marshall observed, food was more valuable to them than money under the circumstances. The citizens, both loyal and rebel, began coming to the Federal lines begging for food. As soon as the 97th Ohio was put back on full rations, its various companies donated portions of their food to feed the local population, only a few days after their foraging had stripped the countryside of food.

Union soldiers did not always have things their own way. A group of foragers, some of whom had live chickens tied to their horses, rode into the yard of a house occupied by six or seven "secesh" women and dismounted. While the soldiers teased them · and listened to their bitter anti-Yankee tirades, one of the women snuck around the house and shook her apron at the horses. The horses began running, the chickens began squawking, and the soldiers chased the animals down the road, as the women yelled after them, "Go it, you yankeys, run. there's your Yankee trick."[119]

Sometimes civilian resistance to foraging was more deadly. Sgt. Charles Crook Hood found the grave of a fellow soldier on a Tennessee farm. John Mulharon and some other soldiers had gone to a farmer and demanded food. The family had told the soldiers "there was nothing in the house." "John then insisted and probably behaved very badly in threatening to do some damages to his family or premises and was about to carry his threats into execution when the farmer shot him through the head and killed him instantly." The outraged soldiers began breaking the windows of the farmer's house, and the family fled. The soldiers burned the house down; dug a grave in a fence corner; and buried Mulharon "without any ceremony."

Hood found the boards that marked the grave almost fallen down; his captain ordered that a proper headboard be made. As Hood and another soldier worked on the headboard, the regiment's colonel came by, inquired what they were doing, and ordered them to return to their company, "saying at the same time that such a man as that did not deserve to have his grave marked"—a very harsh judgment in light of the Civil War soldier's fears of anonymous burial. Sergeant Hood, with the connivance of another captain, snuck back, carved the soldier's name, company, and regiment upon a board, and raised it over the grave.[120]

As Hood's story makes clear, there were those in the Union army who thought looting citizens' property and threatening their lives were disgraceful. An Ohio officer said, "I did not think that those who were battling for the Sacred Cause of the Union could be so forgetful of all that makes them civilized and descend to the level of the barbarians." A New Hampshire soldier was shocked to see soldiers in Fredericksburg looting the town even as the shells fired by the opposing army passed over their heads. A regular army officer reported that "every house" was "ransacked & plundered"—the soldiers searching for money and tobacco. They dragged furniture out into the streets and broke it into pieces. The officer said his "heart felt sick" when he thought of families returning to find their homes destroyed, and of how the enemy, embittered by such wanton pillage, would "fight like tigers in defence of their own homes now threatened with a similar fate." Such behavior struck some Union soldiers as no better than that of the rebels.[121]

Some soldiers felt particularly sorry for the women. One acted as a wagon guard to a forage train, watching soldiers killing "lots of hogs, Guinna hens, Turkeys, Ducks, Chickens, & Geese" and gathering honey and sweet potatoes. The soldiers took anything they wanted, even stealing from slaves. "I tell you it looks hard to see a hundred or two men cleaning out everything they can lay their hands on & the women looking on seeing it all. some boys take even to the wenches dresses or walk right into the house take books Jewelry or clothes & even if she ask's them to spare anything it makes no difference." Another soldier, serving in the Shenandoah Valley, could not stand "to see men go thrue the poor helpless womans houses and take everything they own and sometimes abuse them in thay try to protect themselves." He believed all women deserved more respect, even rebels. And a third soldier in Georgia said, "I have seen women crying & begging for them to leave a litle for the children, but their tears were of no avail." He concluded, "Some of our soldiers are a disgrace to the service."[122]

Despite the regrets that the third soldier felt, he also argued, "Such is war & the sooner the aristocracy or rather the ones that brought it on feels the effects the sooner we will have peace." And another soldier who disliked witnessing the destruction of civilian property shrugged off Yankee behavior in a most time-honored way. "But they would Do the Same with us if they would Get the chance."[123]

Union officers, while not entirely powerless to prevent vandalism and looting, certainly found it difficult. As the war went on, and the notion that the will of the South must be broken became more accepted, the officers did not try. But the soldiers led the officers here, not the other way around. One officer wrote from Mississippi in the fall of 1862, complaining of some Union soldiers "who seem to be possessed with the idea that in order to carry on war men must throw aside civilization and become savages." Soldiers had stolen a carriage and horses and were riding in the middle of a marching regiment. A passing general officer saw them and ordered them out of the carriage. They refused. Grabbing a gun from one of them, he forced them to "unhitch the horses, take off the harness, and putting it on themselves, he made them draw the carriage back to the owner more than two miles." The stern-tempered general was W. T. Sherman.[124]

In January 1865 Sherman's army began its march from Savannah north into South Carolina. The troops marched through pine groves and small towns—a half-dozen houses, a church—that had been partially burned. A pair of blackened chimneys might rise from a burned house near the roadside; these the soldiers called "Kilpatrick's Monuments." Burning cross ties could make a railroad line a "long line of fire," that one volunteer called a "Beautiful sight." One night a strong wind spread fire through fences and houses and into the pine groves so that "the whole country for miles was brilliantly lighted up." The same soldier exhibited his streak of romanticism again: "The scene was a grandly sublime one; to witness that destructive element, as it climbed to the very tops of the tall dead pine trees, filled with turpentine and rosin as they were—with the strong wind fanning the fierce furious flames, as they madly leaped from one combustible object to another sparing nothing before them, but the very earth itself." The sparks and smoke filled the sky. South Carolina, "the 'Mother State of Secession,' where it was nurtured and fostered, until it kindled into flame," was suffering an appropriate fate.[125]

Apparently, setting fire to buildings and watching them burn was highly satisfying. Much of this satisfaction derived from humans' undeniable fascination with fire. Some of it came from the romantic admiration of spectacle; fire was sublime. But the burning of houses was also inspired by the desire to punish wicked Southerners and to revenge the fear that warfare and a hostile environment caused. It is probably not simply a coincidence that in American conceptions of hell, the sinful and the unregenerate were punished by an eternity of fire.[126]

Fire transformed the Southern landscape. A Connecticut soldier observed sourly of Donaldsonville, Louisiana, "this place would be quite pleasant if it had been all burned up." During the war many Union soldiers took the opportunity to do just that: to burn up the unredeemed. Destruction, after all, was the first step to building a purified South, a more American landscape.[127]

The burning of Southern homes and plantations expressed anger and contempt felt toward all Southern society. In one sense, burning a plantation destroyed the world of the planter, as in another sense did freeing his slaves. One soldier wrote that the war had humbled the Southern slaveholder and made the South unlivable: "the blackness of ashes mark where many a comfortable dwelling stood. . . . and the arastocry of the south that once rode in golden chariots are now forced to come into our lines mounted on a long eard mule to beg a little salt." Vandalism was a symbolic victory over a corrupt and foreign society.[128]

A corrupt and foreign society. What to do with the defeated South became the great national question after the war. Different men answered it according to their different kinds of knowledge. There was the knowledge of statistics and newspapers, of ideologues and politicians. The more intimate knowledge that the soldiers shared, however, was not the knowledge of the printed word or the politician's speech. This was the knowledge of the land—plowed fields, trees bearing fruit, well-tended farms—and of labor—the artisan's tools, the well-built houses. The soldiers judged the South they saw by this kind of knowledge. They compared the South to the North and found it lacking. They found a region untidy and unindustrious, a white population untrustworthy, and a black population unworthy of freedom.

The soldiers saw in the South primarily that which they came expecting to see. The view from the road was not necessarily the best one to judge a society by; the conqueror's perspective obscured certain realities. The very foreignness of the landscape may have made men eager to interpret it too hastily. And the threat from a strange and hostile countryside encouraged men to stick together in their own military communities. The Northern soldier was in a position to see the South, but he was hardly in the position to master the workings of its intricate society. Travelers rarely learn everything they would like to know about the places they visit, and in any case, the soldier was only incidentally in the South as an observer.

After the war was over, Winslow Homer celebrated the returned

Union veteran in a painting whose message a too-hasty viewer might miss. A man with his back to the viewer is cutting wheat with a scythe. Unlike the stylized drawing "The way Our Union Boys are raised," this painting makes one feel every aching muscle and every drop of sweat that the harvestman suffers. But it is not merely a painting of an agricultural laborer. In the heat of the sun, he has shed his coat—a worn military blouse—and it lies next to an army-issue canteen he has brought back from the war. Homer's picture is named "A New Field." The Union soldier has returned to America.

FIVE

The Confederate Experience

I Prologue: Lee's Invasion of Pennsylvania, 1863

In the summer of 1863 Robert E. Lee led his Army of Northern Virginia across western Maryland into Pennsylvania. This invasion provided Confederates one of their rare chances to inflict the kind of damage suffered by the South upon their enemies in the North. Lee did not go North rejoicing in the possibility of bringing fire and sword to the land; he did hope that the invasion would bring a speedy end to the war by weakening Northern morale, by impressing Britain and France enough that they would intervene in the American war, and, just possibly, by inflicting a decisive defeat over the Army of the Potomac. If the campaign produced nothing else, at least he could furnish his army with desperately needed supplies at Northern expense for a while.[1]

Many of the soldiers had been in Maryland the year before, during the Antietam campaign. From a Northern viewpoint, this had been an invasion of Maryland, but the Southerners preferred to think of it as an attempt to liberate the state. Maryland, after all, was a slave state with strong Southern sympathies, one of the first victims of Lincoln despotism. Southern soldiers discovered that Maryland was not a hotbed of secession feeling. Much of that state was staunchly Unionist. Some Confederates were dismayed to learn that Union sentiment prevailed even in certain parts of Virginia.[2]

Consequently, in June 1863 most soldiers had more modest expectations than they had had the year before. One wrote home sardonically, "We were received with even fewer demonstrations of joy than when we entered last year." Some Maryland women wore red, white, and blue ribbons. The male civilians avoided contact with the rebels.[3]

Still, there was much to admire about Maryland. Soldiers praised it as "a fine country for wheat, corn, clover, grass and cattle." The farms were beautiful; the houses well-built and comfortable. "People are nearer on an equality here, than in many other sections of the country," one Confederate noted approvingly.[4]

Others looked less favorably upon the state. James B. Sheeran, the Catholic chaplain of the 14th Louisiana, thought western Marylanders possessed no "grace of manners, high-toned sentiment, or intellectual culture"; he compared them unfavorably with Virginians. "Indeed," he concluded, "with all their wealth they appeared little advanced in civilization."[5]

On the evening of June 21, a dozen men in Ramseur's brigade were baptized. A witness commented, "it is the first Soldiers I have seen Baptized since I've been in service, & its a nice thing to see Soldiers baptized." Ramseur's brigade was encamped near Hagerstown, near the Confederate positions during the Antietam campaign less than a year before. The converts were baptized in Antietam Creek, the scene of the bloodiest single day of the war. The same day as the baptism, Thomas Harlow revisited the battlefield. He found hogs rooting dead bodies from shallow graves and eating the flesh from the bones.[6]

Whatever they thought about Maryland, when Confederates left it behind for Pennsylvania, they knew they had become an army of invasion. Some men did not relish the idea of aggressive warfare. A Virginian wrote his wife that "we had no business here to my notion"; it made him "feel just like I was at some one's house that would drive me off." One Confederate who had been raised in Chambersburg refused to fight in Pennsylvania.[7]

Others delighted in crossing into Northern territory. One group of soldiers asked a local inhabitant to identify exactly where the Maryland-Pennsylvania line was. Straddling the line, they drank toasts from a canteen. Sgt. C. C. Cummings also requested a citizen to draw the boundary line for him. Once it was drawn, Cummings leaped from Maryland into Pennsylvania.[8]

Pennsylvania was a revelation to many Confederates. They praised the fine wheat, the unsurpassed farmland, the neat and tidy houses and barns. They admired the numerous small towns, with their brick and stone buildings. Perhaps the most unusual reaction that seeing the North produced came to Jerome Yates, a Mississippi soldier. His family had recently lost many of their slaves. He had been embittered by this, but after he returned from Pennsylvania, he wrote to console his mother and sister "since I have seen how well people live without Negras I am tempted to wish I never had one. I seen something of private life in a free State while in Penn." Apparently the fine crops and comfortable dwellings persuaded him that agricultural wealth could be produced in the absence of black slaves.[9]

All of Pennsylvania did not please the Confederates. One dismissed Greencastle, "a very pretty little town," as inhabited by "the sorriest set of Yankees . . . and the largest collection of ugly dirty looking women I ever saw." Another, who had praised the state's agricultural methods, claimed that the citizens were too frequently unattractive; "Whilst looking admiringly at a sweet cottage and pretty yard, I often pictured to myself some sweet, bright-eyed creature within, when lo! a slatternly square-faced, thick-lipped round and clumsy looking woman would make her appearance with a pail of water on her head!" But he did confess that Pennsylvania had some, if not enough, pretty girls.[10]

Gen. Dorsey Pender thought Pennsylvanians "the most miserable people" he had ever seen. "They are coarse and dirty and the number of dirty-looking children is perfectly astonishing." He dismissed the inhabitants as "louts." A North Carolina lieutenant summed the people up as "Generly Ugly." And a Virginian thought the Pennsylvania Dutch "simple ignorant & degraded." Thus Southerners ridiculed their enemies for the same sins that Northerners found in the South. "Ugly." "Dirty." "Slatternly." "Coarse." "Ignorant." "Degraded." These terms, that sound so descriptive, are really the ways in which Americans customarily think of their enemies. They are ways of making war.[11]

Some Confederates were shocked by the difference between the Northern state and Virginia. Here they found hundreds of healthy men not serving in the Union army, while in Virginia almost all white men of age had gone to war. Francis Dawson said, "it gave us a realizing sense of the strength of the enemy to see that they could have so large armies in the field and leave so many lusty men in peace at home." Some soldiers asked a local woman, "Why, our men and our boys are all in the army, why aren't these?"[12]

Unlike the inhabitants of northern Virginia, the farmers of Pennsylvania were not used to the movements of large bodies of troops. Their reactions to relatively mild Confederate behavior amused the soldiers. One Virginian later remembered the consternation of one Pennsylvania Dutch farmer as the Confederates passed through his farm. "As our guns occupied the road the infantry had turned into the field and had trodden down a belt of wheat the width of a column of fours, and the men had swarmed into his little front yard to get water, making some muddy disorder." Witnessing this spectacle, the farmer went to two Confederate officers and said, "I have heardt and I have readt, of de horros of warfare, but my utmost conceptions did not equal dis."[13]

Indeed, the citizens of Pennsylvania who had the courage to talk to the rebels seemed to be torn between fear and curiosity. "Crowds of ladies" visited the camp of the Louisiana Guard Artillery, where "they were treated with the greatest respect." They told one Louisianian "that they had never seen a cannon and that it was the first time that they had ever seen a large body of soldiers." Other Pennsylvanians assured the invaders that they were Copperheads and offered the soldiers bribes of food. At Turkstown a delegation of ladies met the Confederates to ask if they planned to burn the town; they were told the Confederates "did not enter Pennsylvania for the purpose of destroying private property or warring against women and children." Most people seemed "frightened out of their senses." A farmer and his son degraded themselves in Confederate eyes by going into the road and dragging away obstacles so that the invading soldiers could march by easier.[14]

Some citizens took a bolder attitude. One Confederate recorded that some "deluded wretches" predicted most of the Army of Northern Virginia would not return home alive. Another soldier wrote his wife "this Country looks upon us with evident contempt"; he hoped to teach the citizens a lesson. Some girls wore miniature Union flags; "Others more indecent hold their noses and make faces." A woman chased soldiers out of her garden with a stick. One Chambersburg woman told a Confederate officer, "You are marching mighty proudly now, but you will come back faster than you went." Asked to justify her prediction, she explained, "Because you put your trust in General Lee and not in the Lord Almighty."[15]

Confederates prided themselves on their self-restraint at such taunts. A South Carolina officer reported, "Our men go on and pay no attention to them. They only laugh at them when they make themselves ridiculous." This was the laughter that came to men who were triumphant—and men who had not yet had to worry about guerrilla warfare and a treacherous population.[16]

Union soldiers felt ashamed that Northern citizens did so little to resist the Confederate invasion. Some advocated for the North what was so frequently most condemned in the South: guerrilla warfare. A Pennsylvanian in the Army of the Potomac observed bitterly, "Look at the difference. They ride through Penna. without molestation—while we cannot go a hundred yards outside of the picket line without being fired at." Virginia swarmed with guerrillas, but Pennsylvania could boast of none. Another Pennsylvanian said that if the people of the state did not "respond to the Governor's call and at once take arms and go to the defense of the Old Keystone," they "are not worthy of having a free government." If their patriotism failed them—and he feared it might—he would just as soon see the rebels "destroy everything as they go." But he hoped invasion would arouse Northern patriotism.[17]

When Confederate troops reached Carlisle, Pennsylvania, they raised the Confederate flag over the town while a military band played "Dixie." One soldier wrote home from the U. S. Barracks at Carlisle his approval of Lee's policy of not molesting enemy private property; as he put it they were not allowed "even to pluck off a *cherry* by the wayside." He thought this was the correct policy as it would show the Northern citizens "we are gentlemen."[18]

Many Confederates shared this attitude. Maj. Franklin Gaillard explained that if the army was allowed to loot, the men would become demoralized. "Many of them think it very hard that they should not be allowed to treat them as their soldiers treated our people." He argued that the taking of horses and other goods by proper authorities would "tax the people here and make them feel the war," without private initiative on the part of the soldiers. He

expressed perhaps the most important reason for Confederate re-
straint by saying, "But we must not imitate the Yankees in their
mean acts."[19]

During the invasion many Confederates clung to their moral
superiority over the thieving Yankees who looted the South. What
better way to prove to the world and themselves their virtue and
self-restraint than to treat the natives of Pennsylvania with forbearance and to respect private property? Surely by such conduct
Southerners could demonstrate their right to independence.

Such motives led the soldiers to restrain themselves more than
they otherwise would have. Under Lee's strict order and their own
desires to prove their virtue, the Confederate soldiers did behave
well in Pennsylvania. And the good impression they sought to give
was strengthened by the simple fact that minor interference with
civilian property—the sort that had damned the raw soldiers of
the North in 1861—no longer caused widespread condemnation
in 1863. After the war the myth grew among Southerners that the
Confederate army had indeed been stainless and that the Gettysburg campaign had been marked by gentlemanly propriety.[20]

Joseph Hilton boasted that rather than burning Northern towns,
Confederate troops saved them. Retreating militia had burned a
bridge outside of one town, and the fire spread; Confederates put
it out. Since then, however, Hilton had heard that Yankees had
visited his hometown—and had shown no gentlemanly scruples
toward Southern civilians. Hilton predicted that the next chance
the soldiers had to torch a Northern town they would be happy
to take.[21]

Chaplain Sheeran praised the conduct of Confederate soldiers
in Pennsylvania. While some of them "helped themselves to poultry,
vegetables, milk, etc.," they did not destroy private property wantonly as Union troops did down south. He thought this behavior
"redounds more to the honor of our army than a dozen victories
over the enemy on the battlefield." He also believed it amazed
Northern civilians. "Knowing what their army had done to us;
that they had burned our towns, laid waste our lands, driven helpless women and children from their homes, destroyed our implements of husbandry, that we might not be able to cultivate our
lands, they very naturally expected that our soldiers would treat

them in a similar manner." Sheeran said many Northerners told him that by good behavior the Confederate "had made many friends among them."[22]

After the war the self-congratulation concerning the superior morality of Confederates during the Gettysburg campaign would disgust the realistic John Singleton Mosby, partisan leader and postwar Republican. Mosby did not deny that General Lee attempted to restrain Confederate troops during the invasion of Pennsylvania; he objected to sentimental Lost Cause rhetoric that failed to portray the military necessity that lay underneath the order. "General Lee's order was issued, not from any feeling of tenderness toward the Pennsylvanians, but to preserve the morale and discipline of his army." Gen. James Longstreet had told the English observer James Fremantle much the same thing at the time. "Whilst speaking of entering upon the enemy's soil, he said to me, that although it might be fair, in just retaliation, to *apply* the *torch*, yet doing so would demoralize the army and ruin its excellent discipline. Private property is to be therefore protected."[23]

Unfortunately for the Lost Cause's purity, a great many Confederates did not live up to their mythic responsiblities in 1863. They acted just like Yankees. Like every other campaign of the war, the Gettysburg campaign saw its share of casual looting, intimidation of civilians, and more reprehensible crimes.

Confederates boasted of their consumption of produce of "the corpulent Dutch farmers": eggs, butter, chickens, green apples apple cider and apple butter, cherries, and honey. They admitted to "playing sad havoc with their Horses and Cattle." Still, another insisted that the soldiers took only "things edible." "Oh how the farmers of Pennsylvania suffer for our boys remember Butter." Even officers' black servants enjoyed the looting.[24]

Some soldiers wanted to go further than the rather forgivable "crime" of eating the chickens and apples of Pennsylvania farmers. One soldier said they were "itching to retaliate." Gen. Dorsey Pender wrote his wife, who disapproved of the invasion, that "Our people have suffered from the depradations of the Yankees, but if we ever get into their country they will find out what it is to have an invading army amongst them. Our officers—not Gen. Lee— have made up their minds not to protect them and some of our chaplains are telling the men they must spoil and kill." Before the invasion, H. C. Kendrick, a devout Christian, advocated a war of retaliation. The Yankees had pillaged and destroyed; "I don't think we would do wrong to take horses, burn houses, and commit every depredation possible upon the men of the North." That indicated the far limit of Kendrick's desire for retaliation: he would not countenance ill-treatment of the women of the North. Such conduct would be degrading and make a travesty of his own upbringing. Shepherd Pryor hoped that the army could stay in the North long enough to "make the yanks feel the sting of war." "I assure you those people up here never knew anything about this war until now our army is subsisted entirely off this country." He did not imply a special vengeance—just the constant presence of armies such as the South had enjoyed.[25]

Soldiers burned Thaddeus Stephens' foundry—fit treatment for the property of "a bitter enemy of the South." Confederates also committed acts that were simply thievery, taking money, watches, and clothes in a manner later associated with Sherman's march through Georgia. Major Gaillard, who had feared the effect on morale if the soldiers went unrestrained, regretted the "immense amount of plundering" and thought that "Our army would have been demoralized had we been victorious and remained long over there."[26]

At the same time many Confederates were congratulating themselves on the propriety of their conduct toward Pennsylvania civilians, the men of Jenkins' cavalry were gathering together runaway slaves and free blacks to ship southward to slavery. In Chambersburg Rachel Cormany saw panic-struck contrabands fleeing before the rebel army. When the Confederates arrived she witnessed the rounding up of black women and children, who were "driven by just like we would drive cattle." She recognized some of the blacks as local free people. William S. Christian, who had come to Pennsylvania seeking revenge but found himself so moved by the scared and humble citizens that he endeavored to protect their property, was offered his choice of "a lot of negroes." He had no way to send any home; his "humanity revolted at taking the poor devils away from their homes"; he turned them loose. But other soldiers hoisted black children up to their saddles and rode away with them, and bound black men were marched along with the column, along with stolen pigs, chickens, geese, and horses. Christian, despite his pity for Union citizens, had no scruples about taking a good horse from a local family; he reasoned that after all, their soldiers had taken his. Apparently some Confederates regarded rounding up blacks as fair—and profitable—retaliation for the Union troops "running off" slaves in the South.[27]

This attempt to enslave blacks would not enter the mythology of the Lost Cause. What Southerners remembered of the 1863 campaign was how close they came to victory—the closeness would be exaggerated—and the gallantry of their troops toward Northern civilians. The one made Southerners misty-eyed; the other made them self-righteous.

A comparison of Lee's march into Pennsylvania with Sherman's March to the Sea suggests some differences in Southern and Northern strategy. Whatever its failures, Lee's policy of respecting civilian rights made sense. The Confederate army could not conquer the North. The South needed to persuade the North and foreign nations to respect the Confederacy, to treat it as a nation. Good behavior was a step to earning respect; as Chaplain Sheeran hoped, good treatment would make "many friends among them."

In 1864 the North did not need to prove its respectability; it needed to demonstrate its power. If the South hoped Northern civilians would learn to respect it enough to recognize its independence, the North simply wanted the South to fear it enough to surrender. The March to the Sea succeeded in terrorizing many Southerners.

There is another irony. It is unlikely that many Northerners grew up obsessed with the horrors of Lee's invasion of Pennsylvania. Sherman remained a Southern bugaboo for a hundred years, and now his famous March is an emblem of "total war." Sherman, however, sought to demoralize the South and its army so that they would recognize the inevitable. Lee, who tried to spare citizens, needed a victory on the battlefield, a victory that would cost human lives, not livestock.

The invasion of Pennsylvania and the threat to Washington were directed at Northern opinion. While some Confederates sought revenge, Confederate policy sought a change in Northern attitude.

Sherman's March was also designed to promote defeatism, but this change carried along with it implciations of an altered society. Plantations had been burned, slaves had been freed, and the South, once returned to the Union, was to adopt civilized institutions. Northerners desired social change in the South, while Southerners, if they could obtain the security of an independent nation, could leave Northern society untouched.

There was another difference. Sherman's March, in which the soldiers were not restrained, freed black men and women from slavery. During Lee's invasion, in which the soldiers were more tightly bound, black men and women were returned to slavery.

Southerners would not remember this. They would prefer to cling to the illusion of purity that defeat offers. But the fact is that except for a few days the Confederate army was never an army of occupation; it escaped the burdens of such duty and the temptations of looting and burning its enemy's towns and countryside. The Gettysburg campaign reveals that had they had the chance, Confederates would have rivaled Yankees in the work of destruction.

The Confederate Soldier and the Crisis of the South

In April 1863, Lt. Leonidas Lafayette Polk of the 43rd North Carolina Regiment (C.S.A.) took part in an expedition into the eastern half of his home state, an area that had been held intermittently by Union forces. Elected to the state legislature as a Unionist, Polk had nonetheless volunteered very early in the war and regarded himself as a man of Southern sentiments; he was a slaveholder loyal to his state. By the spring of 1863, however, Lieutenant Polk had considerable misgivings about the Confederate war effort. Speculation and corruption were creating a "rotten aristocracy" in the South; wealth kept the rich man from the army while the poor boy was forced into service. And while Polk recognized the need for military discipline, he resented the restrictions placed upon his freedom: "A man ceases to be himself when he enlists in the ranks."

The expedition of April 1863 came close to demoralizing Lieutenant Polk entirely. He wrote his wife that he could see no point in the campaign except conscripting men of eastern North Carolina.

What particularly saddened him was that he himself was obliged to round up men and force them into the army.

> While performing my duty as enrolling officer I witnessed scenes & compelled compliance with orders which God grant I may never do again. To ride up to a man's door, whose hospitable kindness makes you feel welcome & tell him, in the presence of his faithful & loving wife & sunny-faced children, that he must be ready in 10 minutes to go with you, and see the very looks of sadness and dispair seize the wife & a cloud of apprehension cover the smiling faces of his children—their imploring looks and glances—the tears of sorrow—the Solemn silence—the affectionate clasping of hands—the fervent kisses—the sad & bitter Goodbye—the longing glance at the place most dear to him on earth, as he slowly moves out of sight—this is indeed a sad & unplesant task. When we left doors on the road crowded with the faces of frightened & crying & helpless women with the question, "For God's sake are you going to leave us at the mercy of the Yankees" made me ask often what have we gained by this trip?

Three months later Lieutenant Polk was wounded at the battle of Gettysburg. Recuperating in a Petersburg hospital, he continued his frequent letters to his wife. He expressed his doubts about a growing peace movement in North Carolina; he feared that the North would offer no terms except a return to the Union and the abolition of slavery. Still, he admired "the good old Republican spirit evinced by the plain spoken Sons" of North Carolina, and he longed for peace. In the fall of 1864 he left the service and returned to the state legislature to which he had been elected as a soldiers' candidate. In the interval between his election to office and his resignation from the service, he was court-martialed for cowardice, an accusation he believed to be politically motivated. He was found innocent.[28]

L. L. Polk was not the paradigmatic Confederate soldier, that statistical average and sum of impresssions known as "Johnny Reb." Nonetheless, his wartime career displayed elements common to the experience of most Confederate soldiers. Thousands of Southern white men in the Confederate army shared his dislike of discipline, his love of the South, and his hatred of speculation and class favoritism—as well as the experience of soldiering and defeat. They marched away to war and left behind friends and family whose lives would be plunged into chaos. They opposed an enemy whose equal skill and bravery were combined with superior resources, whose armies invaded and conquered the South. They served a government unable to protect its people or adequately supply its soldiers. They fought a war while the South underwent the revolution of emancipation. In the end it was not just the soldiers but a whole society that was defeated. This shared experience, too complex to be expressed by the rhetoric of Lost Cause orators, the fancies of filiopietistic neo-Confederates, or the condescension of historians who write of "deference" and "planter hegemony," created loyalties to that sectional fiction—the Confederate nation—while it also revealed the class bias and racism at the heart of Southern society. To understand the Confederate soldier, one must move beyond sentimentality or simplistic class analysis to a realization of the complexities of the wartime experience.[29]

In 1861 Southerners plunged into a war that revealed the strains and cracks within their society. The demands that the war placed upon the Southern people were not shared equally; those whom Bell Wiley called "the plain people of the Confederacy" bore a disproportionate share. The Confederacy, which was born of the crisis of the Old South, died, in part, from its own contradictions.[30]

Secessionists claimed, for instance, that the Confederacy would be a bulwark against modern Yankee incursions of power on the autonomy of individuals and small communities. Yet the new government actually encouraged the operation of the market, the growth of industry, and the encroachment of a national government upon individuals and into communities. It tried to control agricultural production and the labor force. Taxes and impressment of food brought farmers into contact with the agents of the state much more frequently than had been the case in the antebellum South. The Confederate Conscription Act of 1862 was the first in American history. Individual autonomy was more threatened by the

Confederacy than it had ever been by the United States. Politicians such as Zeb Vance of North Carolina and Joe Brown of Georgia gained tremendous popularity among Southern whites by their attempts to place the doctrine of state's rights between the Confederate citizen and Jefferson Davis's government at Richmond; at least one historian of the Civil War has claimed that the Confederacy died of states' rights.[31]

Nor was the Confederacy a classless white man's utopia; it proved class-ridden and dominated by the interests of the well-to-do. Conscription, for example, clearly favored the wealthy over the poor. The original conscription act of 1862 was a crazy patchwork of exemptions that placed the burden of service primarily upon poorer men. The "twenty-nigger" law, the most notorious, provided exemptions for planters owning twenty or more slaves and for overseers of large plantations. Such class legislation was justified by its supporters as necessary for the functioning of the Southern economy, but it created considerable resentment among small slaveholders and nonslaveholders alike. James Skelton voiced a popular sentiment when he wrote his sister Emily, "I do not think it is right for me to go through the hardships of camp life and the danger of Battle and others living at home enjoying life because they have a few negroes. . . ." And his brother, A. H. Skelton, a conscript, wrote his sister from a camp near Vicksburg in January 1863, "so here we all go to Hell together and I dont care damn how soon the Big fis was made to eat the little ones anyhow dont this Lat [exemption] Law [beat] all the laws that you ever did see they intend to kill all the poor men and the fools go in to it just like they ware a bliged to do it now if they are a mind to do t all Right But if they ware Like me I would see them in Hell before I would do it." There was nothing one man could do by himself against such injustice, he told his sister, and he had only one final resistance to the Confederate state: "I can think." And independent thought provided the only possible basis for opposition to the planter class during or after the war.[32]

Another provision of the conscription law that favored the wealthy was that which permitted the draftee to hire a substitute in his place. This purchase of substitutes offered a loophole for men of means who were not entitled to any other kind of exemption and encouraged a sort of grotesque speculation on the part of poor men: if they had nothing else to trade in, they had their own bodies. Substitutes, like conscripts, rapidly developed a bad reputation among the Confederate volunteers: they joined the army for reasons of greed rather than patriotism. The inefficiency of this system led to its abolishment in December 1863. An Alabama soldier wrote in his diary, "the substitute business has kept a great many able bodied men out of the service   their is sixty thousand men exempt on account of haveing furnished substitutes and I doubt wether there is twenty thousand substitutes in the serves   certainly not more for it has been conducted so loosly that one man can act the rascal and go Substitute as many times as he is a mind to." The "looseness" was due to the inefficiency of the Confederate government, not the law itself, but the inequitable distribution of hardship was inherent in the law.[33]

Mechanics working on government projects were also exempt from the draft. They were glad to claim these exemptions as the realities of war became more widely known. One Virginian working in Wilmington, North Carolina, and avoiding conscription considered "my mechanical proclivities the greatest blessing God has conferred on me." Without them he would have been drafted. "How a Southern soldier lives and generally dies you know without my telling you." Like many another "poor boy," he could not have afforded to hire a substitute.[34]

The Confederate conscription act was reformed in 1864 to extend the exemption to smaller planters and to eliminate many other exemptions, but the impression the earlier act made persisted. As Charles A. Wills wrote on June 12, 1863, "it looks like the will never be peace anymore for poor people   the rich is getting out of the war on every hand," and the cliché "a rich man's war and a poor man's fight" proved an enduring one.[35]

In general, the Confederate supported conscription, while regretting its abuses. The abuses, however, did represent a fundamental problem of the Confederacy, one that grew as the war went on. The Confederate volunteer regarded himself as a defender of a democratic and virtuous society, and he believed in the honesty and integrity of Confederate authority. The war took its toll in suffering, the war took its toll in death, and the Confederate soldier had to endure terrible privation and bloodshed. But added to the physical burden was the incompetence of the Confederate state and the corruption rampant in Confederate society. Confederate authority failed the Confederate soldier.

The conscription laws ultimately affected almost all white men. They provided the prod that could cause the otherwise reluctant citizen to volunteer and the war-weary veteran to reenlist. The sweeping nature of the laws revealed the distress of Southern society. They do not stand alone, however, as ways in which the besieged Confederacy interfered with the lives of its citizens. Impressment—whether of agricultural produce, of farm animals, or slaves—was another widespread and arbitrary action of the Confederate state that directly influenced the lives of soldiers and their families.

Jestin Hampton was one of many soldiers' wives who had to worry about impressment. During the winter of 1864 she wrote her husband, Thomas, that a regiment of cavalry had passed through her county gathering horses and cows and slaughtering geese, chickens, and ducks, "all without leave." Sent out to seize horses for the government, they examined the Hamptons' yellow horse, but did not take it, because, as they explained to Mrs. Hampton, "they thought it not right to take soldiers property." Thomas, in answering her letter, advised her, if government officers returned to take the horse, to ask them "to put them selves in the condition I am and say if they thought it would be right for me to be acting as they are with my little family and property scarcely enough to keep them from suffering." He hoped they would not take "a soldiers little property."[36]

Not long after this a Confederate soldier stationed at Andersonville Prison wrote home to tell his wife to manage the wheat thrashing in such a way the government would not get all of what little they had raised; his wife may well have felt frustrated by his failure to suggest ways in which that object could be accomplished. But this soldier too conformed to a common pattern. Just as Confederates did not want members of their families drafted into the service, they did not want their families to suffer because of impressment.[37]

On the face of it, soldiers' opposition to impressment was irrational. Impressment was designed to supply the armies. The Confederate supply system was notoriously inefficient, and the soldiers in the field frequently went without. With rations short, the soldiers might be expected to support any measure that might improve their diet. The Confederate soldier practiced a sort of informal and illegal impressment wherever he went. The cavalry in particular, with their greater mobility and relative freedom from supervision, were adept at stealing food from Confederate citizens. In September 1864 William Nugent wrote that the soldiers of the Army of Tennessee would "steal and plunder indiscriminately regardless of age or sex." One soldier wrote from Big Shanty, Georgia, "They talk about the ravages of the enemy in their marches through the country, but I do not think that the Yankees are any worse than our own army." He described soldiers robbing the wife of a Confederate soldier even though she had distributed all her milk and buttermilk to them. The Confederate soldier did not intend to go hungry if food was available.[38]

As the Confederate soldier well knew, impressment was an even greater failure than conscription. The Confederate rail system was forever breaking down. Food collected in Georgia for the Army of Northern Virginia might lie rotting in boxcars on a railway siding until the end of the war. Taking food from a soldier's family did not necessarily do anything to feed the soldier. One can think of few things that would do more to convince a soldier of the almost criminal incompetence of his government than hearing that his family back home was near starving because the government had impressed their foodstuffs for the army while he himself was on less than half rations in the lines around Petersburg. Stealing food from civilians at least conferred a real benefit to the soldier.

Impressment had an arbitrary quality that offended a soldier's sense of justice. James Walker helped impress food in Tennessee but did not enjoy the job. "it looks hard," he wrote, "to see women that maid corn by their own labour & now hiding it in their lofts to keep for Bread & see us go & take every bit out of their houses. . . ." He himself did his best to see that they left the people enough to live on until harvest, but he recognized that no matter how careful the impressment officer might be, impressment was fundamentally unfair. "I have never deprived them of enough for Bread in any instance if they did not have more than enough . . . but it is hard to let others Judge what will be enough for to subsist one till harvest and if they miss harvest they are bound to starve. . . ." Like conscription, impressment did not spread its burden equally on the Southern people.[39]

Even Northern soldiers, even though they believed that the supplies they impressed came from a rebellious population that deserved punishment, felt guilty about taking food from Southern civilians. Confederate soldiers, when they gathered corn from the cribs or a family's supply of bacon, were depriving their fellow countrymen. But the Confederate soldier did not always feel sympathetic toward Confederate civilians. Many Confederates engaged in activities that disgusted the men in the field and disillusioned their families back home. Widespread corruption marked the Confederate experience. In the chaos of the time, profiteering and speculation were rampant. Men made fortunes—bright, glittering, and insecure—by trading with the enemy, engrossing necessities, speculating in gold, Confederate currency, and Yankee greenbacks, and running the blockade. Rhett Butler was not purely a creature of Margaret Mitchell's imagination. These profiteers were the men L. L. Polk referred to as the emerging "rotten aristocracy."

Any war creates opportunities for corruption. Far from being an exception to this rule, the Civil War democratized temptation by providing opportunities at all levels of Southern society. The success of the Northern blockade drove up prices in the South and caused the growth of a large class of hoarders and speculators. The decline in value of Confederate money as the war went on led to the establishment of a black market in gold and in U.S. dollars. Most important of all was the thriving trade with the enemy. Trade with the enemy ranged from the poor farmers who sold pies and milk to the Union soldiers to rich speculators in cotton, high officials who did business with officers equally high up in the Union army.[40]

Probably most Southerners were not involved in speculation or trade with the enemy. But a great many of them were, and the news was not slow in reaching the soldiers in the field. The result was that as rations and clothing became meager for them, they could picture stay-at-homes growing prosperous. Indeed, the conviction spread among many Southerners in and out of service that rampant speculation was an obstacle to negotiating a peace settlement: too many men were making money from the war. Jestin Collins Hampton wrote her husband that the war was being fought for profit: "I do believe every soldier on each side ought to run away and go home and let them that wants it carried on for the purpose of speculation carry it on themselves I hear of some saying they would not have it stopped for know price I do think hanging would be too good for such men."[41]

Mrs. Hampton's letter to her husband crossed one he had written to her the day before in which he, seemingly in anticipation of her letter, tried to reassure her about the Confederacy. "Jestin," he wrote, "we are Involved in this war for liberty and I consider that we ought to endure everything for the sake of our cause. . . . it is true there is a great many trifling men are engaged in speculating and Robing the innocent but the mass are Right and if we do our duty we are certain of Victory in my opinion." Others' reactions to the wartime corruption were less patriotic; they were inclined to give in to the contagion themselves, particularly when they could see the families of Confederate officials involved in the dirty business. A Mississippi soldier advised his wife in March 1864 to tell her father to sell his cotton to the Yankees. "Gen. Adams wife sold cotton to the Yanks while we were after those Yanks that went out under General Sherman this is true, she went to Big Black Bridge and sold cotton got such articles as she wished, as many did, some stole government cotton and carried to Vicksburg, that was not right, it is bad enough to sell what belongs to us. . . ."[42]

The cotton trade, the source of the greatest wartime profits, was so pervasive because the Confederate government, out of necessity, winked at it. Even a man of such rectitude as Robert E. Lee advocated trading cotton to Southern civilians for supplies, knowing that the high price paid for cotton in the North would be the reason the citizens would be willing to make the trade. Proposing such a scheme to the secretary of war, he wrote, "I do not consider the objection that some of the cotton would find its way to the enemy as worthy of being weighed against the benefits that we would derive from adequate supplies of articles of prime necessity to the army." Fighting a war requires money; the South's main source of wealth was its cotton; when the blockade closed trade with Europe, the South inevitably traded with the North.[43]

Whatever the merits of this trade with the North, the realism that underlay it was not likely to inspire the patriotic. And no one could deny that the trade was profitable for those who undertook it. A Texas soldier in Louisiana wrote that the trade, whose existence was notorious among the soldiers, caused great discontent. "the men say they do not believe in fighting and trading with our enemies at the same time and that they derive no benefit from it and think the trade is carried on for the benefit of the high officials." To verify their suspicions, the soldier noted that among a lot of smuggled goods that had recently passed near the camp was a shipment of coffee that made its way to division headquarters. He claimed that the existence of this trade had brought several regiments to the verge of mutiny.[44]

The extensive corruption, together with unpopular governmental actions, such as impressment and conscription, resulted in widespread disaffection. Furthermore, this seemingly powerful and arbitrary Confederate government proved notoriously incompetent, and its conscription and impressment policies were failures. In the later years of the war, the armies in the field were almost always undermanned and underfed.

John Marley's regiment was drawing one third rations in April 1863: "a little meete and corne meal not fit for your horses to eat." The men were "loussy and allmost naked." Furloughs had been stopped. Marley predicted that if rations did not improve and furloughs granted, half of the regiment would desert; five men had deserted already. J. C. Owens said in that same April, "we are whiped now for the briggade quartermaster has quit trying to get rashons." In the spring of 1864, one soldier reported the troops were living on "dry cornbread and a combination of spoilt bones & fat which the commissary calls bacon." Around Petersburg men were dying of pneumonia for lack of shoes; one soldier claimed "our Quartermaster has got about two hundred pair now which he bought but is not allowed to issue them because they cost a little over the Government price." A lieutenant complained he could not get replacements for his missing weapons and that he went into battle "with nothing on but a belt Haversack & canteen." "If I am spared in the next fight & we are successful I may capture a sword & Pistol." By February 1865 soldiers in the lines around Petersburg were reduced to living on one pint of meal and two spoonfuls of sugar a day. "We are all whip," one soldier wrote home.[45]

Moreover the Confederate government could not maintain a stable economy. In January 1864 one soldier noted that Confederate "blue-backs"—bonds—were "about the cheapest article going," selling at five dollars a hundred. The Confederate Congress he thought too incompetent to do anything to improve the situation; "if they had to draw Soldiers rations while they staid in Richmond I think they would hurry through a little faster." Another soldier said more simply, "our Congress are a set of blockheads." Governmental incompetence had destroyed his loyalty to the Confederacy, although honor prompted him to continue serving. "I do not pretend to be patriotic for I have been deviled so as to make it ebb all I ask for is an untarnished name for my family and self."[46]

Runaway inflation made soldiers' pay almost worthless. A Georgia soldier just back from leave wrote from Petersburg in the autumn of 1864 to regret he could not stay home until the fall fruit was ripe. Around Petersburg *poor* peaches sold for a dollar and a half a dozen; good ones cost two to five dollars a dozen. Apples brought much the same prices as good peaches; watermelons could not be had for less than six dollars and sold for as high as fifteen dollars apiece. This meant that "The common private soldier earns enough in one month to buy a pretty fair watermelon, perhaps as much as he and his friends can eat."[47]

Confederate soldiers who brought in recruits were rewarded with leave. Hezekiah Rabb sent his wife two hundred and fifty Confederate dollars in January 1864, to be used to get him a recruit. "I don't want Confederate money to keep me from home," he told her. "I think I could enjoy myself 200 or 300 dollars worth while I am at home if I could get a recruit." This was not simply a testimonial to the joys of home; it was also a revelation of the worthlessness of the Confederate dollar.[48]

Military service, then, did not provide the wherewithal for a man to support his family. In 1864 a Mississippi cavalryman heard that all soldiers over fifty years old were entitled to their discharge. He advised his father to claim his "and hire some land and go to farming." "that is the only chance I see for him to get us something to eat for next year for money is now worth nothing at all."[49]

Confederate authority failed the mass of Southern white people. As the war dragged on, and as evidence of Confederate incompetence, corruption, and class bias mounted, there was a gradual withdrawal of support on the part of many Southern whites. This withdrawal, which Paul Escott has labeled "the quiet rebellion of the common people," defeated the attempt to establish a Southern Confederacy.[50]

In view of this "quiet rebellion," the loyalty of the Confederate soldier becomes harder to explain. After all, most Confederate soldiers came from the common people; Confederate authority failed the Confederate soldier as surely as it did the civilian population. Why did the Confederate soldiers continue to give their loyalty to the army and the government at Richmond long after victory could be expected? Why did not the discontent of ill-treated soldiers lead to some sort of revolt against the authorities, an abandonment of the cause? The fact that the soldiers remained loyal to the Confederate cause long after large numbers of their class had abandoned it suggests that the military experience itself was involved in the formation of Confederate loyalties.

Not all Confederate soldiers remained loyal until the end of the war. Desertion was a constant problem. When convinced that the cause was hopeless or that his family needed him more than the army did, the Confederate soldier voted with his feet. Desertion had reached epidemic levels by the time Lee, Johnston, and Kirby Smith actually gave up the fight. Indeed, one may speculate that had they waited much longer they might have had nobody other than their personal staffs to surrender when the time came.[51]

The Confederate army was initially composed of volunteers, men who supported the Confederate cause because they believed in it and believed in the possibility of its success. When the possibility of success became less convincing, formerly brave and diligent soldiers deserted. In April 1864 an officer reported that two men had deserted—both good soldiers, one "the best in the Regt" whose bravery was a byword. Two men of the 17th South Carolina Infantry in the trenches around Petersburg deserted when they heard the news of Lincoln's reelection. They "could not stand the idea of hardship of four more long years of war." Two weeks later another man deserted while on picket; he had been "a good soldier" until then.[52]

Needless to say, however, volunteers alone did not make up the Confederate army—and some volunteers had been reluctant ones. J. G. Daniels claimed to express the sentiments of a majority of Confederate soldiers in a remarkable song he wrote while home on leave in the summer of 1863. He had been too young to vote in the secession election in Georgia, but found himself volunteering a few years later for fear of conscription.

> The cesessionists then, did carry the day;
> And often time I have heard them say;
> All the blood spilt, I will drink;
> Now what do you recon, these men does think.

> There thoughts I'm sure I do not know;
> But to the war, they hate to go;
> And if the blood that's been spilt, they have drinked it all;
> I'm sure their stomachs can never stall.

> The men that was going to drink the blood,
> Are not the men that wades the mud;
> Oh! No they'd rather stay at home;
> And send the inocents to distant lands to roam.

According to Daniels, the innocents were not wholehearted in their support of the Confederacy.

> The number of men in that company is ninety;
> And the cesesion boys are mighty scanty;
> In the whole company I only know of one;
> With him the rest just have there fun.

> I am here at home today;
> Where I wish I always could stay;
> Where I can get plenty thats good to eat
> And go to see the girls so sweet.[53]

Daniels personally had no doubt where he would prefer to be.

If a large segment of the Confederate army had no real belief in the cause, it is hardly surprising that as the war and the war's reverses continued many of them left the army. Conscripts in particular gained a reputation for desertion. For example, in March 1863 a conscript deserted from Edmund Patterson's company while on picket; he took off his boots, walked barefoot through the snow, and waded a three-foot-deep river. Patterson, confessing he found it hard to condemn the conscript, said, "I hope he didn't catch cold." "I can't see how any man in the South could feel justified in staying home at such a time. But still if I felt so, and was opposed to the war on principle, I would not fight. And if conscripted, I don't know but that I would do as he did, leave between two days without telling anybody goodbye." The conscript in question, however, had been pro-war. "He liked the war, but didn't like to do his share."[54]

Efforts to desert were not always successful. A deserter had two options: He could try to cross into Union lines, in which case he could not be reached by the Confederate authorities, or he could remain within Confederate lines and make his way home or to some other place he might lose himself. If he went back home, it was likely that the provost marshal would arrest him and send him back to the army; many deserters and draft dodgers hid out in the woods. But it was also possible for deserters to organize and resist the often ineffectual Confederate government. Armed conflict broke out throughout the Confederacy, particularly in the hill country. James Bracy wrote home in 1863, "there is a 100 men gon up in Robeson to day after some deserters and conscripts   it seems it is hard times when it take one half of the men to keep the other half from running away."[55]

Such resistance is often interpreted as a sign of Union sympathy and no doubt often was. Some Confederates died for their willingness to express Union sentiments. One soldier repeated as true a story that men of a Mississippi regiment, distrusting one of their fellow's loyalties, disguised themselves as Union soldiers and waited for him in the woods; when he met them and said he desired a Union victory, they killed him.[56]

Far more men deserted, however, because they felt they had done their share of duty and were entitled to go home. Desertion did not necessarily demonstrate a repudiation of the principles of the cause or the authority of Confederate leaders. There seems to have been little of that during the war, and this helped create the postwar phenomena of the Brigadiers, the Party of the Fathers, and the Lost Cause. Instead, desertion often occurred because the commitment to the Confederacy was too lukewarm to endure hard weather, and because loyalty to family was even stronger than loyalty to a dubious Southern nationalism.

The Texas soldiers whom David M. Ray witnessed deserting after the fall of Vicksburg and Port Hudson were "very bold"— they deserted in large groups and took their guns with them. Ray said that "a crowd of them came by our regt and halloed for all men who wished to go to Texas to fall in." And when they heard that the Richmond government had removed Joseph E. Johnston from command, the soldiers defending Atlanta began to "openly talk about going home." "They refuse to stand guard or do any other camp duty and talk open rebellion against all Military authority," Capt. Samuel T. Foster observed, "and at all hours in the afternoon can be heard Hurrah for Joe Johnston and God D—n Jeff Davis." Neither case necessarily reflected latent Unionism or class consciousness. In the first case, the threat of separation from their families led the soldiers to desertion; in both cases, what soldiers judged to be the incompetence of the Confederate States of America disgusted them.[57]

Even those Confederates who hunted deserters frequently felt pity for them. Lt. James Green arrested a deserter who was on his way to his nearby home. Green permitted the man to visit his wife and nine children before he returned him to military authorities. And even when men had no sympathy at all for deserters, they questioned the value of unwilling soldiers to the army; one officer observed that "men who are caught and forced into the ranks are not to be relied upon at all." One group of soldiers tracked a deserter to his home; to capture him they had to shoot him; his wounded arm was amputated. As worthless as that newly crippled deserter was to the Confederate army, he might have symbolized the kind of soldier a beaten cause could coerce from an unwilling populace.[58]

Nonetheless, the crippled deserter is not the most common image of the Confederate soldier. Many soldiers served until the end of the war. The Confederate soldier became a folk hero because of his bravery and endurance, and this heroic myth had a basis in fact. Many Confederate soldiers had been volunteers; volunteers are more likely to stand the hardships of war. Furthermore, the very hardships themselves and the mixture of pride and resentment they produced set soldiers apart from the civilian population. This feeling, combined with the shared dangers of battle and hardships of the march, helped produce the Confederate soldier's *esprit de corps*. His suffering proved his patriotism and thus raised his self-esteem.

From volunteerism and the shared misery of combat and campaigning came another aspect of Confederate loyalty. With the exception of Jefferson Davis, the Confederate authorities who inspired the most devotion both during the Civil War and after were the army officers—and even Davis's popularity seems to have been more a product of his postwar imprisonment than it was of his service as the Confederate head of state. The military experience created loyalty in the soldier to those who suffered by his side, whether officers or common soldiers, and a corresponding distance from those civilians who stayed at home.

Jerome Yates, the soldier for whom the invasion of Gettysburg was such an eye-opener, provides an example of the relationship of the soldier to the stay-at-home. His mother wrote him from Mississippi to ask if she should take the Oath of Allegiance. He was reluctant to give his approval, but said, "under certain circumstances I do not look up it as Binding in the least where people is in a destitute condition & that is the only way to save what they Have or get something to Eat." It was acceptable for a woman to take the oath, but any man who took it was "as good a Yankee as Abe has got." He advised her to do what she thought was best; she took the oath. A few weeks later Yates learned his brother-in-law had been arrested by the conscript officers for trading cotton with the Yankees.[59]

During the war desertion did not simply mean desertion from some abstract entity called the Confederate States of America; it meant abandoning the men with whom one had fought. It meant becoming one of the stay-at-homes. Jerome Yates had no desire to emulate his brother-in-law; he was partially ashamed of his mother. He owed his loyalty to his fellow soldiers. And after the war the veteran's loyalty often stayed with the men who had served with him in the Confederate army.

Confederate loyalty was also based upon a distinctive world view. Nineteenth-century Americans were committed to politics in a way almost incomprehensible to twentieth-century Americans; they had not yet been taught cynicism. Nonetheless, the Confederate soldier's understanding of the political world—and of the world at large—was based on Christianity, and on a Christianity almost entirely conceived of as personal morality. Evangelical Protestantism, which produced the religious ethos of both the North and South, placed individual salvation as the most important single goal of the religious life. Salvation was manifested through a conversion experience and through a subsequent godly life. The emphasis was on personal morality, not on larger social institutions. Sin, which would earn God's displeasure, was a personal matter.[60]

This emphasis on personal morality set many Confederates to searching their own souls in the dark years of the war, rather than examining their institutions with a critical eye. A wave of revivals swept the Confederate armies during the winter of 1863–1864. Pious Confederates—like pious Yankees—could interpret the war as God's punishment for a guilty nation, and hope that repentance would bring peace. The hand of God could be seen in Confederate defeats. One soldier wrote his wife in July 1864, as Johnston's army faced Sherman's across the Chattahoochee River, "it seems like the Lord has turned his face from us and left us to work out our own destruction. . . ." But just as divine displeasure could explain military defeat, the possibility of divine favor could lead men to continue the struggle long after it seemed rational; this soldier went on to offer hope in the form of a prayer, "Oh that he would give the people to see the error of there ways as he did the children of Isreal and save us from everlasting destruction."[61]

As late as February 1865, Captain Hampton could write his wife Jestin that God would bring the South victory. He died on March 20, 1865, of wounds received at the battle of Bentonsville; his last words were a message to his wife and children: "Tell them I love them but must leave them. Tell them all to meet me in Heaven." Evangelical Protestantism's fascination with the children of Israel encouraged hope in ultimate victory no matter what the odds; its emphasis on personal morality encouraged men to look for the causes of misery and defeat in their own shortcomings and vices, not in social institutions. One soldier predicted there would be no peace until the Confederate army had become "soldiers of the cross."[62]

Another reason for the continued loyalty of the soldier to the cause was that of racial solidarity. Nervous politicians in the North had argued that the Emancipation Proclamation would help unite the white South: they were right. In particular, Confederate soldiers hated black troops and murdered black prisoners. While much had been made of the "revolutionary" proposals to arm Confederate blacks that were entertained and reluctantly acted upon in the final days of the war, it is not at all clear that the average Confederate soldier would have ever accepted these desperate measures. They certainly did not accept blacks as legitimate foes.

Private Smith of the 51st Illinois watched black troops charge the Confederate lines at the battle of Nashville. The Confederates, whom Smith thought to be wavering at the point when the black soldiers entered the fight, went into a "frenzy" at their approach. Smith said they fought "like demons, slaughtering the poor blacks fearfully." Reenforcements reached the Confederate lines and coun-terattacked, "yelling, no quarter—to niggers." The black troops were forced to retire "but brought some rebel prisoners back with them, and left behind a most unmerciful number of their dead.

"The rebels who were captured by the colored troops, gave up with a very bad grace," Smith observed, particularly the officers. Smith thought that the officers regarded it as a disgrace to be captured by men "who, perhaps were their former slaves, and whom may be, they had laid the lash over their black backs before the war." Smith observed an incident that confirmed his belief as to Confederate attitudes: "One rebel captain who was marching to the rear, siezed the gun from the hands of one of his guards and shot the negro down, but was promptly run through the body by a sword in the hands of a white officer just behind him."[63]

The massacres at Fort Pillow and the Crater are well-known

examples of the Confederate soldiers' virulent hatred of black troops, but their steady hatred was revealed in unspectacular day-to-day hostilities as well. In the lines around Petersburg, where black troops were used, a Pennsylvania regiment found it advisable, when replacing a black regiment on picket, to call over to the Confederates "that the 2nd Pa was back again." A soldier in that regiment explained to his mother that when white troops were on picket, an informal truce was maintained, but when black troops were on picket, the Confederates opposite kept up a constant fire. "they hate a niger worse than they hate a coperhead Snake." This should not have surprised her, as he had already told her that the Confederates took no prisoners when it came to black troops.[64]

The final reason for Confederate loyalty is the simplest. During the war the primary alternative to Confederate rule was Yankee rule. Whatever the sectional rancor before 1861, fighting a war does not engender love for one's opponents. Even if the sufferings of the white men and women might be traced ultimately to those who led them into secession, they were frequently inflicted by the soldiers of the North.

Fighting in a familiar yet foreign country helped define the Union war experience; resisting an invader distinguished the Confederate experience. When they burned or pillaged the Southern countryside, Union soldiers gave Confederates more reason to hate them. The psychological strain that invasion and occupation placed upon the Union soldier matched the rage and despair that enemy occupation and defeat placed upon the Confederate.

A Louisiana soldier wrote from Alexandria—"or what was the town of Alexandria"—that the sight of the destruction inflicted by the Yankees horrified him and almost made him hope "this cruel and unholy war" would continue until every Northern "city town and hamlet" was destroyed. A Texas soldier in Tennessee wrote, "It almost steels a man's heart against mercy to see the fair habitations of this once proud and prosperous State smouldering in desolation." He described burned houses, fences, and forests; wagons chopped to pieces; slaughtered pigs and cattle left by the roadside; "helpless women and children" stripped of the "last bushel of meal and pound of meat." The Union army, unable to defeat the Confederate soldiery, was making war on "unoffending women and children." "One cannot avoid the conclusion that they have given up all hope of subjugation [subjugating] the country and now resort to every means to satisfy their revenge." And a Virginian cavalryman, viewing what remained of a fine plantation house—"the blackened & broken walls & a fragment of its elegant Portico"—called it a witness "of the ruthlessness of those who would win us back to the bond of brotherly love." It is hardly surprising that this soldier happily rode in Jubal Early's 1864 Pennsylvania raid and approved of the Confederate burning of Chambersburg.[65]

A Confederate soldier fighting near Atlanta addressed the grave of a Union soldier. "Old fellow, you have travelled a long ways to secure a very small spot on earth, when you might have purchased ten thousands times as much nearer home and much cheaper than you got this. You were not satisfied to remain at home, and let us alone; you must come South to murder our citizens, burn our houses, desolate our homes and lay waste our country; to make war upon women and children, turning them out to die of cold and want, without the slightest compunctions of conscience." He concluded gladly, "You for one have met your just reward, which is a grant of land from the Confederates of three feet by six, in an obscure spot, where your friends if you have any, will never be able to find your body for there is nothing to mark the spot except a small hillock of red clay, which a few hard rains will wash away and it will disappear forever." In a less rhetorical fashion, another soldier summed up the attitude of many Confederates who had seen the devastation left by the Union army when he said, "I would hate to be a yankee now & fall into the hands of a southern private."[66]

Yankee treatment of Southern civilians generated the most Confederate resentment. Soldiers complained of Northern soldiers cursing gray-haired old men, threatening women and children, and "running off" unwilling slaves. Killing civilians aroused the greatest hatred of all. In Guntersville, Alabama, Union shelling killed the mother of a Confederate captain, "a helpless old woman who could not escape out of the range of their shells as fast as the others." Men who knew of this death could not easily forgive the North.[67]

No matter how bad Yankee murder was, Confederate soldiers feared something worse. Appeals to Southern men sometimes made it clear that the ultimate Yankee threat was rape. In 1862, when soldiers were asked to reenlist for the duration of the war, one company was asked, "Can it be that you are *men* and yet with the enemy besmeared with the blood of your brothers knocking at your very doors, you will leave these defenseless women to be violated before the eyes of aged Fathers, unable to protect them?" Sgt. Edwin Fay, a particularly paranoid man, instructed his wife to meet the Yankee "Demons" "pistol in hand." Fay believed the Union soldiers capable of any cruelty; "at a house where there were two beautiful young ladies near Vicksburg, they took two negro women in the parlor before their young mistresses & sent in soldier after soldier until they had actually killed the negro women by *violation*." Fay, admittedly dissatsified with army life anyway, offered to come home in June 1862 "if you desire it." "For I hold my first duty is to my family, my country is secondary."[68]

Love of one's family and hatred of the invader could be a potent reason for Confederate service; it could also be the reason for desertion. On one hand, Harry Lewis, scion of a well-to-do Mississippi family, hated the life of a soldier. "But as it is, I joyfully embrace it as the only *means* of preserving all that is near and dear to me—home, family, friends and country." Only by going out and fighting could a man protect his family from the ruin the Union army spread. When this officer died in June 1864, his brother wrote his mother, "he died that we might live free men, and that the lives of our dear ones at home might be passed free from insult and oppression." On the other hand, if soldiers became convinced that the Confederate army could not protect their families, they might go home to give what protection husbands, fathers, and sons were able to offer.[69]

The desire to return to one's loved ones grew stronger when communication with home was cut off by the presence of Union armies. The uncertainty was difficult to bear. "I do not know why it is so but since the battle of Missionary Ridge," wrote a Georgia soldier to his sister, "I think of my old home and all the friends of my youth twice to where I did once before." His wife lived behind the new Union lines and he could not write her. The army could not trust soldiers from Louisiana and Texas who were cut off from their families after the North took control of the Mississippi to go on furlough—if they slipped across the river, they rarely returned to the army.[70]

Not hearing from home made soldiers anxious and worried. Furthermore, while the idea of marauding Union soldiers burning and looting an abstract Confederate population inspired patriotism, the knowledge that Union soldiers were in the midst of one's home community produced fears about quite specific people—children, wives, and mothers. The surgeon of the 43rd Georgia found it very hard even to imagine being cut off from his family while Sherman's armies invested Atlanta, "not knowing what insults and suffering you might have to indure." "I know you will be cared for as long as there is anything in the country to be had but who knows what hour every thing may be swept away and nothing left to subsist upon and again who can protect you from the *base* insults and injuries the fiendish villains may offer." The inability of the Confederate government to protect its people strained the loyalties of its soldiery.[71]

Soldiers had not only Yankees to worry about. If not hearing from home frightened men, news from home sometimes confirmed their worst fears. What did the soldier think whose friend wrote him that his wife was "in A very low state of health not Able to attend to anything at all"; that she and the rest of the family had not recovered from the measles; and that "I see now way for your family to make A crop without your assistance for A short time there being no one there that understands planting a crop nor no one that is Able to attend to it if they did understand it[.]" Under such circumstances, the soldier's Confederate loyalties, no matter how strong, might prove weaker than his love for his family.[72]

As the war went on, it became harder for some soldiers to deny the likelihood of Confederate defeat. Virginian Charles A. Wills was disillusioned by May 1863. He wrote his wife that almost every man in his company wanted to go home because "every man is tired of fighting offisers and all it is too late when they get killed." He thought they would desert if their families began to suffer from want of food. As for himself, "the yankeys hasent done me any harm and I have no harm against them." May 28 he said was an election day in Virginia; he would not vote "unless I can vote for a peace party."[73]

In December 1863 a soldier wrote from Tunnel Hill, Georgia, that he and most other soldiers were tired of the war and thought the Confederacy could not win. "their is a good many that ses tha ar going home." A few months later, in February 1864, J. S. Gooch, stationed near Fort Fischer, said that "iff we cant get piece as we want it we had better take it thee Best way we can get it." If the Confederate government would not end the war, he said, the Confederate soldiers would. "our men are going to thee yankies every night."[74]

In May 1864 a Georgia conscript in camp near Atlanta wrote there was no point in sending the new regiment to the front; with Johnston falling back, "in a few moore Days the front will come to us." In June 1864 W. A. James said it was "nothing but folley for our leaders to contend with the North any longer." The Union army had overwhelming numbers. "War is a dredful thing," he wrote his wife, "but their never was such A war as this & I sincearly hope their never will be Again." For men with clear sight, no amount of patriotism could hide the fact that the Confederacy was doomed. If Lee's army was pitifully small when he surrendered to Grant, it was still bigger than the Confederate government had any right to expect. The Confederate soldier endured the crisis of the Old South with more loyalty than the Confederacy deserved.[75]

The Confederate experience left behind a legacy of bitterness, a legacy of defeat. This bitterness might fuel resentment toward the Southern upper class. More often, however, it expressed itself in hatred of blacks and of Yankees. As the Civil War became the defining Southern memory, Southern whites developed a myth of Confederate unity and nobility of purpose that transcended the reality of their experience. In the sanctioned memory of the war, the Confederate soldier achieved an odd kind of victory. Defeat itself became glorious.

It did not seem so in 1865. For some soldiers, Confederate defeat had been almost unthinkable; it was not an algebraic solution, logically obtained by contrasting Northern and Southern resources; it was a mystery to be explained only by God's will. If the South had been defeated, the Southern people were at fault—a conclusion that some accepted in 1865 but that would be denied in later years. In view of the social crisis the Confederacy underwent, it was not too farfetched to blame defeat on the people's lack of will. A Confederate surgeon summed up much of this attitude immediately after the war. He had retained his optimism as late as March 1865, but was forced to admit in June, "The war is over, and we are a Subjugated people, perfectly right, just as it should be, we are too damned worthless and corrupt to be in any other condition."[76]

Confederate Defeat and Southern Morale: A Note

The story of Confederate defeat and its attending social crises has suggested to some historians that the Southern people were not fully committed to the cause of Southern independence. Indeed, when one reads that the planter class put their economic interest ahead of Confederate success, that the yeomen rapidly became disaffected, and that the slaves welcomed Union victory, one is left wondering just who did support the Confederate cause.[77]

I have argued that the internal social crisis contributed a great deal to Confederate defeat—and to the demoralization of the Confederate soldier. In that sense, I agree that no history of the Confederacy that focuses only on Northern military superiority can account for the South's defeat.

On the other hand, before we pronounce Confederate defeat the result of the Southern people's lack of commitment, certain statistics must be remembered. In his *The Civil War Day By Day,* E. B. Long estimates that of a potential military population of roughly a million, three-quarters of a million served in the Confederate army some length of time; roughly two hundred and fifty thousand of these men—approximately one Confederate soldier out of every three—died during the Civil War.[78]

Clearly, service in the Confederate army does not necessarily represent unalloyed loyalty to the Confederate cause. Nonetheless, these figures are striking, and no amount of juggling can make them disappear. What bearing do they have on the question of Confederate morale?

One can use these casualty figures, for example, when considering one of the most subtle and provocative assessments of the Southern will to fight, Kenneth M. Stampp's "The Southern Road to Appomattox." In this essay Stampp makes a particularly interesting comparison between the South's will to fight during the Civil War and during Reconstruction. During the war Southerners fought a conventional war and lost; during Reconstruction, they fought something very much like a guerrilla war and won. In one case, a brand-new nation and the institution of slavery rested on the war's outcome; in the other, the doctrine and practice of white supremacy. I believe he is right about the superior commitment Southerners felt to white supremacy as opposed to the Confederacy and even slavery. The sort of guerrilla activities they engaged in, however, never exposed them to the risk of a war like the Civil War. It is true that Southerners in 1861 did not take up the kind of guerrilla warfare that might have worn out Northern opposition; on the other hand, it is not clear that the Southerner defending white supremacy in 1866 would have been willing to suffer the same casualties that the Confederate armies suffered; after all, one can hardly say that since the South lost one out of every four white men to defend slavery, they would have been willing to lose one out of every three to defend white supremacy.

If sheer sacrifice of life is worth anything in judging a people's will to make war—and it certainly is—then those of us who question Southern will will have a considerable challenge. It is a commonplace in American military history that the highest percentage of military deaths to the population is to be found in the Confederacy; the next highest in the Union. No other war came close to inflicting the same casualties in proportion to the population; in fact, no other war killed so many Americans. But the percentage of Northern men who served in the Union armies, the percentage of Northern men who died in battle or in military hospitals, is remarkably lower than those among Southerners. One in four white men of military age in the South died compared to one in ten in the North.

Southern society could not bear the strains that the Civil War experience created. But the North did not have to stand up to the same strains. If one out of every four Northern men had died in service, would the Northern will to war appear weak and uncertain?

It would not do to exaggerate the social upheaval that the North did undergo during the war. Certain aspects of the Northern war experience, however, suggest that Northern society would have had difficulty prosecuting the war had as high a proportion of its wealth and population been at risk. The New York draft riots; widespread draft dodging, bounty-jumping, and desertion; the resistance of the Democratic Party's peace wing to the war; the increased reliance on the draft, foreign-born volunteers, and recruitment of Southern freedmen to man the Union armies—all these suggest that the demands of the Civil War might have disrupted Northern society as well as Southern.

There are signs, on the other hand, that the Union army itself maintained its morale even if that of the civilian population was slipping. In the 1864 Presidential election, the Union army voted overwhelmingly for the man whose victory meant a continuation of the war; in the spring of 1864, when the three-year men's enlistments ran out, most veterans of the Union cause chose to remain in the army.

Nonetheless, judging from what resistance to the Lincoln adminstration and military service did emerge, the North was fortunate it could fight its war without making the same demands on its population that the Southern people faced. For example, Northerners were not faced with an army of occupation. No Northern deserter could plead that he went home to protect his family from Confederate soldiery. The Northern economy did fairly well during the war—Northern greenbacks did not become worthless. In fact, the North did so well that its Congress did not have to devote all its attention to war matters. Instead, Republicans began passing the kind of legislation that would be characteristic of the Gilded Age.[79]

Northern desertion provides an interesting comparison. In absolute numbers, far more Union soldiers than Confederate ones deserted—just as the Union army was roughly two and a half times the size of the Confederate army, it could boast of two and a half times as many deserters. And only in the North did bounty-jumping—enlisting in order to receive a bounty and then deserting, sometimes in order to enlist again—emerge as a profession.[80]

Nonetheless, while I devoted a long section to Confederate desertion, I have only touched on Northern desertion—for the simple reason that Northern desertion did not cripple the Union war effort. Southern desertion, on the other hand, helped destroy any chance of a Confederate victory. Northern desertion did not demoralize Northern society as Southern desertion did Confederate society; Northern deserters did not control large blocks of territory as Southern deserters did.[81]

In any case, it is difficult to conclude that the North had a will to make war superior to the South's, when the war placed a lighter burden on its society than it did on Southern society. Perhaps all one can conclude is that the North had a superior will to fight the war it had to fight than the South had to fight its war.

SIX

The End of the War

From the very beginning of the war, men predicted that its conclusion was imminent. In fact, such predictions were made before the war began, as Northern politicians assured the people that the South was bluffing and Southerners guaranteed bloodless secession. A few days after the Confederates had fired on Fort Sumter, a Northern man who later joined the army predicted that Southerners would not go much further along their "suicidal course"; they found the North far more united than they had bargained for. Occasional dissenters from the prevailing orthodoxy warned that the war would be a long, grueling struggle. A Rhode Island colonel—a veteran of the Mexican war—greatly surprised one of his captains by predicting a twelve-year war. But the men who went to war rarely believed these grim realists. They could not have gone to war so eagerly if they had.[1]

When the South persisted on its "suicidal course," when the Northern cravens volunteered for military service, men continued to hope for a short war. Hoping, they could always find reasons to believe that the war was almost over. Soldiers learned the realities of war far better than did civilians. Nonetheless, perhaps because they were far more exposed to the hardships and dangers of war, many of them were ready to believe that the dangers would cease in the immediate future. One Confederate admitted that he believed the war would end soon, "probably, in part, because I have become so anxious for it to terminate."[2]

"War will end . . ." The soldiers said this time and time again, sounding like millenarians forever pushing the end of the world back a few days. It would end by Christmas 1861; it would end after the fall of Yorktown in May 1862; it would end with a resounding Confederate victory by July 1862; it would end near New Year's Day 1863; it would end by the spring of 1863. In May 1863 some Confederates in the Army of Tennessee even welcomed the predictions of coming peace offered by spiritualist table-rapping. The optimism persisted until, eventually, reality caught up with expectations and the war did end.[3]

The various ways in which men expected the war to end revealed their understanding of the way the world worked. One idea—it might be better called an image—prevalent in both armies was the one big battle that would bring the war to a climax. Just as nineteenth-century Evangelicals believed that one emotional upheaval—the conversion experience—could save one's soul, Civil War soldiers often believed that the next major battle would decide the war.[4]

In part this mentality characterized an age fascinated with Napoleonic warfare. Napoleon's battles—particularly his defeat at Waterloo—had been both bloody and decisive. But underneath men's understanding of military tactics was a fiercely Christian mentality. The next big battle would be a bloodbath—the tactics of the war ensured that. Men believed that when enough blood was shed, a guilty nation would have done its penance. Furthermore, men expected that the war would end with a grand climax—that the nation would be redeemed at one stroke, that the enemy would retire after one final charge, that the side with courage and righteousness would triumph after it had manifested its superiority on the field of battle.

In fact, with the exception of the almost ludicrous battles of Franklin and Nashville, where very great quantities of blood were shed as the Union army turned back an insane attempt by John Bell Hood to liberate Tennessee and invade Ohio—battles dignified only by the blood shed—the last months of the war saw no great battles. There were no Shilohs, Chancellorsvilles, or Gettysburgs. Instead, there was the monotonous but deadly conflict in the trenches around Petersburg, the almost unopposed sweep of Sherman's army through Georgia and the Carolinas.

Nonetheless, the image of battle retained its hold on the American soldier. While writers would later use battle as the very embodiment of meaninglessness, the men who lived through the battles of the Civil War found it hard to believe they were not decisive; what else could explain such pain, sacrifice, and bravery? And men whose faith in God was threatened by war's random horrors looked for peace as divine acknowledgment that they had suffered enough to expiate whatever sins had brought on the war.

The prospects of salvation and of peace became understandably confused in the minds of men. The peace that Christ brought to the soul became associated with the peace that the war's end would bring to civil society. As the war dragged on, its close seemed to demand a miracle of grace as much as an individual's redemption. A Confederate soldier assured his friend that "you need not be afraid of saying too much to me on the subject of a hope in Christ it givs me pleasure to rad a letter from you on that subject I hope this war will soon end." Clearly, this soldier expected that the spread of religion and "a hope in Christ" were somehow related to his hope for peace.[5]

Soldiers on both sides believed that God had sent the war as punishment for America's sins. One Union soldier wrote that "this war is sent by our Lord and if the People are punished enough for ther national sin that it will soon be settled." Lt. Benjmen F. Ashenfelter of the 35 Pennsylvania Volunteers thought, "so as the Nation becomes Humbled in the sight of God the war will end and no sooner." God might measure punishment in blood and suffering, but He would end the war whenever He pleased; He made the calculations of generals and politicians irrelevant—they were instruments in His hands.[6]

Pious abolitionists in the Union ranks thought the war a punishment for slavery. Orra B. Bailey wrote, "we as a nation have committed a great sin in cultivating and propping this institution up untill it has become so powerful that it has almost over thrown the Government." But after the Emancipation Proclamation, Bailey hoped that "the clouds that have envelopd us for the last two years will be spedily clear and that we come out of this civil war purified and more united than we ever was." Once the North had recognized the true meaning of the war and transformed it into an antislavery conflict, surely God would bring a speedy victory. "their is a passage in the bible that reads in this wise the wicked are Gods sword or in other words, the means that the wicked take to streghen their cause is in Gods handes the means of their overthrow[.] now the rebels have taken up their sword to uphold slavery now possibly that is the only way it could be rooted out."[7]

Andrew Sproul, an Irish-born Presbyterian soldier, believed that God "will carry on the war untill that he will make all flesh free." Capt. Burrage Rice believed the duty of the Union army was not just to defeat the rebellion but to transform Southern society. "Not only civilization but christianization should go hand in hand with our armies," he noted in his diary in October 1861, adding, perhaps prematurely, "& as we proclaim 'Liberty to the man,' should also proclaim a way of deliverance for the souls of men." While Charles Wellington Reed did not call on God's pleasure to end the war, he certainly thought a national commitment to emancipation a necessary step to Union victory. "the prospect of our ultimate success seems better than ever. we now know what we are fighting for, and that's what half didn't or wouldn't know before." In August 1864 Pennsylvanian John Harmer's faith in Union victory was so great he said if the rebels "whip Grant and drive Sherman to the Ohio and burn the citties of Pa. I will still believe that they must be finally destroyed. I cannot believe that Providence intends to destroy this Nation."[8]

Other soldiers viewed the prospect of divine aid with more cynicism. The Sixth Ohio Cavalry—"the Bloody Sixth"—had to be marched to religious services. After one sermon Sgt. Albinus Fell said, "I think the damned old cuss of a Preacher lied like *Dixie* for he sayed that God has fought our battles and won our victorys. now if he has done all that why is it not in the papers and why has he not been promoted." Fell concluded that if God really was "doing all the fighting, they might as well discharge the *sixth* for they won't fight under his command worth a dam."[9]

The Yankees who relied upon divine favor might have been surprised—perhaps outraged—by Confederates who thought that God would bring them victory once the people had been brought to repentence. Richard Webb, a North Carolina chaplain, had been conducting revival meetings when he proposed marriage; he thought he would be home soon. "I am of the candid opinion that this will be the last year of this cruel war, and my opinion is based on the fact that God has given us so many tokens of good in converting so many hundred soldiers, and still the work goes on all through this army. I don't believe that God will deliver us over into the hands of our enemies while we take Him to be our refuge and strength." Shortly before Appomattox his cry was "O Lord get to thyself a great name, in this our extremity, by a deliverance from our enemies, that in addition to other motives gratitude may propel our hearts to love and serve thee!" H. C. Kendrick believed that the people of the South were "destined to freedom, as the christian is to inherit eternal bliss in a future state"[10]

Even if God could not be relied upon, Confederates could still hope for a sudden victory. Confederates thought the Northern population might use the political process to repudiate the war. As far as Southerners could see, Lincoln and his party had inaugurated a reign of terror in the North; surely even Northern-born Americans would resist tyranny while they were still able. Some Confederates placed their faith in the Presidential election of 1864.[11]

By and large, Northern Peace Democrats did not cherish the notion of a disrupted Union; they saw peace as the first step to national reconciliation. Furthermore, even though the 1864 Democratic Convention adopted a peace platform, the party's candidate—the military hero Gen. George McClellan, who had been far more discredited among the Union soldiery than anyone realized, and whose acceptance of the nomination disgusted many of the admirers he had left—repudiated the platform. Nonetheless, Confederates thought Lincoln's defeat would herald an independent South and the end of the war. The very ambivalence of the Democratic Party encouraged the hopeful. A Texan soldier wrote, "I have a yankee paper now before me of a late date (St. Louis *Republican*) which contains the Chicago platform, which is very good I think, but can be construed in two ways, this will only have a tendency to unite the war democrats with those for peace & the peace party. . . . I am forced to believe that we will have peace by next spring."[12]

Yankees feared what rebels hoped. Most Union soldiers supported Lincoln in 1864 and viewed McClellan's candidacy as a threat to the Union. A Massachusetts soldier, living in the dangerous but dreary trenches around Petersburg, said that the election of McClellan "would be the worst thing that was ever done for the country and the Rebels say that is what they are depending on most." It might mean the close of the war, but it would ensure the survival of slavery.[13]

David Seibert, a Pennsylvanian, thought Lincoln's reelection would give the Confederate cause "a Great *Blow*." He hoped that Lincoln's victory would be a landslide. A Wisconsin soldier stationed in Louisiana thought that a Republican victory would soon bring the war to an end. "Nearly all the soldiers are for Lincoln—Abraham," he wrote. "If he is elected, I can assure you that there will not be much fighting afterwards, just a few guerillas may hold out, the others will realize that it is impossible to fight on." Even the officers who were in the Confederate prison in Danville, Virginia, in November 1864 voted in favor of Lincoln in a mock election— 276 to 91.[14]

Republicans in and out of the army could be vicious when they campaigned against McClellan. Gen. Edward A. Wild sent Edward W. Kinsley, captain of the black 54th Massachusetts, a letter he might make public if necessary. It proclaimed McClellan "the most treacherous traitor of them all," a tool of slaveholders throughout the war, a member of the Copperhead Knights of the Golden Circle, a general whose reputation had been manufactured by the farseeing Jefferson Davis long before the war, a man who systematically returned slaves to slavery, guarded rebel property while exposing that of Unionists, sabotaged the federal cavalry, and lost every campaign he ever fought. At the bottom of this public letter, General Wild wrote a private note. "Dear Kinsley, I do not think this is quite prudent. But if you get me into a scrape, you must shoulder the consequences."[15]

But even men who had no Republican loyalties found it hard to trust McClellan. Wimer Bedford was an Illinois captain who hoped to resign from the service to go into the cotton trade in New Orleans. "Don't like the Nigger [business] or the Yankees—I mean the down Easters—*anyhow*." Soon after Lincoln's reelection Bedford resigned his commission. Even so, during the fall of 1864, Bedford said he could support McClellan only if he could be "sure he was a war man."[16]

At least one shrewd commentator would be thankful when the fall elections were over. He was in Butler's army. As long as the political excitement continued, he explained, Butler would have his army on the move to keep his name in the newspapers.[17]

The election of 1864 disappointed Confederates. Reelecting Lincoln, with an overwhelming soldier vote, the North demonstrated its resolve to continue the war. As the enlistments of many Union three-year regiments ran out, most Northern soldiers "veteranized"—an even greater revelation of their commitment to the Union cause. In effect, the soldiers of the Union army had been allowed to vote on whether or not their service—their fighting, suffering, and dying—would go on. The very fact that the nation permitted them their say must have confirmed the ideology of freedom and Union they fought to defend.[18]

The election of 1864, divine intervention, the enemy's cowardice, a climatic battle—none of these ended the war quickly. The Civil War was as bloody as any war Americans ever fought. As bloody as slavery. As bloody as might be expected in a nation whose identity came from a patriotic war. The hand of God might be so bloody. The other hopes of meaning and design and sudden victory should have died long before Appomattox. But men's hopes supply armies as much as food and ammunition do.

One final means by which some Confederates thought they might achieve their independence was the enlistment of black soldiers. Gen. Patrick Cleburne was the first major figure to propose recruiting slaves. By December 1863 Cleburne had recognized that the Confederate armies had exhausted the white population of the South. If more soldiers were needed to defeat the North, they must be recruited among the blacks. Blacks would not fight unless they and their families were freed. Cleburne proposed emancipating all Southern slaves. Furthermore, Cleburne argued that freeing the slaves "would at once take the wind out of the sails of Northern Abolitionists and cause them to cease the war, for they would no longer have food upon which to keep fanaticism alive." And once the moral issue of slavery had been resolved, the European powers, who could not aid the South "without helping slavery," would support the Confederacy. Cleburne persuaded other Confederate officers to sign a petition advocating Confederate emancipation. Capt. Thomas J. Key thought that such a step would "make or ruin the South." The authorities in the Army of Tennessee and in the government at Richmond suppressed the petition and ordered Cleburne's silence on the issue of emancipation.[19]

It took another year for the Confederate government to call for black enlistments—and even then the call was accompanied by no sweeping promises of universal freedom. Whatever the official policy, most Confederate soldiers, when they paid heed to the proposal at all, remained dubious about black Confederates. In February 1865 Douglas Cater wrote that his fellow soldiers argued frequently about the wisdom of arming blacks. "I remain silent 'cause I can't tell if it will do." Most Confederates probably agreed with the soldier who wrote, "we had better give it up but there is a talk of bringing the nigers out but I dont think that wil do[.]"[20]

The idea that after the Emancipation Proclamation and with Union victory so near at hand, Southern blacks would volunteer for the Confederate army was preposterous in any case. In February 1865 a Union soldier who interviewed Confederate deserters heard that the rebels "are now drilling Negroes in Petersburg for their army." He drew the correct conclusion. "if they go to depend on them they will soon explode the Bogus shell of the Confederacy."[21]

Even until the end, some rebels suffered from what can only be termed insane Confederate optimism. James McMichael was in a Union prison when he heard the news of Lee's surrender. He noted in his diary that "now for the first time I consider our cause hopeless." The news of Johnston's surrender arrived two weeks later. He did not know what to do but thought it best to stay true to his oath of allegiance to the Confederacy. Not until May 7 did he feel justified in taking the Oath of Allegiance to the United States and leaving his military prison—and even then he feared his friends would view his actions as disloyalty. Abbie Brooks met a Confederate, a former prisoner of war, en route to his home in Kentucky in May 1865. He "cried because he had to take the oath to go home and see his wife." He had been a prisoner for two years, refusing to take the oath the whole time.[22]

Confederates needed to believe in ultimate victory, as they greatly feared the consequences of defeat. In 1864 John Paris, the chaplain of a North Carolina regiment, preached a sermon on the execution of twenty-two Confederate deserters. He encouraged Confederate soldiers in their loyalties not simply by appealing to their moral sentiments, but by presenting what peace terms the tyrants in Washington would offer. He predicted that Southern lands would be sold to pay the public debt the North incurred during the war, that the blacks would not only be freed, but be given equality as well, that the voting rights of Southern whites would be taken away, that governors, judges, and even ministers would be appointed by the federal government or military authorities, and the South would suffer "the deep and untold mortification of having bands of negro soldiers stationed in almost every neighborhood to enforce these laws and regulations." In brief, a Northern victory would bring about a revolution in Southern society.[23]

When the news of Lee's surrender reached his regiment, Paris reported that "Excitement among the officers and men is intense. Many propose to fight out to the bitter end, rather than to surrender. Others are determined to take to the bushes and then take care of themselves." Perhaps the predictions of their chaplain helped create this excitement; in any case, Paris himself was not free from it. Until a higher officer convinced him that flight was "an act incompatible [with] my relationship to the regiment," he planned to "take to the woods," and "reach my family if possible."[24]

David M. Ray, however, heard rumors that Andrew Johnson promised that the rebellious states would have the same rights as they did before the war—that there would be no revolution. He confessed that he thought this "very doubtful." Indeed, while the terms the North would enforce were "a source of deep anxiety to every true heart," he knew that "we will have to submit with the best grace possible." They had no choice. "It seems to be the opinion of almost every one that the war is about over, that we are *beaten;* it is useless to disguise the fact that the majority of the soldiers are whipped and discouraged and think it useless to fight longer."[25]

When Ray decided to accept defeat in May 1865, he represented most Confederates. It was not until later that Southern whites came to believe that they could continue to resist federal policy. But even in 1865 some Confederates' responses to Lee's surrender bordered on the fatuous. Cavalry Gen. Thomas T. Munford, who rode away from Appomattox to avoid participating in the surrender, sent Col.

Gustavus Dorsey an order advising him of the temporary end of the war: "You must tell your noble boys, who have so long and nobly upheld our banner, to make Virginia their homes until an opportunity is offered to strike again." Munford predicted the South would "never submit to Yankee rule." "My hope *is* that the Yankees will oppress us so heavily that the people will soon rise again. . . . Tell your brave men to keep away from the Yankees, look out for homes and *wives* in Virginia and we will yet want men and firm hearts to fight against our ruthless foe." Dorsey read the order aloud to his troopers and disbanded his battalion.[26]

At the battle of Resaca in May 1864, the 105th Illinois captured a Confederate battery. From underneath one of the gun carriages a big, red-haired man with no shirt fearfully emerged. He wore a tattoo on one arm that read "Fort Pillow." His captors read it. He was bayonetted and shot instantly. Another regiment in Sherman's army was reported to have killed twenty-three rebel prisoners, first asking them if they remembered Fort Pillow. The Wisconsin soldier who recorded this incident claimed flatly, "When there is no officer with us, we take no prisoners." They would revenge their brother soldiers.[27]

Fort Pillow, a federal outpost in Tennessee, had been captured by Confederate Gen. Nathan B. Forrest in April. Many in its garrison were black. The Confederate forces slaughtered them after their surrender. One Confederate who heard of the massacre wrote "General Forest captured Fort Pillow and about six hundred the most of them was Negroes he didn't [take] any of them prisoners killed every one of them I think that was the best thing he iver done in his life." Union soldiers regarded the Fort Pillow incident as proof that, as one put it, the rebels were as savage as Indians. At Resaca and elsewhere they retaliated.[28]

White soldiers recognizing black soldiers as brothers would have been a revolutionary idea—so, for that matter, would widespread refusal on the part of the Union army to take prisoners. Mutual respect among whites and blacks was just what those who advocated black soldiers hoped for. Like emancipation, black service in the Union was to be a step on the road to equality for all races.

But while some white soldiers witnessing black military participation lost their racist contempt for blacks, few were converted to the cause of black equality.

By the end of the war, blacks made up one-tenth of the Union army. Blacks enlisted for a broad range of reasons. Some simply because they were American patriots—although their love of their country is hard to explain. Others, perhaps most, wanted to join the war against slavery. Most black soldiers had been slaves. Those who had labored in Dixie fled to Union lines or welcomed Union armies; they volunteered so that they could thank the government that freed them, they could help free others, or they could feed themselves and their families—or go back and free their families. Others volunteered for a personal freedom. If they lived in loyal slave states—Kentucky, Maryland, Missouri—they freed themselves and their families by their enlistment. Freedom: their own, their families, their race. If whites wondered how blacks could be fitted into American institutions, they should have considered how American the values were that black volunteers espoused.

Black soldiers also hoped to persuade Americans that they deserved the same rights as other men. Those who performed the duties of a citizen were entitled to the privileges of citizenship; and no duty was more fundamental than defending one's nation. At the time, black leaders and whites who were sympathetic to black rights assured those who volunteered that they would earn the respect of other Americans. While in the army blacks fought not only Confederates but entrenched American racism. Initially, the government paid them less than white troops, segregated them into all-black regiments, treated them more as uniformed, ill-paid laborers than as soldiers, and appointed almost no black officers. Blacks protested this unequal treatment and succeeded in overturning some—but not all—of the racist policies. As one of their white officers told them, they were fighting for their "manhood." By the end of the war black soldiers believed they had proved it.[29]

But America ignored the proof. While the Fourteenth Amendment rewarded blacks with full citizenship, its protection was rapidly stripped away. And when Northerners celebrated their victory, they rarely remembered the black soldiers who contributed to it. The popular memory of the Civil War had very little room for black agents; the North remembered the boys in blue giving blacks their freedom, not black soldiers helping to free their race. Somehow the attempt to force respect for black rights and prowess by military service failed. Somehow blacks could be soldiers but still not worthy of citizenship.

Blacks sought a role—soldier—that white men feared degraded them. Blacks wanted soldiering to raise them in the eyes of America: the man who could serve his country as a soldier earned the right to citizenship. White soldiers saw black service as a threat—instead of raising blacks to the status of the soldier, it might reduce soldiers to the status of blacks. That logic informed the racist responses of soldiers to the proposal of black recruitment. Most soldiers initially opposed the idea of black soldiers. As one said, "We don't want to fight side by side with the nigger. We think we are a too superior race for that." Another echoed him, saying, "I will Never fight by the side of A Nigger & that is the feeling of the army where ever I have been." After he first saw black troops, one sergeant described them as "regular Congoes with noses as broad as plantations and lips like raw beefsteaks." Another soldier warned, "it will ruin the army." He went on to say, "if a negro regiment were to come and camp near an old regiment out here, the men would kill half of them." Not only were these men racist; they knew full well how America regarded blacks. If blacks could be soldiers, did it mean soldiers were no better than blacks?[30]

As the war went on and the number of the dead grew, white soldiers reconsidered their opposition to black enlistment. Frequently soldiers who supported the idea of black troops did not do so because of any confidence in blacks, but because black participation would save the lives of white men. They agreed with James Miller: "i would a little rather see a nigers head blowed of then a white mans." Or they believed, as a Michigan soldier did, that even though blacks were inferior, Confederate viciousness would inspire in them a courage born of desperation: when surrender means certain death, men—even blacks—fight all the harder.[31]

In some cases, actual service with black soldiers reduced white prejudice against them, although often racism was impervious to any contradicting evidence. The healthiest response to black soldiering was simple recognition that blacks, like whites, could fight well. A New Jersey soldier said, "When I was home I used to run down colored troops as bad as any one but one month in Virginia has entirely cured me of that as they did all the fighting in our corps and fought well." He was pleased that their presence saved "us the honor of being shot at by the Jonnies," but his evaluation of black ability sounds honest. Another soldier incidentally praised black troops while unwittingly revealing what had come to define good soldiering: "The 54th Mass Regt of Blacks were on picket that night and behaved very well, many of them were killed."[32]

Unfortunately, men had more complex ways of judging black performance, ones that did not simply compare black and white achievement. Men could argue that blacks made good, even superior, soldiers compared to whites—but that there were fundamental differences in the way they soldiered. Whites drew two distinctions between white and black soldiers. Blacks were said to make better soldiers because they were more subservient; they were said to make better soldiers because they were more savage. Discipline and savagery, as we have seen, were desirable traits in a soldier. They were not necessarily desirable in citizens.

One of the first things that white soldiers praised in their black counterparts was their ability on the parade ground. Many whites thought that blacks took to drill in a way no other soldiers did. "The best drilled regiment I ever saw on dress perade," was a typical description. A soldier and abolitionist said of the black garrison he visited "a better and nobler looking set of men I have never seen with Uncle Sam's uniforms." Whites associated this readiness to accept discipline and subordination with slavery. Obedience to their masters had prepared blacks for obedience to their officers. But whites also believed that blacks had innate characteristics that well suited them for drill and discipline; their "peculiar docility" for example. The spectacle of well-drilled soldiers—a symbol of manly self-discipline and patriotism if they were white—meant slavish subservience if they were black.[33]

At other times, whites created the image of black soldiers as irresistible savages—the savage enemy that rebels had earned. Charles M. Maxim advocated the use of black troops because they were the best counterpoise to rebel barbarity. Disgusted by reports that Confederates kept explosives underneath their military prisons to set off in case of escape, he concluded that the Southern people had become "thoroughly debased and bloodthirsty." "The negro is the one to fight such a people." Years of cruelty toward the black man would encourage him to reciprocate in kind. Lucien P. Waters, the man called the Abolition Sergeant, saw black cavalry in action in Louisiana. These "dire avengers" sought "to square accounts with their old master." "Remembering the cruel lash of lore, & the merciless treatment for their unrequited toil & stewardship, they could with difficulty be made to give quarter." Waters viewed black ferocity benignly: "I did not blame them." Men like Maxim and Waters wanted black soldiers to act out their violent fantasies of revenge. They hoped that black soldiers would exceed the limits they thought proper for white soldiers. A New Jersey officer who praised black soldiers for refusing to take prisoners added, "I wish we had a hundred thousand such soldiers added to the army of the Potomac."[34]

The image of black soldiers as beasts—"they fight like tigers"— allowed white soldiers to project their own savagery upon other soldiers. Black soldiers were the perfect foe of rebels because both were savage; virtuous Union soldiers were incapable of such barbarious behavior. Conversely, the image of black soldiers as slaves in uniform obeying a new set of masters gave men unhappy with their own submission to authority an example of more total subservience. Compared to black soldiers, white soldiers regarded themselves as specimens of independent volunteers. White soldiers judged black soldiers in ways that assuaged their own psychological dilemmas. The most troubling aspects of soldiering, the ones that they feared rendered the soldier unfit to be a citizen, were the ones they associated most with blacks. Blacks could not win. Had they made poor soldiers they would have been called unworthy of citizenship—but their successful military service was interpreted in such a way that it in itself meant black citizenship was suspect.[35]

During much of Reconstruction, blacks made up the bulk of the federal forces in the South. Black soldiers and veterans were the backbone of the Republican Party in many parts of the South. But in the end, the federal government, responding to pressure from Southern whites, withdrew black troops from the South. And Union veterans with black skins did not, as a rule, vote in the late-nineteenth-century South. Blacks continued to serve in the United States Army—they were the "buffalo soldiers" of the Indian Wars—but without the full trust of white Americans in general or of white veterans in particular. The service of 179,000 blacks in the Union army had not persuaded them of the justice of black citizenship or even the worth of black soldiers.

In 1865, as the end of the war approached, one Illinois volunteer flirted with the notion of joining the regular army, expecting to be sent west to keep order among the Indians and the Mormons. His family protested and he decided he would return home when the war was over, for military life was too idle for his taste. Even so, he feared the possibility that the regular army would become primarily composed of its various black units: "you must have a better opinion of the Negro than I to leav our government to their Protection," he cautioned. "it must be well watched after peace"[36]

The war did not lack a climax. Instead of a decisive battle closing the war, April 1865 witnessed the assassination of Abraham Lincoln by John Wilkes Booth. The Union cause gained its final martyr, and the Civil War concluded in a fashion almost unimaginable to the people of the day. In a sense, Lincoln's murder was the last act of terrorism and Booth the ultimate guerrilla.[37]

The news of Lincoln's murder aroused extreme grief and rage among Union soldiers, emotions they were barely able to control. Southerners who portrayed Sherman's progress through Georgia and the Carolinas as one great atrocity, a mode of warfare on civilians never seen before, no doubt would have been surprised by the reaction of Sherman's army to the news of Lincoln's death. "I have heard only one sentiment expressed, & it seems to be universal throughout the army. Woe to the South if this Army is compelled to pass through it again." Despite Southern insistence that Sherman's march represented the height of inhumanity, it seems clear that Sherman's soldiers had no trouble at all imagining what further vengeance they might inflict upon the South if they cared to. There were reports of soldiers in Nashville killing men who expressed satisfaction with Lincoln's death.[38]

Lt. Christopher Keller's first reaction to the news of Lincoln's death was disbelief. It took several days and official confirmation for the men of his company to accept that the man Keller had called "the *people's* candidate" was gone. When that fact had sunk in, Keller claimed the iron had entered his soul: "My only fear now is that the war will end and we have no opportunity to avenge his death upon the vile traitors." "The battle cry will be 'Lincoln' and woe to the rebel that falls into our hands." His grief and rage were real, but by May 10 he was commenting on the good feelings between the paroled Confederate soldiers passing through Montgomery and the Union troops stationed there.

Keller also recorded that the citizens of Montgomery professed "great sorrow for the death of the President," sorrow he judged sincere. But he had little sympathy for their sorrow, because he thought it selfish. Now that they were beaten, they would rather the kindhearted Lincoln head the federal government than the severe Andrew Johnson. "Johnson is a southern man and knows exactly what a rebel is."[39]

Lincoln's forbearance to the South was a common theme. One soldier wrote, "It will go hard with them now! While Lincoln was President, they could expect mercy but none now." He too pitied rebels falling into Union hands; by his moral arithmetic "the blood of a hundred thousand of the cursed and hell born Rebels, and their allies could not compensate" for Lincoln's death. After April 1865 the Union soldier embraced a sentiment that would become a national faith: Lincoln was the South's best friend. John F. Brobst wrote of the South, "They have slain Mercy and now they must abide by the sterner master, Justice." Lincoln's assassination revealed that the South did not deserve mercy—in fact, that it had rejected mercy. Lincoln's mercy, much like the grace of God, was freely offered, and to the Union soldier, those who did not take it were damned.[40]

Just as some soldiers interpreted the war itself as payment for a nation's sins, men found divine cause for the events at Ford's Theatre. In fact, some wondered if Lincoln's death had been a most appropriate if bitter punishment, since one sin the North had committed was idolatry. "We had almost made Lincoln a God and now he has been taken from us." For Charles Calvin Enslow the meaning in this was clear: God meant to teach the North that He, not mortal man, gave victories. Yahweh had punished Gideon's pride.[41]

Other men also saw the hand of God in the President's death. Capt. George Anthony announced that if the news of Lincoln's death had been accompanied by "a proclamation of extermination with a call for Volunteers for 10 years or the war," nine-tenths of the army would have enlisted. Anthony regretted Lincoln's death, but he thought it would save the North from "mistaken philanthropy and a false mercy toward our enemy." Now the North would be ready to do what must be done, and revolutionize the South by stripping leading men of citizenship. Indeed, if extermination was necessary to wipe out treason, Anthony was at the service of his country.

Captain Anthony feared the overtender hearts of his Northern brethren precisely because he had discovered such weakness in his own breast. "I confess that I was fairly frightened at my own feelings as I saw the Army of Lee with its gray headed leader drawn up for surrender to us as their conquerers. the awful magnitude of the crisis the remembrance of the weeping and wailing the treasure and blood their crimes had cost were all sunk in a spirit of forgiveness and of mercy and had it been left to me I much fear that then and there I should have restored to full citizenship every man from Gen Lee down and I have much reason to believe that my feelings were shared by most officers and men who saw with me." Providentially, the crime of Lincoln's assassination, "a crime so much greater than before," would "nerve us up to the placing of justice before mercy."[42]

Some Southerners reacted to Lincoln's death in ways that confirmed Yankee rage. The mother of a Texas soldier wrote her son, "we have heard that Lincoln is dead (I reckon that would be good news if it is only so) but we have heard that so often I am afraid it will turn out like it has before." People who seceded upon Lincoln's election and who had fought "Lincoln hirelings" for four years could hardly be expected to mourn his death.[43]

At least one Southerner—a prisoner in the North—found hope in Lincoln's death. He proclaimed the assassination "a cowardly act, doubtless the work of some fanatic radical." Whatever his moral qualms, he still welcomed the murder. "Yet it assures us our independence, for Lincoln's clemency—dictated by Seward's policy—were greatly to be dreaded. The red republican Johnson will give our people that union which would otherwise have been wanting, in desperate circumstances." He had the same expectations of Johnson as his Northern counterparts did, even if he would not have called Johnson's severe policy justice.[44]

Other Confederates feared the Unionist Johnson as well. After hearing the news, one Confederate in a Northern prison admitted, "The sad fate of President Lincoln affects us greatly, but though I trust we all feel proper abhorence for the deed the principal cause of our feeling the matter so strongly is the question of how it will affect us." In general, the Confederate soldier did not welcome assassination as a means of making war.[45]

The martyred Lincoln was one symbol; the craven Davis was another. The victorious Union soldier dreamed of how the traitor might best be punished. John F. Brobst assumed that Davis would be executed—"he must go up some ten feet above the face of the earth and perform on a tight rope for the benefit of a society called the Loyal People of America." This he thought the appropriate finale to a war caused by "petty politicians and fire eaters." Charles M. Maxim wanted Davis hung for his complicity in Lincoln's assassination, rather than for treason. He reasoned that even though treason was as great a crime as murder—"for treason is murder"—it was a political crime that might attract sympathy, particularly from foreign nations. Davis's execution as a common murderer would diminish such sympathy. One of the most original—and possibly lucrative—ideas for the disposition of Jeff Davis came from an Illinois soldier. Charles Calvin Enslow proposed placing him on exhibition in a cage near the Lincoln monument in Springfield or taking him through the North "as a show," the proceeds of which would be given to a "Soldiers' Orphan Asylum."[46]

The most notable aspect of the vengeance Union soldiers demanded is that it was not exacted. While the trial of those accused of plotting Lincoln's death was a shameful affair, there were not widespread arrests of former Confederates. The Union soldiers who remained in the South did not run amok, satisfying their desire for revenge. Instead, Union soldiers proved oddly willing to sympathize with their former enemies—so long as the defeated rebels acted as if they recognized their defeat.

In April 1865, after Lee's surrender but before Davis's capture and a certain end to the war, a New York major reported that he saw Confederates in Petersburg "sporting gray uniforms with the most imperturbable coolness." Outside of the city, in the Union camps, Lee's veterans would visit the Yankee soldiers, and rebs and Yanks "would sit quietly around the fires and smoke and talk over the war and the prospects for peace."[47]

In June 1865 a Northern soldier in Virginia watched white farmers at work in their fields, hoeing corn and cutting early hay. Some of the men had been planters before the war and the work was new to them. The Northerner concluded with satisfaction that such men "will now have something else to do than to concoct treason & secession." Sloth and luxury had threatened to destroy American values; now that Southern whites were hard at work, the South might rejoin the Union. Union soldiers were pleased with the changes they had brought to the Southern landscape. They were so pleased that most of them were ready to leave the South and return to their families in the North.[48]

The failure of Reconstruction was foretold in letters written by those Union soldiers left in the South after the surrender of the Confederate army. Many of them could not see why they were there after the war was over; some could understand why they were there but did not relish the duty; and some gave explanations that suggested they had little sympathy with Reconstruction policy. Almost all wanted to go home.

One Northern soldier wrote from Raleigh in April that "us *veterans*" would be kept in the South until the formerly rebellious states could elect officials. Another soldier thought that the civil authorities of the South would not be able "to keep the peace" until the withdrawal of the Northern troops, "as a soldier would make no account of a constable or policeman in the South." Henry Pippitt explained to his mother that they were stationed at Dinwiddie Courthouse in May 1865 "to protect citizens and thier property and make the lazy nigers work." Two months later they were at Petersburg. From there he reported that he longed to come home, but that they could not turn over the government of the city to local authorities until the latter could protect themselves from the freedmen. "the nigers are geting worse and worse every day down here. thier where 2 shot ded by the New Yorkers last evening." He personally had not yet been disturbed by an impudent freedman, "but I pitty the niger that does lay his hand on me. death is his portion." Despite the fact he had fought in the trenches around Petersburg and had seen black troops in action, at the war's end, Pippitt was still "down on A niger worse than a dog."[49]

"Father perhaps you would like to know what we are doing here now I will tell you," Henry W. Gay wrote home to Maine in August 1865. "We are keeping the Niggers from killing the whites." That was his understanding of the duties of the 15th Maine, and it was not as farfetched as it may sound. The regiment Maine was assigned to keep order on local plantations. They guarded the owners and former masters when they returned to their land; they forced the blacks to sign labor contracts, a necessary job, Gay explained, since "the Niggars are so ignorant that they will not signe unless a Soldier goes and makes theme do it."

Frankly, Gay did not think these duties sufficient reason for him to remain in the South or in the army. The Civil War volunteer rarely became a soldier: he would accept military service in wartime but not in peacetime. Peace-keeping did not strike the Civil War veteran as an important role. "I tell you it is not much like the Soldering that we had last year, but I do not like to be a Solder in peaceable time there is not eny fun in it."[50]

In May 1865 Lt. Christopher Keller anticipated that the next job that would face the U.S. army was fighting the French, whom he termed "frog-eaters" and "garlic-eaters," in Mexico. He and the men of his company, however, were not marching toward the Rio Grande where the real enemy of the United States lay waiting. Instead, they were doing provost duty in Montgomery, Alabama, where the days went by slowly and they waited for their discharge. He complained, "it *seems* as though we could do no more good here. Of course we know that such is not exactly the case but there is no stimulus for our patriotism now as there was before and we feel more discontented," even though they were "pleasantly situated."

Toward the end of the month, he wrote a letter to his parents "full of nothing of importance to us or of interest to you." In it he mentioned that freed slaves from the surrounding countryside crowded Montgomery as their former masters had driven them from the plantations; that most blacks had no employment and were "coralled" and fed by the army; and that "Last Sunday some negroes came in town from some point east of here, four of whom had their ears cuts off and one an old woman had a piece of her scalp taken off besides." A local white man had committed "this instance of rebel barbarity" because the blacks "were going to the Yanks," and he wished to "put the Yankee mark on them." By June, Keller had decided that there was simply no reason to keep Union soldiers in Montgomery.[51]

Union soldiers had not enlisted to destroy slavery; they certainly had not enlisted to defend black rights. Military duty during Reconstruction seemed to them to have nothing to do with preserving the Union or protecting their families. Like most American volunteers after a war, they felt their duty was done and that they were entitled to go home.

Ironically, at the same time that Northern soldiers expressed the sentiments that doomed Reconstruction, the shock of defeat left Southern soldiers more willing to accept changes in the South than they would ever be again. They had been defeated and they knew it; they believed that the North had the power and the will to create a revolution in Southern society. They would not have been able to resist—the weary soldiers of 1865 were not ready for partisan warfare.[52]

Capt. Samuel T. Foster, after entertaining several ludicrous schemes for continuing the war, asked himself some hard questions in April 1865. "Who is to blame for all this waste of human life?" "And what does it amount to? Has there been anything gained by all this sacrifice? What were we fighting for, the principles of slavery?"

The principles of slavery no longer seemed worth fighting for. He was surprised at the way "mens minds can change so sudden from opinions, of life long, to new ones a week old." Some defeated Confederates had begun to question what Alexander Stephens had called "the cornerstone of the Confederacy."

"I mean that men who have not only been taught from their infancy that the institution of slavery was right; but men who actually owned and held slaves up to this time,—have now changed in their opinions regarding slavery, so as to be able to see the other side of the question,—to see that for man to have property in man was wrong, and that the Declaration of Independence meant more than they had ever been able to see before. 'That all men are, and of right, ought to be free' has a meaning different from the definition they had been taught from their infancy up,—and to see that the institution (though perhaps wise) had been abused, and perhaps for that abuse this terrible war with its results, was brought upon us as punishment." He added, "These ideas come not from the Yanks or northern people but come from reflection and reasoning among ourselves."

According to Foster, a few soldiers wished to continue the fight. But most of them were "ready to submit to anything that comes up." They were willing to submit to those things that Chaplain Paris had predicted. "We do not suppose, nor expect to be allowed to vote any more, as long as we live. We also expect that all the lands in the Confederacy, will be taken away from the white people to pay their war expenses then given in small 160 acre lots to the negroes." In fact, they were willing to submit to a harsher Reconstruction policy than the North ever adopted.

Foster also reconsidered his opinion of Southern blacks when he saw black children on their way to a school run by Northern teachers. He stopped a twelve-year-old student and asked her what she studied. She showed him her reading, grammar, arithmetic, and geography books. He examined her on the texts. She proved proficient at grammar, geography, and arithmetic. "I never was more suprised in my life! The idea was new to me." Contemplating this "neat and clean" schoolgirl, he saw the possibility of a future in which educated blacks competed as equals with whites, and in which men and women were judged by their character, not their color.[53]

Capt. Thomas J. Key had a simliar experience on his way home to Arkansas. In Paducah and Nashville he saw black girls "on their way to school with their books, slates, etc." He concluded that

"There has been a marked change in social and domestic circles since the revolution began," and hoped that education would develop the moral sensibilities of the black race.[54]

Whatever the prospects of a new social order, the war did not change certain realities. As early as spring 1863, one Confederate had warned his father not to sell his land, no matter how much he needed the money. "The Yankees can run away with everything else but land." Everything else had included slaves—had included the institution of slavery. Despite Captain Foster's predictions, the federal government did not strip white landowners of their property to redistribute it to the freed people. Even without slaves the Southern planter class retained its economic base. And the egalitarian, color-blind future has been a long time in coming. But it is not necessary to argue that Captain Foster was typical of all Confederate veterans to believe that the federal government could have made more demands of the defeated South than it actually did.[55]

An Iowan cavalryman in Augusta, Georgia, who saw many rebel veterans pass through during April and May 1865, said that Confederates and Federals spent a great deal of time together, already talking over old battles. On May 8 he attended an auction where the soldiers of the lately warring armies mingled freely. The auctioneer, with what fantastical notions of turning a profit it is hard to imagine, bought up Confederate currency at the rate of $100 C.S.A. to $1 in silver. The Iowan saw an ex-Confederate lieutenant pay $500 in Confederate money—"all his wages for the last seven months in the army before Richmond"—for a box of cigars. The Confederate had lost his right arm during that period; the Iowan concluded, "that was a costly box of cigars."[56]

Sometimes Union soldiers' comments about the Confederate veterans returning home revealed the fears they had about their own future reception up north. An Indiana soldier who saw how the citizens of Macon, Georgia, treated Southern veterans thought that "it is a shame the way they treat their own soldiers, who have been in the army for long years fighting for the confederacy they hoped to gain." Three years ago, he said, Southerners had promised to honor those who fought for their cause. "But those promises are now forgotten and they are treated worse than beggars. I issued

rations to 78 men from Lee's army passing through here—home—
there own state, who had eaten nothing for 48 hours; had been
refused a bite to eat because they were ragged and dirty." The
ingratitude of the South to these ex-soldiers disgusted him. But
could he be certain that the civilian population back in his home
would be any more grateful?[57]

The 105th Illinois regiment was marching down the sidewalk in
Chicago in June 1865. These veterans of Sherman's army were
ordered off the sidewalk and into the street. Cpl. James A. Congleton asked, "Could a greater insult have been offered us?" He
thought it lucky for the policeman that most of the men in the
regiment did not realize what was going on—otherwise that policeman would have been killed. "We had our guns and also quite
a good supply of cartridges also our bayonets and it is Safe to add
that the whole Police force of Chicago would not have forced us
from the walk." Congleton believed such shabby treatment typical
of the mean-spirited civilians. Too cowardly to join the Confederate
army and fight openly against the Union, they intended to denigrate
the soldier now that the war was over.[58]

The Army of the Potomac and the western armies that fought
with Sherman paraded the streets of the capital at the end of the
war. "As I listened to the steady footfall again I experienced the
odd feeling of excitement, and the fancy of the dreaded 'Mill'
grinding to atoms Kings, & Kingdoms, Emperors & Empires, Tramp,
tramp, slow but sure," one soldier wrote, "I thought that tramp
of freemen is grinding to dust tyrants and tyranny." Even as this
Grand Review celebrated the Republic's victory, it pointed up the
distance between soldiers and civilians. One soldier commented
that the people seated in the reviewing stands and on the tops of
houses looked down on the passing soldiers through their opera
glasses as though the soldiers were "some wild Beasts." The Capitol
was bedecked with flags and banners. One motto in paticular struck
Col. Charles S. Wainwright: "The only debt we can never repay:
what we owe to our gallant defenders." Presumably this admission
was meant to be flattering, but it made the colonel wonder, "whether
having made up their minds that they *can never* pay, they will not
think it useless to try."[59]

The end of the war revealed feelings in the soldiers that surprised even themselves. Charles Maxim wrote home that the realization that he would never go into combat again made him feel "lonesome." There was no other time, he confessed, when one's emotions were at such a pitch. More than that, going into battle, one felt an emotion that was different from any other emotion, one for which Maxim lacked a name; he could only describe it negatively. It was not "very pleasurable," "not wicked," and "not painful." This excitement was what led a man on "when he almost knows it is death to go any farther."[60]

Soldiers did not exactly miss the fighting; they knew what war was. But men missed the "fun." "It is much more lonesome here now than when the war was going on," James M. DeHaven wrote his mother in June 1865. Now they saw "the same thing every day," and this was boring compared to the marches of the war when they traveled through the countryside. Men wondered how life would feel without the camaraderie of the army. Would they be isolated—"lonesome"—in civil society? How much had war changed them?[61]

There was little official concern about the reintegration of the soldier—Union or Confederate—into his community. In general the soldier was expected to find his own way. After the Grand Review, Sherman bid his troops farewell "with the full belief that as in war you have been good soldiers, so in peace you will make good citizens." And the American volunteer, who had taken pride in his soldiering but had never entirely lost his identity in it, in general merged into postwar society—if not painlessly, then with pains that were not often discussed.[62]

The soldiers of the Union had the Grand Review to welcome them back to American society. From the nation's capital they went home. The soldiers of the Confederacy performed no such civic ritual as they returned to civilian life, but soon enough the Lost Cause would develop its oratory and its political allegiances. Both had gone to war to defend liberty as they conceived it. Both had fought enemies they called savage—and had encountered savagery within themselves. The North now had to face the responsibilities of victory; the South had to accept the bitterness of defeat. Yet in many ways both turned away from these realities, one by ignoring responsibility, the other by creating the consoling myth of the Lost

Cause. White Americans North and South reluctantly considered the question of black rights, because the war had brought a new liberty that most had not thought of in 1861: emancipation. All had experienced a war that surpassed anything they had imagined.

The soldiers who had fought had shared the political culture of America in the last years of the old Republic, whether they embraced its Northern or its Southern expression. Between 1861 and 1865, they had created a new American history, a potent source of myth and identity. Now they brought home whatever lessons might be learned from the war, whatever patriotism, brutality or cynicism it might have created, and whatever memories that might be self-consciously celebrated or half-unconsciously repressed. Theirs was the knowledge from which the new America would be built.[63]

Abbreviations

AHS	Atlanta Historical Society.
CHS	Connecticut Historical Society.
DUKE	Duke University.
EMORY	Emory University.
HNOC	Historic New Orleans Collection.
LC	Library of Congress.
LHC	Louisiana Historical Center. Louisiana State Museum.
MHC	Michigan Historical Collections, Bentley Historical Library, University of Michigan.
MHS	Massachusetts Historical Society.
NC	North Carolina Collection, University of North Carolina.
NYHS	New-York Historical Society.
PU	Princeton University.
SCHOFF	Schoff Collection, Clements Library. University of Michigan.
SHC	Southern Historical Collection, University of North Carolina, Chapel Hill.
TULANE	Tulane University.
UG	University of Georgia, Athens.
USAMHI	U.S. Army Military History Institute.
UT	University of Texas, Austin.
UV	University of Virginia, Charlottesville.
VHS	Virginia Historical Society.
VSL	Virginia State Library.
WM	The College of William and Mary in Virginia.

Notes

1. WARS FOR FREEDOM

1 Henry H. Seys to Harriet Seys, September 14, 1861. Henry H. Seys Letters. SCHOFF.

2 Paul Joseph Revere to John, November 11, 1861; tribute to Colonel Revere on his death, 1863. Paul Joseph Revere Papers. MHS.

3 Samuel Smeetze to Mary, March 13, 1864. Confederate Papers (Miscellaneous). SHC. See Bell Irvin Wiley, *The Life of Johnny Reb: The Common Soldier of the Confederacy.* (Indianapolis, 1943), 15–18, for an account of Confederate volunteering.

4 Thomas L. Carson to Daniel Davis, May 14, 1861. Confederate Miscellany. EMORY. Thom [?] to Ma, May 10, 1861. Confederate States of America Archives. Army-Miscellany. Officers and Soldiers Letters. DUKE. James A. Roberts to Cousin Griff [Robert G. Williams], March 4, 1861. Robert Williams Collection. UG. 1861 Memorandum book. April 19, 1861. Mansfield Lovell Papers. LHC.

5 W. Gordon McCabe, quoted in Douglas Southall Freeman, *Lee's Lieutenants* (New York, 1944), III, 673.

6 William Pegram to Mary Evans (Pegram) Anderson, February 18, 1861, May 3, 1861. William Pegram to Virginia Johnson (Pegram) McIntosh, November 10, 1860. Pegram-Johnson-McIntosh Papers. VHS.

7 William Pegram to Virginia Johnson (Pegram) McIntosh, August 1, 1864. William Pegram to James West Pegram, March 17, 1865.

8 Rufus W. Cater to Cousin Fanny, September 1, 1860, September 19, 1860, June 26, 1861. Douglas and Rufus Cater Papers. LC.

9 F. Jay Taylor, ed., *Reluctant Rebel: The Secret Diary of Robert Patrick, 1861–1865* (Baton Rouge, 1959), 86. For a discussion, for example, of wealth distribution in upcountry South Carolina, see Lacy K. Ford, Jr., "Social Origins of a New South Carolina: The Upcountry in the Nineteenth Century." PhD dissertation, University of South Carolina, 1983, 44–48, 55.

10 James Oakes, *The Ruling Race: A History of American Slaveholders,* (New York, 1982), 228–30. Ford, "Social Origins of a New South

Carolina," 339–44. Steven Hahn, *The Roots of Southern Populism: Yeoman Farmers and the Transformation of the Georgia Upcountry, 1850–1890* (New York, 1983), 40–41, suggests that the concentration of wealth in the 1850s was characteristic of the staple-producing regions, rather than the Southern upcountry. See also Hahn's discussion of the loyalty of nonslaveholders to the slave system, 85–91.

11 Oakes, *The Ruling Race,* 232–42. Henry C. Harper Diary, July 14, 1861. Confederate Miscellany. EMORY.

12 J. Mills Thornton interprets secession as the last crisis of the Jacksonian era—the heir of the war against the monster Bank, a symbolic crusade fueled by the tensions created by the expanding market economy. While this interpretation ignores the fact that secession was also an attempt on the part of the slaveholders to cement the loyalty of the nonslave-holding class to the South's "peculiar institution," it does help explain why many Southern whites supported secession. J. Mills Thornton III, *Politics and Power in a Slave Society: Alabama, 1800–1860* (Baton Rouge, 1978). For a discussion of the economy of the Old South, see Gavin Wright, *The Political Economy of the Cotton South: Households, Markets, and Wealth in the Nineteenth Century.* For the premarket sector, James A. Henretta, "Families and Farms: *Mentalitie* in Pre-Industrial America," *William and Mary Quarterly,* 35 (January 1978) 3–32; Michael Merrill, "Cash is Good to Eat: Self-Sufficiency and Exchange in the Rural Economy of the United States," *Radical History Review,* 4, (Winter 1977), 42–71; Gavin Wright and Howard Kunreuther, "Cotton, Corn, and Risk in the Nineteenth Century," *Journal of Economic History,* 35 (September 1975), 526–51; Hahn, *The Roots of Southern Populism.* See also Forrest McDonald and Grady McWhiney, "The South from Self-Sufficiency to Peonage: An Interpretation," *American Historical Review,* 85 (December 1980), 1095–1118. For commercialism associated with Yankee values, see Ford, "Social Origins of a New South Carolina," 367, 483. For an example of non-slaveholders' attitudes toward slavery, see Frederick Law Olmsted, *A Journey in the Back Country, 1853–1854* (New York, 1970), 197–204.

13 H. C. Kendrick to sister, November 15, 1861. H. C. Kendrick Papers. SHC. Francis Dunbar Ruggles Diary, September 6, 1862. Francis Dunbar Ruggles Collection, HNOC.

14 William M. Cash and Lucy Somerville Howorth, eds., *My Dear Nellie: The Civil War Letters of William L. Nugent to Eleanor Smith Nugent* (Jackson, Miss., 1977), 45–46.

15 Lieutenant Lomax to Lt. George Bayard, April 21, 1861. Copy from *The Confederate Veteran,* Lomax Family Papers. VHS.

16 Clyde Lottridge Cummer and Genevieve Miller, eds., *Yankee in Gray: The Civil War Memoirs of Henry E. Handerson With a Selection of his Wartime Letters* (Western Reserve University, 1962), 21–22, 8–29, 112.

17 Address delivered by Dr. B. M. Palmer to the Washington Artillery from the steps of City Hall, May 27, 1861. Louisiana Historical Association Collection. TULANE. Memorandum Book of C. C. Bier, May 27, 1861. LHC.

18 R. Henderson Shuffler, ed., *The Adventures of a Prisoner of War, 1863–1864, by Decimus et Ultimus Barziza* (Austin, 1964), 58–60.

19 The historian W. R. Brock sums up the value of the Union well when he says, "No one who thought about these matters in the northern states doubted that the idea of American nationalism was bound up with the ideals of human betterment. This explains the intensity of emotion that focused upon the word 'Union'; it was not a mere political arrangement but the only way in which an American could summarize his romantic concept of national existence." *Conflict and Transformation: The United States, 1844–1877* (Baltimore, 1973), 132. See Bell Wiley's discussion of Union volunteerism, *The Life of Billy Yank: The Common Soldier of the Union* (Baton Rouge, 1983), 17–21, 37–40. "A Stirring Incident of the Federal War, 1861: A Drama Written by a Mr. Kellog Taken Prisoner at the First Battle of Bull's Run Virginia and confined at the Old Tobacco Factory Richmond And played by Him and his Fellow Prisoners of the 38th New York Volunteers and other Regiments." NYHS. For an insightful discussion of the relationship between the Revolution and American nationality, see Charles Royster, "Founding a Nation in Blood: Military Conflict and American Nationality," Ronald Hoffman and Peter Albert, eds., *Arms and Independence: The Military Character of the American Revolution* (Charlottesville, 1984).

20 Caleb Blanchard to wife, January 18, 1863; June 11, 1863. Caleb Blanchard Papers. CHS.

21 Samuel Storrow to father, October 12, 1862. Samuel Storrow Papers. MHS. Henry H. Seys to Harriet Seys, November 7, 1862. Henry H. Seys Papers. SCHOFF. Orra B. Bailey to wife, November 19, 1862. Orra B. Bailey Papers. LC. Levi E. Kent Diary, January 1, 1862. SCHOFF.

22 John Wesley Marshall Journal, September 7, 1862. LC.

23 Caleb Blanchard to wife, December 20, 1862; March 17, 1863; February 12, 1865. Caleb Blanchard Papers. CHS. Eric Foner, *Free Soil, Free Labor, Free Men: The Ideology of the Republican Party Before the Civil War* (New York, 1970). Paul W. Gates, *The Farmer's Age: Agriculture, 1815–1860* (New York, 1960), 94–98, 272–75, 293. For a provocative discussion of the impact of the Market Revolution on Northern thought during the sectional conflict, see Avery Craven, "Coming of War Between the States: An Interpretation," *Journal of Southern History*, II, #3 (August 1936), 303–322. See also Richard Hofstader, *The American Political Tradition and the Men Who Made It* (New York, 1960), 93–136; Leonard P. Curry, *Blueprint for Modern America: Nonmilitary Legislation of the First Civil War Congress* (Nashville, 1968); Kenneth M. Stampp, *And the War Came: The North and the Secession Crisis, 1860–1861* (Baton Rouge, 1950); David Brion Davis, *The Slave Power Conspiracy and the Paranoid Style* (Baton Rouge, 1969).

24 August J. Barr to wife, September 18, 1862. Harrisburg Civil War Round Table Collection. USAMHI.

25 See Bell Irvin Wiley's account of antislavery soldiers and the general antipathy toward abolition in the Union army, *Billy Yank*, 40–44.

26 A. C. Wilcox to Cousin Mary, May 31, 1864. New York 81st Infantry

Folder, Civil War Miscellany. USAMHI. For an account of antebellum Northern racism, see Leon F. Litwack, *North of Slavery: The Negro in the Free States, 1790–1860* (Chicago, 1961); Eugene H. Berwanger, *The Frontier Against Slavery: Western Anti-Negro Prejudice and the Slavery Extension Controversy* (Urbana, Illinois, 1971).

27 Rufus Mead, Jr., to friends, May 27, 1861; Rufus Mead, Jr., to folks at home, November 14, 1861. Rufus Mead, Jr., Papers. LC.

28 John Fleming, Civil War Recollections, 12. NYHS.

29 See the discussion of the "Treasury of Virtue" in Robert Penn Warren, *The Legacy of the Civil War: Meditations on the Centennial* (New York, 1964), 59–63. John Fleming, *Civil War Recollections*, 81.

30 Henry J. Johnson to Clara Johnson, June 30, 1862; January 14, 1863; March 14, 1863; April 8, 1863. Henry J. Johnson Letters. SCHOFF.

31 Carl N. Degler, *The Other South: Southern Dissenters in the Nineteenth Century* (New York, 1974).

32 James Fenton Diary, 74. PU. Jasper N. Barritt to brother, September 14, 1864. Jasper N. Barritt Papers. LC.

33 Ashley Halsey, ed., *A Yankee Private's Civil War by Robert Hale Strong* (Chicago, 1961), 1, 7.

34 Oscar Osburn Winther, *With Sherman to the Sea: The Civil War Letters, Diaries, and Reminiscences of Theodore F. Upson* (Bloomington, Ind., 1958), 13–19.

35 Sidney O. Little to Sarah P. Durant, December 19, 1862. Sidney O. Little Papers. SCHOFF. C. E. Taylor to father, July 14, 1861. Confederate States of America Records, Case I. UT.

36 Confederate Soldier's War Diary, May 25, 1862. Folder I, Case I. Confederate States of America Records. UT.

37 Bell Wiley says that flag presentations "were almost identical throughout the length and breadth of Dixie." *Johnny Reb,* 21. See Wiley, *Billy Yank,* 28–30, for an account of Union flag presentations. Address of C. R. Hanleiter on receiving Banner presented to the "Jo Thompson Artillery," September 1861. Cornelius Redding Hanleiter Collection. AHS.

38 Philip A. Lantzy to father and mother, July 27, 1861. Harrisburg Civil War Round Table Collection. USAMHI.

39 William W. Hassler, ed., *The General to His Lady: The Civil War Letters of William Dorsey Pender to Fanny Pender* (Chapel Hill, 1965), 16.

40 William M. Collin Diary, February 22, 1862. LC.

41 W. J. Underwood to B. Y. Hunter, July 9, 1861. Underwood–Key Family Papers. AHS. Newton Wallace Diary. July 4, 1862. NC.

42 Clipping in scrapbook, Confederate Papers, Miscellaneous. SHC.

43 "drawn off by Wm. Yandle this 13th of August, 1864. for George Lenord at Camp Jackson." Confederate States of America Archives. DUKE.

44 For a discussion of Confederate ideology, see Paul D. Escott, *After Secession: Jefferson Davis and the Failure of Confederate Nationalism* (New York, 1976), 168–95. On the Confederate Constitution, see Charles Robert Lee, Jr., *The Confederate Constitutions* (Chapel Hill, 1963).

2. ENEMIES AND SAVAGES

1   There is a great body of literature on English–Indian relations in the colonial period. See, for example, Richard Slotkin, *Regeneration through Violence: The Mythology of the American Frontier, 1600–1860* (Middletown, Conn., 1973), and James Axtell, *The European and the Indian: Essays in the Ethnohistory of Colonial North America* (New York, 1981).

2   Charles Royster, *A Revolutionary People at War: The Continental Army and American Character, 1775–1783* (Chapel Hill, 1979).

3   John Frederic Holohan Diary, June 5, 1861. Private possession. Ned Holmes to father, August 14, 1862. Ned Holmes Letters. MHS. George Bates Starbird to Marianne Starbird, January 11, 1863. Starbird Letters. SCHOFF. Allan Nevins, ed., *A Diary of Battle: The Personal Journals of Colonel Charles S. Wainwright* (New York, 1962), 59. Bell Wiley discusses Confederate attitudes toward Union soldiers in *The Life of Johnny Reb: The Common Soldier of the Confederacy* (Indianapolis, 1943), 308–321; Northern attitudes toward Confederates in *The Life of Billy Yank: The Common Soldier of the Union* (Baton Rouge, 1983), 346–61. As is so often the case in these two works, the attitudes, actions, and beliefs described are almost identical North and South.

4   James I. Robertson, Jr., ed., *The Civil War Letters of General Robert McAllister* (New Brunswick, N.J., 1965), 48–49.

5   Robertson, *McAllister*, 126.

6   Francis Boland to John Brislin, June 14, 1862. Harrisburg Civil War Round Table Collection. USAMHI. See also Frederick D. Williams, *The Wild Life of the Army: Civil War Letters of James A. Garfield* (Michigan State University, 1964), 244.

7   William W. Hassler, ed., *The General to His Lady: The Civil War Letters of William Dorsey Pender to Fanny Pender* (Chapel Hill, 1965), 18.

8   Confederate Papers (Miscellaneous). SHC. Hanleiter War Diary, December 23, 1861. Cornelius Redding Hanleiter Papers. AHS. Albert Moses Luria War Journal, August 19, 1861. Albert Moses Luria Papers. SHC. For a Confederate's belief of Southern victory at 13 to 1 odds, see W. W. Edwards to Thomas V. Humphris, November 30, 1861. Confederate Miscellany. EMORY.

9   William Ellis Jones Diary, August 9, 1862. SCHOFF.

10 Samuel Lockhart to mother, July 5, 1864. Confederate Papers (Miscellaneous). SHC.

11 Andrew Devilbliss to Mary, October 14, 1861. Andrew Devilbliss Letters. Civil War Miscellaneous Series. TULANE. See Diary of Unknown Prisoner at Johnson's Island, 1864–1865. Louisiana Historical Association Collection, April 26, 27, 1864, TULANE, for a Confederate's complaints about "Boston missionary enterprise" on the Hawaiian Islands and Yankee anti-Catholic sentiment.

12 H. J. H. Rugeley, ed., *Batchelor-Turner Letters, 1861–1864: Written by Two of Terry's Texas Rangers* (Austin, 1961), 15–16, 35. See also James W. Silver, ed., *A Life for the Confederacy: As Recorded in the Pocket Diaries of Pvt. Robert A. Moore* (Jackson, Tenn., 1959), 28, 122, 125. One Confederate soldier who helped bury some Union sol-

diers wrote, "I printed Abolitionist on a Oak Board and stuck it at his head for the Yanks to see if they should come after we left." Bell Irvin Wiley, ed., *"This Infernal War": The Confederate Letters of Sgt. Edwin H. Fay* (Austin, 1958), 180.

13 Wirt Armistead Cate, ed., *Two Soldiers: The Campaign Diaries of Thomas J. Key C.S.A. December 7, 1863–May 17, 1865, and Robert J. Campbell, U.S.A., January 1, 1864–July 21, 1864* (Chapel Hill, 1938), 70, 138–39, 164. For additional comments on miscegenation, see John G. Barrett, ed., *Yankee Rebel: The Civil War Journal of Edmund DeWitt Patterson,* (Chapel Hill, 1966), 171.

14 Osmun Latrobe Diary, December 11, 1862; December 16, 1862; May 10, 1863. VHS.

15 John S. Barlett to sister, May 3, 1863. John S. Barlett Papers. CHS.

16 John R. Morey Diary, July 14, 1863. MHC. Harry Lewis to Mrs. John S. Lewis, May 7, 1863. Harry Lewis Papers. SHC.

17 George Hall Nicholls to M. G. Nicholls, September 23, 1862. George Hall Nicholls Letters. SCHOFF. J. S. Jenkins to Susan A. Kenny, June 17, 1864. Confederate Miscellany. EMORY. Cf. Bell Wiley, *Johnny Reb,* 311. A Union soldier complained that "The Rebels are so mean and treacherous that they burn all the bridges and tear up the rail road track after they retreat and so we can't get after them." Philip A. Lantzy to family, April 6, 1862. Harrisburg Civil War Round Table Collection. USAMHI.

18 John Fleming, *Civil War Recollections,* 21. NYHS.

19 Albert Moses Luria War Journal, August 19, 1861. SHC.

20 John S. Barlett to sister, January 4, [1862?]. John S. Barlett Papers. CHS. William N. Barnard to Simon Peterson, April 11, 1862. Simon Peterson Letters. SCHOFF.

21 John D. St. John to father, April 14, 1862. Bela St. John Papers. LC. Also, see Sidney O. Little to Elvin Little, June 17, 1863. Sidney O. Little Letters. SCHOFF. Lewis J. Martin to Mrs. C. E. Martin, July 18, 1862. Lewis J. Martin Letters. SCHOFF. Hugh P. Roden to George Roden, Sr. [May 5, 1862]. Roden Brothers Letters. SCHOFF.

22 Thomas J. W. Chattin to Miss. M. F. Chattin, May 22, 1862. Confederate Miscellany. EMORY. Michael L. Hambrick to mother, September 7, 1862. Hambrick Civil War Letters. UG.

23 Rugeley, *Batchelor-Turner,* 29. See also Silver, *Moore,* 40. Hassler, *Pender,* 140. A. C. Hill to Judge T. M. Rector, July 28, 1863, Civil War Miscellany, UT; Journal of G. Briant, February 20, 1863. Briant Family Papers. LSM. Address to soldiers, March 4, 1862, copy in Louisiana Historical Association Collection, Box 2. TULANE. Printed in *Official Records,* Series I, Volume 9, 53–54.

24 Jacob W. Haas to brother, December 18, 1862. Harrisburg Civil War Round Table Collection. USAMHI.

25 Shepherd Green Pryor to Penelope Tyson Pryor, October 3, 1862. Shepherd Green Pryor Papers. UG.

26 Margaret Brobst Roth, ed., *Well Mary: Civil War Letters of a Wisconsin Volunteer* (Madison, 1960), 69. Rugely, *Batchelor-Turner,* 11.

27 For a discussion of Northern opinions of Southern society on the eve of the Civil War, see Kenneth M. Stampp, *And the War Came: The North and the Secession Crisis, 1860–1861* (Baton Rouge, 1950), 253–

59; Eric Foner, *Free Labor, Free Soil, Free Men: The Ideology of the Republican Party Before the Civil War* (New York, 1970).

28 Edward Henry Courtney Taylor to Lottie, April 14, 1862; to family May 28, 1862. Edward Henry Courtney Taylor Papers. MHC.

29 John Fleming, *Civil War Recollections*, 2. NYHS. Robertson, *McAllister*, 94.

30 Paul Ambrose Oliver to mother, June 3, 1862, Paul Oliver to Sam, November 12, 1863. Paul Ambrose Oliver Papers. PU.

31 Williams, *Garfield*, 65. William T. Sherman, *Memoirs* (Bloomington, Ind., 1957), volume 1, 337.

32 John Pierson to wife, August 15, 1862. John Pierson Letters. SCHOFF.

33 Mary Acton Hammond, ed., "Dear Mollie: Letters of Captain Edward A. Acton to His Wife, 1862," *Pennsylvania Magazine of History and Biography*, LXXXIX, 1 (January 1965), 10–15.

34 William G. Dickson to E. Levassor, December 24, 1864; January 20, 1865; March 14, 1865. William G. Dickson Letters. SCHOFF.

35 John S. Copley to Robert Moody, February 21, 1862. John S. Copley Papers. PU.

36 Caleb Blanchard to wife, February 8, 1863. See also his letter of April 12, 1863. Caleb Blanchard Papers. CHS.

37 R. M. Campbell Diary, 21. AHS.

38 Harry Lewis to Mrs. John S. Lewis, May 15, 1863. Harry Lewis Papers. SHC.

39 R. Henderson Shuffler, ed., *The Adventures of a Prisoner of War, 1863–1864, by Decimus et Ultimus Barziza* (Austin, 1964), 102. See also Silver, 137. Albert Moses Luria War Journal, January 1862. Albert Moses Luria Papers. SHC. For another reference to "Yankee despotism," see William M. Cash and Lucy Somerville Howorth, eds., *My Dear Nellie: The Civil War Letters of William L. Nugent to Eleanor Smith Nugent* (Jackson, Miss., 1977), 87.

40 C. C. Bier Memorandum Book, July 18, 1861 [misdated]. LHC.

41 Stephen E. Ambrose, ed., *A Wisconsin Boy in Dixie: The Selected Letters of James K. Newton* (Madison, 1961), 72.

42 Numa Barned to Annie Barned, December 27, 1862. Numa Barned Letters. SCHOFF. See also Felix Brannigan to father, n.d. [first page missing], Felix Brannigan Papers. LC.

43 Charles J. Mills to mother, September 1, 1862. Harrisburg Civil War Round Table Collection. USAMHI.

44 Douglas Cater to cousins Laurence and Fannie, June 1, 1863. Rufus W. Cater to Fannie, June 19, 1863. Douglas and Rufus W. Cater Papers. LC.

45 Caleb Blanchard to wife, October 15, 1862. Caleb Blanchard Papers. CHS. See also Williams, *Garfield*, 37; Nevins, *Wainwright*, 59; Origen G. Bingham to family, September 21, 1862. Civil War Miscellany. USAMHI.

46 Allen Landis to parents, September 27, 1862. Allen Landis and Family Papers. LC. Calvin Mehaffey to mother, May 26, 1862. Calvin Mehaffey Letters. SCHOFF. See also Levi E. Kent Diary, February 14, 1862. SCHOFF. Arthur H. DeRosier, ed., *Through the South with a Union Soldier* (Johnson City, Tenn., 1969), 46.

47 G. Briant Journal, March 30, 1863, April [13?], 1863. Briant Family Papers. LHC.

48 See, for example, David Coe, ed., *Mine Eyes Have Seen the Glory: Combat Diaries of Union Sergeant Hamlin Alexander Coe* (Rutherford, Madison, Teaneck, New Jersey, 1975), 54.

49 William C. McKinley to wife, February 15, 1862. William C. McKinley Papers. LC.

50 Wiley, *Fay*, 102, 158. A. S. Webb reported that Union soldiers captured in Virginia in October 1861 were "fine-looking, well-dressed men." When asked why they had joined the army, the prisoners said "that they were thrown out of employment and had nothing else to do." A. S. Webb to S. A. Webb, October 24, 1861. Webb Family Papers. SHC.

51 Frank Harding to Eddy Harding, May 3, 1862. Civil War Miscellaneous Series. TULANE.

52 William G. Hills Diary, March 1, 1864. LC.

53 Byron Densmore Paddock Diaries, June 24, 1864. SCHOFF.

54 David M. Ray to mother, January 28, 1863. David M. Ray Papers. UT. F. Jay Taylor, ed., *Reluctant Rebel: The Secret Diary of Robert Patrick, 1861–1865* (Baton Rouge, 1959), 101–102. See also Thomas J. Rounsaville to family, February 8, 1863. Civil War Miscellany Papers. USAMHI. This letter also says that deserters claimed if the federal administration continued its emancipation policy, the western states would secede and form their own nation.

55 Henry Grimes Marshall to folks, July 27, 1864; to Hattie, November 25, 1864. Henry Grimes Marshall Letters. SCHOFF. For an account of a Confederate deserter who wished to get home to his friends in New York City, see Marshall to [Jerusha Marshall], May 13 [1864].

56 Roth, *Well Mary*, 60.

57 Coe, *Coe*, 91–92.

58 C. C. Brown to John A. Cato, December 9, 1862. Civil War Miscellany Papers. USAMHI. D. G. Brinton Thompson, "From Chancellorsville to Gettysburg: A Doctor's Diary," *Pennsylvania Magazine of History and Biography*, LXXXIX, #3 (July 1965), 303. Ambrose, *Newton*, 41.

59 The best study of Civil War prisons is William B. Hesseltine, *Civil War Prisons: A Study in War Psychology* (Columbus, Ohio, 1930). Hesseltine argues that the poor treatment of Union soldiers in Southern prisons was due to the gradual collapse of the Confederacy's infrastructure, and that the North, attributing this ill-treatment to conscious Southern malevolence, responded with deliberate and avoidable ill-treatment of Confederate prisoners-of-war.

60 W. P. Harper Diary, November 1, 1863. Louisiana Historical Association Collection. TULANE.

61 William Whatley Pierson, Jr., ed., *Whipt 'Em Everytime: The Diary of Barlett Yancey Malone, Co. H., 6th N.C. Regiment* (Jackson, Tenn., 1960), 92, 93, 100, 101, 108. For another example of a Union guard killing a prisoner—this time for not moving fast enough—see Francis A. Boyle Diary, 10–11. UG. On black guards, see also Diary of Unknown Prisoner at Johnson's Island, March 5, 1864. Louisiana Historical Association Collection. TULANE.

62 Diary of Unknown Prisoner at Johnson's Island, January 14, 1864; May 7, 1864.

63 Pierson, *Whipt 'Em Everytime*, 96. James R. McMichael Diary, 8. AHS. Francis A. Boyle Diary, 6, 9. UG.

64 Francis A. Boyle Diary, 13–14, 20–21. Diary of Unknown Prisoner at Johnson's Island, 1864–1865. February 2, 1864. In the fall of 1862 the Union soldiers at Fort McHenry routinely stole the food and clothing Baltimoreans brought the Confederate prisoners. Caleb Blanchard to wife, November 1, 1862; November [20], 1862. Caleb Blanchard Papers. CHS. Conditions for officers were not always onerous. At Fort Delaware Confederate prisoners could purchase watermelons and beer if they desired. A New York officer imprisoned in Macon, Georgia, said one could live "very comfortably" in prison if one had money. James R. McMichael Diary, 3. AHS. James Gaunt Derrickson Diary, July 12, 1864. SCHOFF.

65 Shuffler, *Barziza*, 99–100. James Gaunt Derrickson Diary, October 13, 1864; October 17, 1864.

66 William M. Collin Diary. August 22, 23, 1862. LC. See below for an account of Andersonville.

67 Diary of Unknown Prisoner at Johnson's Island, 1864–1865. January 8, 1864, March 29, 1864.

68 Point Lookout, Maryland, Prison Camp Records. Box 1: Letters of prisoners. See particularly R. C. Combs, et al., to Provost Marshal, November 11, 1863; John Lucas to Provost Marshal, n.d.; Thos. Curley, et al., to Provost Marshal, October 6, 1863; G. W. Watson to Provost Marshal, October 10, 1863. SCHOFF.

69 Samuel F. Duvall to Captain Patterson. Point Lookout, Maryland. Prison Camp Records. Box 1: Letters to prisoners. SCHOFF.

70 John Ransom, *John Ransom's Diary* (New York, 1963), 65–66, 125–26, 148, 166–67. Henry H. Stone Diary, May 1864–December 1864. Harrisburg Civil War Round Table Collection. USAMHI.

71 S. J. Gibson Diary, July 16, 1864; October 17, 18, 1864. November 10, 1864. LC.

72 James Gaunt Derrickson Diary, July 12, 1864; September 14, 1864.

73 James R. McMichael Diary, 1–2. AHS.

74 Charles Wesley Homsher Diary. LC. John Ransom also mentions the guards' desire for Union buttons, which they called "Buttons with hens on." Ransom, *Diary*, 94.

75 Ransom, *Diary*, 28, 113–17.

76 Ransom, *Diary*, 112–17. S. J. Gibson Diary, July 11, 12, 1864.

77 Joseph Williams to Destramona Williams, July 12, 1864. Robert Williams Collection. UG.

78 Christian Association Records. Francis A. Boyle Papers. SHC.

79 See Henry Wirz Papers, LC. Wirz's defense was that the charges against him were so vague as to be meaningless and that a military court had no proper jurisdiction in times of peace. He also argued that he was covered under the terms of the Sherman/Johnston peace convention.

80 John Faller to mother, December 23, 1861. Harrisburg Civil War Round Table Collection. USAMHI.

81 John William DeForest, *A Volunteer's Adventures: A Union Captain's Record of the Civil War* (New Haven, 1946), 190, 209.

3. From Volunteer to Soldier: The Psychology of Service

1   Charles R. Johnson to Nellie, December 10, 1862. Coco Collection. Harrisburg Civil War Round Table Collection. USAMHI.

2   Charles A. Wills to Mary J. Wills, May 10, 1863. Mary J. Wills Papers. WM.

3   David Donald discusses Confederate attitudes toward authority in his essay, "The Southerner as Fighting Man," in Charles G. Sellers, ed., *The Southerner as American* (New York, 1960), 72–88.

4   Bell Irvin Wiley, ed., *"This Infernal War": The Confederate Letters of Sgt. Edwin H. Fay* (1958), 51, 162. C. E. Taylor to father, July 14, 1861, Confederate States of America Records, UT. J. C. Owens to Susannah Owens, April 26, 1863, Confederate Papers (Miscellaneous). SHC.

5   George Bates Starbird to Marianne Starbird, April 2, 1864. Starbird Letters. SCHOFF. Jacob J. Frank Diary, July 26, 1862. LC. Mary Ann Anderson, ed., *The Civil War Diary of Allen Morgan Geer, Twentieth Regiment, Illinois Volunteers* (1977), 2. See also Samuel Storrow to parents, December 4, 1862. Samuel Storrow Papers. MHS.

6   David C. Bradley to mother, June 21, 1863. Civil War Miscellany Papers. USAMHI. John Fleming, *Civil War Recollections,* 226, 384. NYHS.

7   "Some of Our Hardships," Ms. in Charles Fenton James Papers. SHC. A Northern soldier stationed in Florida wrote, "We have been very busy since coming down here   in the first place we had to tear down all the old Quarters that the N.H. regt left and then build new again you should have seen the Quarters left by the N.H. Regt I would suppose any white folks above staying in such filthy Quarters   you would by staying in the bunks say one hour be so covered with fleas that you could pick them off your clothes by the dozen I am not troubled with the dear little creaturs much in the way of biting but they will get next to my hide and drill in squads." Orra B. Bailey to wife, May 30, 1863. Orra B. Bailey Papers. LC.

8   Paul Vaughan to sister, August 3, 1863. Paul Vaughan Papers. SHC. John Crosby to Abby J. Crosby. June 4, 1863. John Crosby Papers. CHS.

9   J. W. Allen to uncle, October 16, 1861. Confederate Miscellany. EMORY. Matthew Bone to William Bone, October 14, 1861. Adams Collection. UG. H. H. Green to J. M. Davis, May 28, 1862. Malcolm Letters. UG.

10   Neill McLeod to Elisabeth McLeod, July 19, 1862. Neill McLeod Papers. SHC.

11   John A. Hall to A. M. Morrow, May 15, 1862. Confederate Miscellany. EMORY. John Crosby to Abby J. Crosby. May 1 [1863]. John Crosby Papers. CHS.

12   War Journal, August 19, 1861. Albert Moses Luria Papers. SHC.

13   Harry Lewis to Mrs. John Lewis, July 20, 1862. Harry Lewis Papers. SHC.

14   E. H. Hampton to Aldecha Baily, July 14, 1864. Harvey Bailey Papers, Civil War Miscellany Papers. USAMHI. Albinus R. Fell to wife, January

19, 1862; February 10, 1862. Civil War Miscellany Papers. USAMHI. John Fleming, *Civil War Recollections,* 159. NYHS. A Union officer wrote his wife, "We have lost several men of the 10th by Sickness and more must go unless better care can be had for the Sick I do not mind seeing a man shot down in Battle but it is exceedingly painfull to see them suffer for want of proper care in the Hospitals [.]" John Pierson to wife and daughter, June 5, 1862. John Pierson Letters. SCHOFF.

15 Thomas S. Howland to mother, June 10, [?] Thomas S. Howland Papers. MHS.

16 Daniel Faust to sister, May 7, 1863. Harrisburg Civil War Round Table Collection. USAMHI. B. H. Coffman to wife, July 12, 1863. Civil War Miscellany Papers. USAMHI.

17 George H. Allen Diary, December 27, 1862. UT. For a Confederate account of exposed bodies left from the battle of Fredericksburg, see Joseph Hilton to mother and father, March 23, 1863. Confederate Miscellany. EMORY.

18 Alexander Smith Webb to mother, October 31, 1861. Webb Family Papers. SHC. Frank Appleton Badger to mother, October 2 [5?], 1862. Alfred M. Badger Papers. LC.

19 Mike M. Hubbert Diary, June 30, 1862. Confederate States of America Records. UT.

20 Norman D. Brown, ed., *One of Cleburne's Command: The Civil War Reminiscences and Diary of Capt. Samuel T. Foster, Granbury's Texas Brigade,* C.S.A. (Austin, 1980), 115.

21 The soldier's feeling of being set apart—liminality—has long been characteristic of the warrior experience. The soldier has long been seen as both the representative of his society and as a figure foreign to organized society. Traditionally, war is seen as teaching a knowledge that cannot be communicated. The best discussion of this is Eric J. Leed, *No Man's Land: Combat and Identity in World War I* (Cambridge, 1979), 1–38.

22 S. H. Baldy to mother, May 31, 1861. Confederate Miscellany. EMORY.

23 David Herbert Donald, ed., *Gone for a Soldier: The Civil War Memoirs of Private Alfred Bellard* (Boston, 1975), 13.

24 John William DeForest's *Miss Ravenal's Conversion from Secession to Loyalty,* a fine novel written by a Union officer, touches upon this phenomenon and reveals particular bitterness about the place of the veteran in postwar America. For an account from another war, see Ford Madox Ford's *Parade's End.* Soldiers serve as a standing moral rebuke to civilians in times of crisis; one suspects that much of the contempt shown them by civilians springs from the need to project outward the emotions produced by one's own failure to participate in the great struggle. See also Charles Royster, " 'The Nature of Treason': Revolutionary Virtue and American Reactions to Benedict Arnold," *The William and Mary Quarterly,* 3rd Series, XXXVI (April 1979), 163–93, for a discussion of civilian attitudes during the American Revolution.

25 Rudolphe Rey to Miss Lizze DeVoe, June 14, 1865. Rey Papers. NYHS. George Starbird to Marianne Starbird, October 21, 1863. Starbird Letters. SCHOFF.

26 Habun R. Foster to Charles A. Wills, September 11, 1862. Mary J. Wills Papers, WM. Rufus W. Cater to Cousins Laurence and Fannie, June 1, 1863. Douglas J. and Rufus W. Cater Papers. LC.

27 Benjamin F. Ashenfelter to father, September 26, 1862. Harrisburg Civil War Round Table collection. USAMHI.

28 Douglas J. Cater to Laurence, June 24, 1864. Douglas J. and Rufus W. Cater Papers. LC. Clifford Dowdey and Louis H. Manarin, eds., *The Wartime Papers of R. E. Lee* (Boston, 1961), 80.

29 Susan Previant Lee and Peter Passell, in their analysis of Claudia Goldin and Frank Lewis, "The Economic Cost of the American Civil War," *Journal of Economic History* 35 (June 1975), 304–309, reveal some of the limitations of economic history by admitting it cannot explain why the soldiers of both armies fought for so much less money than they should have received in light of "risk premiums" and "loss of future wages." They suggest, in the case of the Union army, "the difference between the actual human capital loss and the required risk premium paid reflected unmeasured non-material benefits the soldiers received in fighting for their cause(s)." *A New Economic View of American History*, (New York, 1979), 224–25. It would be disingenuous of me, however, to pretend that the Confederate and Union soldiers were not very much concerned with money; resentful of better-paid officers, bounty-jumping volunteers, and stay-at-homes who earned enough to buy their way out of the army, the soldiers worried about economic matters frequently. Patriotism does not blind, nor are those who experience it insensible to everything else.

30 John Pierson to daughter, March 26, 1863. John Pierson Letters. SCHOFF.

31 John Pierson to Joanna, July 15, 1863. John Pierson Letters. SCHOFF. See also the letter of a Pennsylvania laborer. "I also feele sorry That I could not send you some Money yet the pay day is past for over a month ago But as long as we are marching and fighting wee wont Draw any money and it wouldent do To draw any money now for wee couldnot send any home in any safety at at preasant for the is no express from here but I hope wee will soon get into camp and get our money I know you would need it veary Bad But I hope your friends will not lieve you suffer you must do the Best you can I hope everything will come rite after all for all that Abel Herrold wouldent Trust you that flower I ecspect the cause is becase he is a copper head and they cant any Thing Better be exspected of such a man as he is for that is coper head princiapels The time I Boated for him I had to wait 18 months for 40 dollars of my pay and he wont trust 5 dollars for a couple of weeks" John Carvel Arnold to wife, June 5, 1864. John Carvel Arnold Papers. LC.

32 Henry H. Seys to Harriet Seys, October 23, 1863. Henry H. Seys Letters. SCHOFF.

33 John Rogers to family, May 15, 1862. Rogers Family Papers. Harrisburg Civil War Round Table Collection. USAMHI.

34 Christopher Howser Keller to George and Esther Keller, October 3, 1862. Christopher Howser Keller Letters. SCHOFF.

35 Harry Lewis to Mrs. John S. Lewis, February 15, 1863. Harry Lewis Papers. SHC.

36 Lyman C. Holford Diary, November 4, 1863. LC.

37 S. H. Eells to friends, June 25, 1862. S. H. Eells Papers. LC.
38 Henry I. Greer to mother, July 16, 1864. Henry I. and Robert Greer Papers. LC. R. S. Webb to mother, May 26, 1864. Webb Family Papers. SHC.
39 Harry Lewis to Mrs. John E. Lewis, August 20, 1863. Harry Lewis Papers. SHC. John Fleming, Civil War Recollections, 50. NYHS.
40 Pellona Alexander to Manning P. Alexander, April 14, 1862. Manning P. and Pellona David Alexander Letters. UG.
41 James T. Miller to Joseph Miller, May 24, 1863. James T. Miller to Robert and Jane Miller, June 6, 1863. Miller Brothers Letters. SCHOFF.
42 James T. Miller to William Miller, June 8, 1863. Miller Brothers Letters, SCHOFF.
43 James T. Miller to Robert and Jane Miller, February 18, 1863. Miller Brothers Letters. SCHOFF.
44 Samuel Storrow to parents, December 4, 1862. Samuel Storrow Papers. MHS.
45 Christopher H. Keller to Caroline M. Hall, September 14, 1862, September 21, 1862; to George and Esther Keller, September 14, 1862. Christopher H. Keller Letters. SCHOFF.
46 Luther C. Furst Diary, Mary 12, 1861, June 1, 1861, June 2, 1861. Harrisburg Civil War Round Table Collection. USAMHI. Frank Appleton Badger to mother, September 21, 1862. Alfred M. Badger Papers. LC.
47 H. H. Green to J. M. Davis, May 28, 1862. Malcolm Letters. UG. Alexander Smith Webb to sister, February 6, 1862. Webb Family Papers. SHC.
48 Ashley Halsey, ed. *A Yankee Private's Civil War by Robert Hale Strong* (Chicago, 1961), 205.
49 Joshua Taylor Bradford Diary, February 7, 16, 23; March 6, 1862. LC.
50 See also Wiley's account of "The Baptism of Fire," *The Life of Johnny Reb: The Common Soldier of the Confederacy* (Indianapolis, 1943), 28–35, and of "The Supreme Test," *The Life of Billy Yank: The Common Soldier of the Union* (Baton Rouge, 1983), 66–95.
51 George M. Decherd to Friend Rehum, January 6, 1862. James W. Redding Family Papers. UT. Bela St. John to brother, May 10, 1863; Bela St. John to parents, July 25, 1862. Bela Taylor St. John Papers. LC.
52 John S. Willey to wife, July 14, 1861; February 6, 1863. Norman Daniels Collection. Harrisburg Civil War Round Table Collection. USAMHI.
53 Habun R. Foster to Mary J. Wills, July 26, 1862. Mary J. Wills Papers. WM. George Henry Bates to William Bates, June 2, 1864. George Henry Bates Letters. SCHOFF.
54 Andrew Devilbliss to Mary, April 16, 1862. Civil War Miscellaneous Series. TULANE.
55 James Henry Hall to Richard M. J. Hall, May 2, 1862. SCHOFF. George W. Crosley to Edna, April 10, 1862. Civil War Miscellany Papers, USAMHI.
56 George W. Crosley to Edna, April 10, 1862. Civil War Miscellany Papers. USAMHI.

57 Shepherd Green Pryor to Penelope Tyson Pryor, October 6, 1861. Shepherd Green Pryor Papers. UG.

58 R. F. Eppes to wife, July 13, 1862. Confederate Papers (Miscellaneous). SHC.

59 A. W. Smith to mother, June 17, 1862. Civil War Miscellaneous Series. TULANE. Joseph Cotten to uncle, August 30, 1861. Joseph Cotten Papers. SHC.

60 John G. Barrett, ed., *Yankee Rebel: The Civil War Journal of Edmund DeWitt Patterson* (Chapel Hill, 1966), 6. Richard M. Campbell Diary, 25. AHS. See also Byron Densmore Paddock Diary, January 1, 1863. SCHOFF.

61 Hugh Roden to George Roden, Sr., November 12, 1862. Roden Brothers Letters. SCHOFF. See also Henry Pippitt to mother, June 20, 1864: "Mother when you go into battle you dont think of being killed all you think of is push a head and kill all you can of the rebs." Henry Pippitt Letters. SCHOFF.

62 Numa Barned to A. Barned [n.d], 1862. Numa Barned Letters. SCHOFF. Wayne C. Temple, ed., *The Civil War Letters of Henry C. Bear: A Soldier in the 116th Illinois Volunteer Infantry* (Harrogate, Tenn., 1961), 30.

63 H. C. Kendrick Papers, fragment, 1863. SHC. Later Donlon and a Confederate soldier exchanged shots while Donlon was on picket. Donlon wounded the rebel in the leg and the Union soldiers caught him. Donlon asked the prisoner for a ring he was wearing "and he gave it to me to remember him with as I had given him a mark he would take to the grave." Donlon sent the ring to his mother to wear until he returned from the war—something he never did, as he died at Andersonville Prison. Michael Donlon to brother, January 14, 1864, May 21, 1864. Civil War Miscellany Papers. USAMHI.

64 Benjamin F. Ashenfelter to Father Churchman, July 29, 1863. Harrisburg Civil War Round Table Collection. USAMHI.

65 William M. Cash and Lucy Somerville Howorth, eds., *My Dear Nellie: The Civil War Letters of William L. Nugent to Eleanor Smith Nugent* (Jackson, Miss., 1977), 185–86.

66 John Frederic Holahan Diary, November 3, 1862. Private possession.

67 Margaret Brobst Roth, ed., *Well Mary: The Civil War Letters of a Wisconsin Volunteer* (Madison, 1960), 111.

69 George Anthony to Ben Anthony, August 15, 1863. George Tobey Anthony Letters. SCHOFF.

70 H. J. H. Rugeley, ed., *Batchelor-Turner Letters, 1861–1864: Written By Two of Terry's Texas Rangers* (Austin, 1961), 50–51. James T. Miller to brother, August 17, 1862. Miller Brothers Letters. SCHOFF. George O. Jewett to Deck, August 16, 1863. George O. Jewett Papers. LC.

71 George O. Jewett to Deck, July 20, 1862. George O. Jewett Papers. LC. Samuel Storrow to parents, February 27, 1863. Samuel Storrow Papers. MHS. E. J. Lee to J. G. Taylor, October 13, 1861; May 20, 1862. Lee Collection. UT. John Thomas to sister, June 17, 1864. Confederate States of America Archives. Army-Miscellany. Officers and Soldiers Letters. DUKE. John to My Dear Pa, August 31, 1864. DUKE. James T. Binion to brother, July 30, 1861. EMORY.

72 Charles H. Richardson Diary, June 10, 1863. LC. Samuel Storrow to parents, January 22, 1863. Samuel Storrow Papers. MHS.
73 Henry Pippitt to Rebecca Pippitt, August 14, 1864. Henry Pippitt Letters. SCHOFF. Franklin Gaillard to Maria, August 12, 1863. Franklin Gaillard Papers. SHC. Samuel Henry Eells to aunt, February 12, 1863. Samuel Henry Eells Papers. LC.
74 Andrew J. Sproul to Fannie, July 4, 1863. Andrew J. Sproul Papers. SHC. Orra Bailey to wife, March 13, 1863. Orra Bailey Papers. LC.
75 Caleb Blanchard to wife, February 11, 1863; March 22, 1863; April 15, 1863; June 11, 1863. Caleb Blanchard Papers. CHS. See also Caleb Blanchard to wife, February 8, 1863; February 26, 1863; March 5, 1863; March 11, 1863; August 15, 1863.
76 Caleb Blanchard to wife, September 28, 1862; November 13, 1862; December 20, 1862; June 11, 1863. Caleb Blanchard Papers. CHS. It is typical of the freedom of discussion common in the Union army—despite Sergeant Blanchard's threats against his soldiers—that in November 1862 Blanchard's regiment held a lyceum in which the question for debate was "is the president justified in removing McClellan?" Caleb Blanchard to wife, November 29, 1862.
77 Joseph Lester to father and sisters, November 1, 1862. Joseph Lester Papers. LC.
78 James Barfield to wife, April 21, 1864. Confederate Miscellany. EMORY.
79 Douglas Cater to Fannie, June 24, 1864. Douglas J. and Rufus W. Cater Papers. LC. Shepherd Green Pryor to Penelope Tyson Pryor, February 23, 1862. Shepherd Green Pryor Papers. UG. James I. Robertson, Jr., ed., *The Civil War Letters of General Robert McAllister* (New Brunswick, N.J., 1965), 106.
80 Joseph Lester to father and sisters, November 1, 1862. Joseph Lester Papers. George Boyd Smith Diary, 5. LC.

4. THE LANDSCAPE OF WAR:
THE UNION SOLDIER VIEWS THE SOUTH

1 David A. Rice to sister, April 2, 1863. David A. Rice Papers. LC.
2 Rhys Isaac observes that the term "landscape" can be "usefully applied to any terrain or living space that has been subjected to the process of a conscious or unconscious design." A landscape is something that can be interpreted by the viewer; it can convey to him information about those who designed it. And humans, seeking to orient themselves in a strange environment, will always strive to interpret the landscape around them. They will do so, necessarily, from their preconceptions and personal experience. Rhys Isaac, *The Transformation of Virginia* (Chapel Hill, 1982), 19.
3 Davis Ashley to parents, December 24, 1861. Civil War Miscellany. USAMHI. George H. Allen Diary, October 4, 5, 1862. UT. Christopher H. Keller to George and Esther Keller, September 14, 1862. Christopher H. Keller Letters. SCHOFF. See also, David Coe, ed., *Mine Eyes Have Seen the Glory: Combat Diaries of Union Sergeant Hamlin Alexander Coe* (Rutherford, Madison, Teaneck, N.J., 1975), 15; Charles Calvin

Enslow to Martha Ann Enslow, October 16, 1862. Charles Calvin Enslow Papers. LC.

4 Henry Glassie, *Pattern in the Material Folk Culture of the Eastern United States* (Philadelphia, 1971).

5 Newton Wallace Diary, February 8–16, 1862; June 22, 1862. NC. David Nichol to father, October 21, 1861. Harrisburg Civil War Round Table Collection. USAMHI. Wilbur Fisk Diary, January 4, 1864. LC. For additional examples of Yankee sight-seeing in Washington, see William J. Carroll Diary, June 6, 7, 1865. MHC.

6 George Henry Bates to [William Bates?], September 21, 1862. SCHOFF. John Faller to sister, August 25, 1861. John and Leo Faller Letters. Harrisburg Civil War Round Table Collection. USAMHI. Lucien P. Waters to parents, July 13, 1862. NYHS. Charles W. Reed to Emma, September 19 [1862]. Charles W. Reed Papers. PU. See also James A. Wiley to friend, May 5, 1862, and June 29, 1862. Harrisburg Civil War Round Table Collection. USAMHI; George H. Allen Diary, October 15, 1862. UT.

7 Diary, April 20, 1865. Jeremiah T. Lockwood Papers. LC. See also Byron Parsons Diary, April 18, 19, 1865. LC.

8 Howard Malcolm Smith to Mary, October 25, 1862. Howard Malcolm Smith Papers, LC.

9 Bill C. Malone, *Southern Music, American Music* (University Press of Kentucky, 1979), 18–37, is an interesting discussion of the national fascination with the South as displayed in popular music. See William R. Taylor, *Cavalier and Yankee: The Old South and American National Character* (New York, 1969).

10 Orra B. Bailey to wife, February 23, 1863. Orra B. Bailey Papers. LC. Christopher Howser Keller to George and Esther Keller, November 23, 1863. Christopher Howser Keller Letters. SCHOFF. John Augustine Johnson Diary, April 10, 1865. LC. Reynolds Griffin to sister, September 4, 1862. Griffin Letters. SCHOFF.

11 E. N. Gilpin Diary, March 25, 1865. LC.

12 John Crosby to Abby J. Crosby, December 14, 1862, January 3, 1863. John Crosby Papers. CHS. Southern mud, apparently, was quite different from the Northern article. One Union soldier described it as "a mud that is most like clay," and said it "will stick to our boots in great loads. very different from the north, when it rains *very* hard the ground is beat down hard so that it is not very mud, but the slow rain makes the top of the ground very soft and deep." John A. Hammond Diary, December 30, 1862. Harrisburg Civil War Round Table Collection. USAMHI.

13 Orra B. Bailey to wife, November 19, 1862. Orra B. Bailey Papers. LC. John Crosby to Abby J. Crosby, August 10, 1863. John Crosby Papers. CHS. See also John Guest to sister, January 12, 1863. Civil War Miscellany. USAMHI. He describes St. Helena's Island: "there is plenty of mosquitoes and flies and A grate many other plagues unmentionable."

14 John Crosby to Abby J. Crosby, April 5, 1863. John Crosby Papers. CHS.

15 John Brinkerhoff Jackson, *American Space: The Centennial Years: 1865–1876* (New York, 1972), 25, 61–62. Drew McCoy, *The Elusive Republic* (Chapel Hill, 1980).

16 Lewis J. Martin to Mrs. C. E. Martin, June 3, 1862. Lewis J. Martin Letters. SCHOFF. Samuel S. Ely to home, April 10, 1864. Albert S. and Samuel S. Ely Papers. PU.

17 Edward Henry Courtney Taylor to Marie, August 16, 1861. E. H. C. Taylor Papers. MHC. Henry Snow to sister, November 4, 1862; to mother, November 24, 1862. Henry Snow Letters. CHS. George H. Allen Diary, November 19, 1862. UT. See also William G. Hills Diary, January 23, 1864. LC.

18 Aida Craig Truxall, ed., *"Respects to All": Letters of Two Pennsylvania Boys in the War of Rebellion* (Pittsburgh, 1962), 75.

19 John Pierson to wife, April 27, 1862, June 5, 1862. John Pierson Letters. SCHOFF.

20 Diary, November 9, 1862. Charles Crook Hood Papers. LC.

21 John Fleming, *Civil War Recollections*, 179. NYHS. Calvin Ainsworth Diary, April 14, 1864. MHC. Samuel Storrow to parents, November 26, 1862. Samuel Storrow Papers. MHS. For other Northern complaints about the size of Southern towns see Samuel Gault Diary, April 9, 1863. HNOC. William H. Aldis to wife, October 29, 1862. William H. Aldis Papers, NYHS. Diary, February 16, 1863. Charles Crook Hood Papers. LC. Truxall, *Respects to All*, 69.

22 "Lack of detailed study makes hypothesis necessary, but one cannot escape the conclusion that the driving forces in northern American society were focused in the small towns." William R. Brock, *Conflict and Transformation: The United States, 1844–1877* (Baltimore, 1973), 134. See 132–34 for an excellent discussion of Northern towns.

23 See James Oakes, *The Ruling Race: A History of American Slaveholders*, (New York, 1982), 91–94, for a discussion of Southern towns.

24 Lavalette Griffin to sister, May 21, 1862. Griffin Letters. SCHOFF.

25 Thomas S. Howland to mother, October 15, 1864. Thomas S. Howland Papers. MHS. Horace N. Snow to Sarah, April 24–25, 1865. Snow Family Papers. DUKE.

26 Christopher H. Keller to George and Esther Keller, November 16, 1862. Christopher H. Keller Letters. SCHOFF. Newton Wallace Diary. May 3, 1862. NC.

27 Newton Wallace Diary, December 14, 1862. NC. Cf. entries of June 27, November 3, November 4, 1862. John Wesley Marshall Journal. June 30, 1863. LC. See also John E. Bassett Diary, October 31, 1862. John E. Bassett Papers. MHS.

28 Christopher H. Keller to Caroline M. Hall, December 13, 1863. Christopher H. Keller Letters. SCHOFF.

29 Francis Jennings, *The Invasion of America: Indians, Colonialism, and the Cant of Conquest* (New York, 1975). Ervin H. Zube, ed., *Landscapes: Selected Writings of J. B. Jackson* (Amherst, 1970), 44–45.

30 Howard Malcolm Smith to Mary, November 4, 1862. Howard Malcolm Smith Papers. LC. Lyman Foster to Mary Foster, January 6, 1863. Foster Family Papers. Civil War Miscellany. USAMHI. Samuel S. Ely to mother, March 26, 1865. Albert and Samuel Ely Papers. PU.

31 Truxall, *Respects to All*, 76, 77, 93. For a similar discussion of fruit culture near Middleburg, Tennessee, see Samuel Henry Eells to aunt, April 2, 1863. S. H. Eells Papers, LC. Eells said that the whites were "too lazy" to cultivate fruit and that the slaves would not do "anymore

than they can help." For a discussion of lazy Southerners, white and black, in North Carolina, see Newton Wallace Diary, May 3, 1862. NC.

32 Coe, *Coe*, 27–28.

33 Horace [Evans] to father. June [18], 1861. Evans Family Papers. Civil War Miscellany. USAMHI.

34 James T. Miller to Joseph Miller, September 7, 1863. Miller Brothers Letters. SCHOFF.

35 Elbert Corbin Diary, May 29, 1864. Civil War Miscellany. USAMHI. Luther C. Furst Diary, May 5, 1863; May 11, 1863. Harrisburg Civil War Round Table Collection. USAMHI.

36 John D. St. John to parents, March 26, 1862. Bela St. John Papers. LC.

37 E. N. Gilpin Diary, April 13, 1865. LC.

38 Samuel L. Conde to young friends, August 15, 1862. Civil War Miscellany. USAMHI. Francis E. Wheaton to brothers and sisters, May 17, 1862. Civil War Miscellany. USAMHI. Edward H. Sentell Diaries, April 14, 21, 1863. NYHS.

39 George Tobey Anthony to Benjamen Anthony, April 26, 1864, May 12, 1864. George Tobey Anthony Letters. SCHOFF.

40 Samuel Ely to family, September 6, 1863. Albert and Samuel Ely Papers. PU.

41 Lawrence N. Powell estimates that twenty thousand to fifty thousand Northerners came to the South to seek their fortunes as planters in the period 1862–1876. His study *New Masters: Northern Planters During the Civil War and Reconstruction* (New Haven and London, 1980) provides a fine account of the reactions of Northern planters to Southern society that can be compared with profit to the reactions of the Northern soldiers. In many cases, of course, the Yankee planter was a former Union soldier.

42 Numa Barned to Emma Barned Dick, n.d. 1862. Numa Barned Papers. SCHOFF. E. H. C. Taylor to sister, August 20, 1863. Edward Henry Courtney Taylor Papers. MHC. Northern attitudes toward the South in the 1860s are remarkably similar to American attitudes toward Mexico in the 1840s. Robert W. Johannsen points out that Americans felt their invasion of Mexico would create in that country a purer republicanism. "The best, perhaps only remedy for the nation," wrote a volunteer, "is to Americanize it." See Robert W. Johannsen, *To the Halls of Montezumas: The War with Mexico in the American Imagination* (New York, 1985), 279.

43 Henry H. Seys to Harriet Seys, February 17, 1862, February 18, 1862, July 12, 1862. Henry H. Seys Letters. SCHOFF.

44 Henry H. Seys to Harriet, August 20, 1863. Henry H. Seys Letters. SCHOFF.

45 Henry H. Seys to Harriet, March 11, 1863; March 17, 1863. Henry H. Seys Letters. SCHOFF.

46 Ashley Halsey, ed., *A Yankee Private's Civil War by Robert Hale Strong* (Chicago, 1961), 63. William L. Winship to mother, March 30, 1863. William L. Winship Papers, CHS. Henry Grimes Marshall to folks, August 23, 1863. Henry Grimes Marshall Letters. SCHOFF. Coe, *Coe*, 91–92. Levi E. Kent Diary, January 28, 1862. SCHOFF. Luther C.

Furst Diary, May 19, 1862. Harrisburg Civil War Round Table Collection. USAMHI.

47 Leslie W. Dunlap, ed., *"Your Affectionate Husband, J. F. Culver": Letters Written During the Civil War* (Iowa City, 1978), 147.

48 Richard C. Halsey to Charles L. Keck, March 10, 1863. Josiah Edmund King Letters. SCHOFF.

49 Orra B. Bailey to wife, June 21, 1863. Orra B. Bailey Papers. LC.

50 George Ward Nichols, *The Story of the Great March* (New York, 1865), 132–133.

51 M. A. deWolfe Howe, ed., *Marching with Sherman: Passages from the Letters and Campaign Diaries of Henry Hitchcock, Major and Assistant Adjutant General of Volunteers, November 1864–May 1865* (New Haven, 1927), 239–242.

52 S. H. Eells to Aunt and Uncle, January 24, 1863. S. H. Eells Papers. LC.

53 William H. Nugen to sister, December 7, 1863. William H. Nugen Papers. DUKE.

54 Diary, November 23, 1864. George C. Lawson Papers (in Robert Shaw Collection). AHS.

55 Frederick D. Williams, *The Wild Life of the Army: Civil War Letters of James A. Garfield* (Michigan State University Press, 1964), 72.

56 Williams, *Garfield,* 122.

57 John Pierson to wife, July 29, 1862, August 4, 1862. John Pierson Letters. SCHOFF.

58 John Pierson to wife, August 8, 1862. John Pierson Letters. SCHOFF.

59 John Pierson to wife, August 11, 1862, August 15, 1862, August 22, 1862. John Pierson Letters. SCHOFF.

60 John Pierson to wife, August 11, 1862, August 15, 1862. John Pierson Letters. SCHOFF.

61 John Pierson to wife, March 10, 1863. John Pierson Letters. SCHOFF.

62 Alva Griest, *Three Years in Dixie,* October 13, 1863. Harrisburg Civil War Round Table Collection. USAMHI.

63 John Wesley Marshall Journal, June 26, 1863. LC.

64 Rufus Mead, Jr., to folks at home, March 16, 1862. Rufus Mead, Jr., Papers. LC. Calvin Ainsworth Diary, October 31, 1863. MHC.

65 John E. Bassett Diary, November 22, 1862. MHS. Margaret Brobst Roth, ed., *Well Mary: The Civil War Letters of a Wisconsin Volunteer* (1960), 46.

66 Joseph Lester to father, December 19, 1862. Joseph Lester Papers. LC. John Crosby to Sam Starr, May 13, 1863. John Crosby Papers. CHS. John S. Copley to Robert Moody, August 10, 1861. John S. Copley Papers. PU.

67 Burrage Rice Diary, December 29, 1864. NYHS.

68 William H. Bradbury to wife, October 10, 1862. William H. Bradbury Papers. LC.

69 George Wetmore to Orpha E. Skinner, July 4, 1863. George Wetmore Papers. CHS.

70 Calvin Mehaffey to mother, May 11, 1862. Calvin Mehaffey Letters. SCHOFF.

71 Calvin Mehaffey to mother, May 11, 1862. May 16, 1862. Calvin Mehaffey Letters. SCHOFF.

72   E. P. Failing Diary, December 4, 1864. Failing-Knight Papers, MHS. Thomas D. Grant to Meg, December 24, 1861, Civil War Miscellany. USAMHI. For another description of an "old plantation hoedown," see Bela St. John to parents, July 25, 1862. Bela Taylor St. John Papers. LC. See also Leo Faller to home, June 2, 1862. Harrisburg Civil War Round Table Collection. USAMHI.

73   For example, see Jabez Alvord Diary, September 19, 1862. LC.

74   Jabez Alvord Diary, May 31, 1863, June 1, 1863. LC. George Schubert to Sophia, February 16, 1863. George Schubert Letters. SCHOFF. Frederic S. Olmsted Diary, May 17, 1863. SCHOFF.

75   Silas W. Browning to wife, February 8, 1863. Silas W. Browning Papers. LC. Alva Griest, *Three Years in Dixie*, November 15, 1863. Harrisburg Civil War Round Table Collection. USAMHI.

76   Arthur H. DeRosier, Jr., *Through the South with a Union Soldier* (1969), 67.

77   George Bates to William Bates, February 24, 1864. George Henry Bates Letters. SCHOFF. J. Kimball Barnes to George Starbird, December 25, 1862; March 3, 1863. Starbird Letters. SCHOFF.

78   John Frederic Holahan, Civil War Diary, April 26, 1862. Private possession.

79   Charles Crook Hood Diary, December 17, 1862. LC. Oscar Osburn Winther, ed., *With Sherman to the Sea: The Civil War Letters, Diaries, and Reminiscences of Theodore F. Upson*, (Bloomington, Ind., 1958), 135. William H. Bradbury to wife, December 12, 1862. William H. Bradbury Papers. LC. Robert Goldthwaite Carter, *Four Brothers in Blue: Or Sunshine and Shadows of the War of the Rebellion, a Story of the Great War from Bull Run to Appomattox* (1913. Reprint: Austin, 1978), 89–90.

80   James W. Hildreth to mother, November 23, 1862, January 4, 1863. Flinbaugh Collection. Harrisburg Civil War Round Table Collection. USAMHI.

81   Howard Malcolm Smith to Mary, March 10, 1863. Howard Malcolm Smith Papers. LC.

82   Nelson Stauffer, *Civil War Diary* (California State University, Northridge Libraries, 1976), September 2, 1862 (n.p.).

83   David Nicholl to father, February 1, 1862. Harrisburg Civil War Round Table Collection. USAMHI.

84   Lucien P. Waters to parents, July 13, 1862. Lucien P. Waters Papers. NYHS.

85   Charles Calvin Enslow to Mattie, October 13, 1863. Charles Calvin Enslow Papers. LC.

86   Reynolds Griffin to Dan Griffin, January 24, 1863. Griffin Brothers Letters. SCHOFF.

87   See, for example, Frederic Olmsted Diary, May 2, 4, 5, 17, 1863. SCHOFF. Lucien P. Waters to parents, [June] 24, 1864. Lucien P. Waters Papers. NYHS.

88   E. H. C. Taylor to sister Anna, June 21, 1862. Edward Henry Courtney Taylor Papers. MHC.

89   Jacob Seibert to father, January 10, 1863. Harrisburg Civil War Round Table Collection. USAMHI. James R. French to parents, April 2, 1863. Albert Wilder Letters. SCHOFF.

90 John Pierson to daughter, March 15, 1863. John Pierson Letters. SCHOFF. James T. Miller to Jane Cramer, February 6, 1863. Miller Brothers Letters. SCHOFF.

91 Williams, *Garfield,* 65–66. Garfield had one final sardonic observation on Lincoln's Emancipation Proclamation. It was "strange," he thought, "that a second rate Illinois lawyer should be the instrument through whom one of the sublimest works of any age is accomplished." Williams, *Garfield,* 207.

92 Thomas S. Howland to mother, December 4, [1862?]. Thomas S. Howland Papers. MHS.

93 S. H. Eells to aunt and uncle, January 24, 1863. S. H. Eells Papers. LC.

94 C. C. Enslow to Martha Ann Enslow [November 15, 1863?], 24–25. Charles Calvin Enslow Papers. LC.

95 William H. Dunham to Henrietta, December 29, 1861, January 14, 1862, June 3, 1862. Civil War Miscellany. USAMHI.

96 George Starbird to Marianne Starbird, October 10, 1862; November 5, 1863; George to Solomon Starbird, October 15, 1862. Starbird Letters. SCHOFF.

97 Diary, January 5, 1865. George C. Lawson Papers in the Robert Shaw Collection. AHS.

98 John William DeForest, *Miss Ravenel's Conversion from Secession to Loyalty* (New York, 1964), 456.

99 Rufus Mead to family, October 25, 1863. Rufus Mead, Jr., Papers. LC.

100 It cannot be emphasized too strongly that Confederate soldiers as well as Union soldiers had to deal with guerrillas. An ambitious attempt to analyze racism, mountain Unionism, and a brutal Confederate atrocity can be found in Phillip Shaw Paludan, *Victims: A True Story of the Civil War* (Knoxville, 1981).

101 James A. Congleton Diary, May 19, 1863. LC. Herman Melville's "Scout Toward Aldie" is a masterful evocation of the feeling of mystery surrounding the Confederate partisan John S. Mosby.

102 Thomas S. Howland to sister, September 1, [186?]. Thomas S. Howland Papers. MHS. Howard Malcolm Smith to Mary, June 11, 1863. Howard Malcolm Smith Papers. LC. Alva Griest, *Three Years in Dixie,* January 3, 1864. Harrisburg Civil War Round Table Collection. USAMHI.

103 Henry Pippitt to Rebecca Pippitt, April 23, 1864. Henry Pippitt Letters. SCHOFF.

104 DeRosier, *Through the South* (1969), 66, 79. See also Caleb Blanchard to wife, May 24, 1863; May 29, 1863. Caleb Blanchard Papers. CHS.

105 Alva Griest, *Three Years in Dixie,* April 8, 1863. Harrisburg Civil War Round Table Collection. USAMHI. For a similar incident, producing a similar emotional response, see Coe, *Coe,* 98. "Some of the scouts were fired upon and driven in today. One man was killed. He was wounded by the first fire and captured by the Bushwhackers, who, to torture their captive, shot him seven times before he expired. The affray has created a spirit of revenge among the boys, and they have gone out in force to avenge the death of their comrade or lay waste the country."

106 William H. Dunham to Henrietta, October 28, 1861, [early January, 1862]. Civil War Miscellany. USAMHI.

107 George Tobey Anthony to Benjamen Anthony, August 4, 1863. George Tobey Anthony Letters. SCHOFF. A similar method of combatting

guerrillas during the Boer War is discussed in the film *Breaker Morant*. The assumption that citizens could control the guerrillas was not entirely correct. In 1863 a group of Fauquier County citizens petitioned Mosby to cease guerrilla warfare because the Union army had threatened to burn their town in retaliation. "Not yet being prepared for any such degrading compromise with the Yankees," Mosby refused. "My attachs on scouts, patrols, and pickets, which have provoked this threat, are sanctioned both by the customs of war and the practise of the enemy," he explained, and offered the civilians some cold comfort: "and you are at liberty to inform them that no such demonstrations deter me from employing whatever legitimate weapon I can." John Singleton Mosby to F. W. Powell and others, February 4, 1863. John Singleton Mosby Papers. UVA.

108   Edward Paul Reichhelm Diary, 2–3. LC. Cf. Sherman, *Memoirs of General William T. Sherman* (Bloomington, Ind., 1957), I, 289. "What few inhabitants remained at the plantations on the river-bank were unfriendly, except the slaves; some few guerilla-parties infested the banks, but did not dare to molest so strong a force as I then commanded." Another soldier on the expedition recorded that one evening they anchored near a planatation, and its house and barn were soon in flames—"a beautiful but destructive scene." He blamed the fire on the slaves. Calvin Ainsworth Diary, December 24, 1862. MHC.

109   John A. Clark to William W. Whedon, August 10, 1863. Clark-Whedon Letters. SCHOFF.

110   Maurus Oestreich Diary, July 25, 1863. Civil War Miscellany. USAMHI.

111   Clyde C. Walton, *Private Smith's Journal: Recollections of the Late War* (Chicago, 1963), 55.

112   Theodore Sage to parents, May 24, 1862. Harrisburg Civil War Round Table Collection. USAMHI.

113   John E. Morris to Jonathan Morris, April 28, 1863, May 19, 1863. John E. Morris Papers. CHS.

114   James T. Miller to Robert E. Miller, July 26, 1862. Miller Brothers Letters. SCHOFF.

115   Alva Griest, *Three Years in Dixie*, November 30, 1862, July 31, 1863. Harrisburg Civil War Round Table Collection. USAMHI.

116   Joseph Lester to family, August 23, 1863. Joseph Lester Papers. LC.

117   Newton Wallace Diary, April 30, 1862, November 30, 1862. N.C. Jacob Seibert to father, December 5, 1863. Harrisburg Civil War Round Table Collection. USAMHI. William H. Dunham to Henrietta, November 20, 1861. Civil War Miscellany. USAMHI. Warren [Beddoe] to Harriet Beddoe, April 11, 1862. Albert A. Andrews Papers. CHS. Albert C. Cleavland to Christopher H. Keller, August 3, 1863. Christopher H. Keller letters. SCHOFF.

118   Marshall M. Miller to family, May 20, 1864. Marshall M. Miller Letters. LC. Joseph Lester to family, August 23, 1863. Joseph Lester Papers. LC.

119   John Wesley Marshall Journal, January 16, 1863, February 8, 1863, July 8, 1863, July 17, 1863. LC.

120   Diary, November 7, 1862. Charles Crook Hood Papers. LC.

121   Henry S. Sherman Diary, May 6, 1863. PU. Isaac C. Richardson to wife, Part 8, December 12, 1862. Isaac C. Richardson Papers. SHC.

John Darragh Wilkins to Mrs. John Darragh Wilkins, December 18, 1862. John Darragh Wilkins Letters. SCHOFF.

122 Bela Taylor St. John to brother, February 10, 1863. Bela Taylor St. John Papers. LC. Daniel Faust to sister, November 2, 1864. Harrisburg Civil War Round Table Collection. USAMHI. David Nichol to father, May 21, 1864. Harrisburg Civil War Round Table Collection. USAMHI.

123 David Nichol to father, May 21, 1864. Harrisburg Civil War Round Table Collection. USAMHI. Philip A. Lantzy to parents, October 13, 1861. Harrisburg Civil War Round Table Collection. USAMHI. The accuracy of Lantzy's argument is touched on in the next chapter.

124 [James W. Denver] to wife, November 29, 1862. Harrisburg Civil War Round Table Collection. USAMHI.

125 W. C. Johnson Diary, January 27, 1865; February 7, 1865; February 8, 1865; February 12, 1865; February 17, 1865. LC. See George C. Lawson Diary, January 30, 1865. George C. Lawson Papers in Robert Shaw Collection. AHS.

126 Paul Shepard explores some of the implications of mankind's love of fire in *Man in the Landscape: A Historic View of the Esthetics of Nature* (New York, 1976), 55–57.

127 John Crosby to Abby J. Crosby, July 27, 1863. John Crosby Papers. CHS.

128 George A. Hudson to Marin, May 7, 1864. George A. Hudson Papers. LC.

5. The Confederate Experience

1 W. S. Nye, *Here Come the Rebels!* (Baton Rouge, 1965) is a fine account of the invasion.

2 William Henry Cocke to family, October 7, 1862. Cocke Family of Portsmouth, Virginia, Papers. VHS. Edward Samuel Duffey Diary, September 11, 1862. VHS. William Pegram to Virginia Johnson Pegram, September 7, 1862. Pegram-Johnson-McIntosh Papers. VHS. William Ellis Jones Diary, September 10, 1862. SCHOFF. Mike M. Hubbert Diary, September 7, 9, 10, 1862. Confederate States of America Records, UT. Joseph T. Durkin, ed., *Confederate Chaplain: A War Journal of Rev. James B. Sheeran, C. Ss. R., 14th Louisiana, C. S. A.* (Milwaukee, 1960), 24. Some Confederates had been pleased by their earlier reception in Maryland. See M. Shuler Diary, September 6, 1862. LC.

3 Hodijah Lincoln Meade to Charlotte Randolp (Meade) Lane, July 19, 1863. Meade Family Papers. VHS. W. B. Bailey Diary, June 22, 1863. TULANE.

4 Samuel W. Eaton Diary, June 23, 24, 1863. SHC.

5 Durkin, *Sheeran*, 47.

6 James E. Green Diary, June 21, 1863. SHC. Thomas Harlow to father and mother, June 21, 1863. Harlow Family Papers. VHS.

7 Charles A. Wills to Mary J. Wills, June 26, 1863. Mary J. Wills Papers. WM. James C. Mohr, ed., *The Cormany Diaries: A Northern Family in the Civil War* (Pittsburgh, 1982), 334–35.

8 John G. Barrett, ed., *Yankee Rebel: The Civil War Journal of Edmund*

DeWitt Patterson (Chapel Hill, 1966), 110. Nye, *Here Come the Rebels!*, (Baton Rouge, 1965), 124.

9 Jerome B. Yates to Ma and Maria, June 17, 1863, August 14, 1863. Confederate States of America Records, Case VII. UT. R. Henderson Shuffler, ed., *The Adventures of a Prisoner of War, 1863–1864 by Decimus et Ultimus Barziza* (Austin, 1964), 43. Shepherd Green Pryor to Penelope Tyson Pryor, July 12, 1863. Shepherd Green Pryor Papers. UG. James E. Green Diary, June 25, 1863. SHC. Iowa Michigan Royster to mother, June 29, 1863. Iowa Michigan Royster Papers. SHC. Florence McCarthy, Jr., to Jane E. McCarthy, July 10, 1863. McCarthy Family Papers. VHS. William Daniel Ross to sister, June 30, 1863. Ross Family Correspondence. VSL.

10 William W. Marston, June 22, 1863. Confederate Miscellany. EMORY. Shuffler, *Barziza*, 43.

11 Wiliam W. Hassler, ed., *The General to His Lady: The Civil War Letters of William Dorsey Pender to Fanny Pender* (Chapel Hill, 1965), 254. James E. Green Diary, June 25, 1863. SHC. Hodijah Lincoln Meade to Charlotte Randolp (Meade) Lane, July 19, 1863. Meade Family Papers. VHS.

12 Francis W. Dawson, *Reminiscenses of Confederate Service, 1861–1865* (Baton Rouge, 1980), 92. Fannie J. Buehler, *Recollections of the Rebel Invasion and One Woman's Experience during the Battle of Gettysburg* (Gettysburg, 1900), 12. (I am indebted to Dr. Charles Royster for this last citation.)

13 Memoir of Frederick Mason Colston. Bryan Family Papers. VHS.

14 W. B. Bailey Diary, June 23, 24, 1863. TULANE. Samuel W. Eaton Diary, June 28, 1863. SHC. Iowa Michigan Royster to mother, June 29, 1863. Iowa Michigan Royster Papers. SHC. Samuel Angus Firebaugh Diary, June 23, 1863. Civil War Miscellany. USAMHI. Florence McCarthy, Jr., to Jane E. McCarthy, July 10, 1863. McCarthy Family Papers. VHS.

15 Alexander C. Jones Diary, June 28, 1863. Louisiana Historical Association Collection. TULANE. George W. Jones to Sarah Jones, June 29, 1863. George W. Jones Papers. DUKE. Franklin Gaillard to Sonny, June 28, 1863. Franklin Gaillard Papers. SHC. Francis W. Dawson, *Reminiscences*, 93. Barrett, *Patterson*, 111. Florence McCarthy, Jr., to Jane E. McCarthy, July 10, 1863. McCarthy Family Papers. VHS.

16 Franklin Gaillard to Sonny, June 28, 1863. Franklin Gaillard Papers. SHC.

17 Paul Fatout, *Letters of a Civil War Surgeon* (Purdue Universities, 1961), 69. Jacob Seibert to father, June 19, 1863, June 27, 1863. Harrisburg Civil War Round Table Collection. USAMHI.

18 Nat to parents, June 28, 1863. P. H. Turner Papers. SHC.

19 Franklin Gaillard to Sonny, June 28, 1863. Franklin Gaillard Papers. SHC.

20 Shuffler, *Barziza*, 58.

21 Joseph Hilton to Miss Lizzie Lachlison, July 18, 1863. Confederate Miscellany. EMORY.

22 Durkin, *Sheeran*, 47–48.

23 John S. Mosby to N. C. Jordan, August 23, 1909. John S. Mosby Col-

lection. DUKE. Walter Lord, ed., *The Fremantle Diary* (Boston, 1954), 195.

24 Joseph Hilton to Miss Lizzie Lachlison, July 18, 1863. Confederate Miscellany. EMORY. Diary, June 28, 1863. Paul T. Vaughan Papers. SHC. Samuel Angus Firebaugh Diary, June 23, 1863. Civil War Miscellany. USAMHI. Alexander C. Jones Diary, June 28, 1863. Louisiana Historical Association Collection. TULANE. Hassler, *Pender*, 254–55.

25 Barrett, *Patterson*, 110. Hassler, *Pender*, 226. During the invasion a soldier in Pender's division wrote, "Our Maj Genl (Pender) has issued such strict orders about straggling and plundering that the people have not suffered from us." John McLeod Turner to Emilie, June 28, 1863. John McLeod Turner Letters. VHS. H. C. Kendrick to mother, June 6, 1863. H. C. Kendrick Papers. SHC. Shepherd Green Pryor to Penelope Tyson Pryor, June 28, 1863. Shepherd Green Pryor Papers. UG.

26 Samuel W. Eaton Diary, June 26, 1863. SHC. Mohr, *Cormany*, 337–38. Franklin Gaillard to Maria Procher, July 17, 1863. Franklin Gaillard Papers. SHC.

27 Mohr, *Cormany*, 328–30. Frank Moore, *Rebellion Record* (New York, 1861–1871), VII, Documents, 1977, 325. W. S. Nye, *Here Come the Rebels!* (Baton Rouge, 1965), 144. For an example of Confederate cavalry recovering blacks from Union troops in an earlier campaign, see Asa J. Wyatt Diary, May [25?], 1862. SHC. The *New York Herald* reported the capture of fifty blacks by the Confederates. As they were marched southward, "the brave citizens of Greencastle turned out, captured the rebel guard, and sent the darkeys on their way rejoicing." *New York Herald,* July 2, 1863, 4. I am indebted to Dr. Charles Royster for this citation.

28 For Polk's biography, see Stuart Noblin, *Leonidas Lafayette Polk: Agrarian Crusader* (Chapel Hill, 1949). For Polk's Civil War service, see the L. L. Polk Papers, SHC, specifically his letters to his wife, January 29, March 9, March 21, March 26, April 19, July 23, 1863.

29 It is a common assumption, for example, that one advantage possessed by the Confederate army during the war was the fact that Southern officers were used to command and that Southern soldiers, trained by a pervasive class-and-caste system, were used to obedience. A recent and very explicit example of these attitudes is to be found in William L. Barney's *Flawed Victory* (New York, 1979). Barney describes Confederate officers as "members of a master class," accustomed to deference from both blacks and poor whites. Emory Thomas comments on the deference shown by poorer whites to their social betters in *The Confederate Nation* (New York, 1979), and argues that while planter hegemony was challenged during the war, it emerged relatively unscathed. An important statement of this thesis is Eugene Genovese's "Yeoman Farmers in a Slaveholders' Democracy," *Agricultural History,* Volume 49 (April 1975), 331–42. (The version of this essay in Eugene Genovese and Elizabeth Fox-Genovese's later *Fruits of Merchant Capitalism* modifies the original thesis considerably.) See also Genovese, *Roll, Jordan, Roll: The World the Slaves Made* (New York, 1976), 91–92. This interpretation of the antebellum South is now being challenged by the growing body of literature dealing with antebellum politics and

the role of the small slaveholder and the nonslaveholder in the South. Among these works are James Oakes, *The Ruling Race* (New York, 1982), Harry Watson, *Jacksonian Politics and Community Conflict* (Baton Rouge, 1981), and J. Mills Thornton III, *Politics and Power in a Slave Society* (Baton Rouge, 1978). The truth of the matter is that in a society as fluid as the antebellum South, there was sufficient possibility for upward mobility that even nonslaveholders might expect to own slaves sometime in the future—thus nonslaveholder support of slavery is perfectly rational if deplorable. After all, Thomas Sutpen, William Faulkner's embodiment of the Old South in *Absalom, Absalom!*, is the son of poor whites.

30 For the Confederacy's internal crisis, see Bell Wiley, *The Plain People of the Confederacy* (Baton Rouge, 1943), and Paul Escott, *After Secession* (Baton Rouge, 1978). Escott's essay "The Failure of Confederate Nationalism: The Old South's Class System in the Crucible of War," in Harry P. Owens and James J. Cooke, eds., *The Old South in the Crucible of War* (Jackson, Miss., 1983), 15–28, treats many of the issues raised in this chapter; I find many of Professor Escott's arguments most convincing.

31 For an account of modernization in the Confederate state, see Thomas, *The Confederate Nation* (New York, 1979); it does not seem to me that Thomas appreciates the relationship between this modernization process—which he calls a "revolutionary experience"—and the prewar conflict between yeomen and planters. Escott, *After Secession* (New York, 1978), has a useful account of the conflict between Davis and Vance and Brown; see also Frank Owsley, *State Rights in the Confederacy* (Chicago, 1925) and May Spencer Ringold, *The Role of the State Legislatures in the Confederacy* (Athens, Georgia, 1966).

32 James M. Skelton to Emily Skelton, February 11, 1863. A. H. Skelton to sister, January 10, 1863. Skelton Papers. SHC. In one sense independent thought was meaningless—for example, there was no general election within the Confederacy as a whole during the war. Nonetheless, men known as soldiers' candidates, such as L. L. Polk, could be elected to the state legislatures, and states such as North Carolina nurtured strong peace movements.

33 January 1, 1864. Diary identified as Bailey Diary. Louisiana Historical Association Papers. TULANE. Substitutes and their families suffered from the common contempt. John Stickleman, a substitute from Virginia, complained that his home country, which distributed food to its soldiers' families, refused to aid his wife because he was a substitute, not a volunteer. John B. Stickleman to Siv, February 26, 1864. Confederate States of America Archives; Army-Miscellany; Officers and Soldiers Letters. DUKE. Conscripts were also despised. For example, Sgt. John C. Murray of the Crescent Artillery was reduced to the ranks for refusing to eat with conscripts. John C. Murray Diary, February 7, 9, 1864. Civil War Miscellaneous Series. TULANE.

34 George to Ma & Pa, January 4, 1863. Anonymous Civil War Letter. Miscellaneous Collections. Louisiana State University Department of Archives and Manuscripts. Thanks to Dr. Charles Royster for this citation.

35 Charles A. Wills to Mary, June 12, 1863. Mary J. Wills Papers. WM.

36 Jestin Collins Hampton to Thomas B. Hampton, February 11, 1864. Thomas B. Hampton to Jestin Collins Hampton, March 18, 1864. Thomas B. and Jestin C. Hampton Letters. UT.

37 Joseph Williams to Destramona Williams, July 24, 1864. Robert Williams Letters. UG.

38 William M. Cash and Lucy Somerville Howorth, ed., *My Dear Nellie: The Civil War Letters of William L. Nugent to Eleanor Smith Nugent* (Jackson, Miss., 1977), 211. F. J. Taylor, ed., *Reluctant Rebel: The Secret Diary of Robert Patrick, 1861–1865* (Baton Rouge, 1959), 168.

39 Jas. Walter to wife Sue, February 22, 1864. Confederate Miscellany. EMORY. See Ella Lonn's discussion of impressment in her *Desertion During the Civil War* (Gloucester, Mass., 1966—reprint of the 1928 edition), 13–14.

40 Lawrence N. Powell and Michael S. Wayne, "Self-Interest and the Decline of Confederate Nationalism," Owens and Cooke, eds., *The Old South in the Crucible of War*, 29–45, treats the effect of greed—more politely called self-interest—on the Confederate war effort.

41 Jestin Collins Hampton to Thomas B. Hampton, November 22, 1862. Thomas B. & Jestin C. Hampton Letters. UT. One Confederate soldier wrote, "have some very discouraging news from our homes in Miss. Some are buying up and selling cotton to the abolitionists. Hope none of my friends or relatives are falling so badly." James W. Silver, ed., *A Life for the Confederacy: As Recorded in the Pocket Diaries of Pvt. Robert A. Moore* (Jackson, Tenn., 1959), 125.

42 Thomas B. Hampton to Jestin Collins Hampton, November 21, 1862. Thomas B. & Jestin C. Hampton Letters. UT. John A. Cato to wife, March 20, 1864. Civil War Miscellany. USAMHI.

43 Lee to Davis, July 5, 1864; Lee to Seddon, February 16, 1864. Clifford Dowdey and Louis H. Manarin, eds., *The Wartime Papers of R. E. Lee* (Boston, 1961), 673, 815.

44 David M. Ray to mother, March 6, 1864. David M. Ray Papers. UT.

45 John R. Marley to father, April 13, 1863. Confederate States of America Archives; Army-Miscellany; Officers and Soldiers Letters. DUKE. J. C. Owens to Susannah Owens, April 26, 1863. Confederate Papers (Miscellaneous). SHC. Robert Greer to mother, April 14, 1864. Henry I. & Robert Greer Papers. LC. Bailey Diary, January 1, 3, 12, 1864. Louisiana Historical Association Papers. TULANE. Henry Greer to father, August 24, 1864. Henry I. & Robert Greer Papers. LC. Brinkley E. Phillips to Mr. Dabney and Mr. Phillips, February 1, 1865. Confederate States of America Archives. Army-Miscellany. Officers and Soldiers Letters. DUKE.

46 Bailey Diary, January 1, 1864. Louisiana Historical Association Papers. TULANE. Isaac Alexander to mother and sisters, February 21, 1864. Isaac Alexander Papers. SHC.

47 T. P. Forrester to Sallie & Mary T. Clark, September 11, 1864. Confederate States of America Archives. Army-Miscellany. Officers and Soldiers Letters. DUKE.

48 Hezekiah Rabb to wife, January 16, 1864. EMORY.

49 William Decatur Howell to mother [March, 1864]. EMORY.

50 See "The Quiet Rebellion of the Common People," Escott, *After Secession* (New York, 1976).

51   The classic treatment of desertion in both armies is Ella Lonn, *Desertion During the Civil War* (Gloucester, Mass., 1966—reprint of the 1928 edition).

52   Harry Lewis to Mrs. John Lewis, April 6, 1864. Harry Lewis Papers. SHC. John Alfred Feister Coleman Diary, November 16, 1864, December 5, 1864. EMORY.

53   From a song written by J. G. Daniel of Co. E. 30th Reg't Ga. Vols., June 29, 1863. EMORY.

54   Barrett, *Patterson*, 96–97.

55   James Bracy to Mary Bracy, May 11, 1863. Confederate States of America Archives. Army-Miscellany. Officers and Soldiers Letters. DUKE.

56   A. W. Smith to mother, October 1862. Civil War Miscellaneous Series. TULANE.

57   David M. Ray to mother, September 11 [1863]. David M. Ray Papers. UT. Norman D. Brown, ed., *One of Cleburne's Command: The Civil War Reminiscences and Diary of Capt. Samuel T. Foster, Granbury's Texas Brigade, C.S.A.* (Austin, 1980), 106–7. Captain Foster, a Texan himself, singles out the Texas troops—men whose families were cut off from the eastern Confederacy—as the most prone to desertion. One occasionally gets the sense that Texans, who had their own unique history with its own patriotic symbols, were the least Confederate of Southerners—although they did not have the strong identification with the generation of 1776 that many Virginians felt.

58   James E. Green Diary, September 9, 1864. SHC. Cash and Howorth, *Nugent*, 203. Thomas Lanham to Miss Amealia, March 22, 1864. Confederate States of America Archives. Army-Miscellany. Officers and Soldiers Letters. DUKE.

59   Jerome B. Yates to mother, August 21, September 13, September 28, October 29, November 17, 1863. Confederate States of America Records. UT.

60   For a fine analysis of evangelical Protestantism and its impact on Southern culture, see Donald G. Matthews, *Religion in the Old South* (Chicago, 1977).

61   J. M. Davis to Miss Mary N. Davis, July 6, 1864. Malcolm Letters. UG. Confederate religion deserves more detailed study. Dr. Drew Gilpin Faust has begun to unravel the complicated strands of Confederate religion; she and I have several disagreements, but her work in this field is challenging and perceptive; historians of the Confederate experience are in her debt. A suggestive study of Yankee religion is James H. Moorhead, *American Apocalypse: Yankee Protestants and the Civil War, 1860–1869* (New Haven, 1978).

62   Thomas B. Hampton to Jestin C. Hampton, February 26, 1865; K. C. Phillips, Reminiscences; Thomas B. Hampton Papers. UT. H. C. Kendrick to mother and father, March 9, 1863. H. C. Kendrick Papers. SHC.

63   Clyde C. Walton, *Private Smith's Journal: Recollections of the Late War* (Chicago, 1963), 195–96.

64   Henry Pippitt to Rebecca Pippitt, June 20, 1864, December 5, 1864. SCHOFF.

65   [Henry] Lee to sister, August 11, 1864. Lee Collection. UT. H. J. H. Rugeley, ed., *Batchelor-Turner Letters, 1861–1864: Written by Two*

of Terry's Texas Rangers (Austin, 1961), 50–51. J. Kelly Bennette Diary, June 20, July 30, 1864. SHC.

66 Taylor, *Patrick*, 201–2. J. C. Salter to sister, July 11, 1864. Confederate States of America Archives. Army-Miscellany. Officers and Soldiers Letters. DUKE.

67 J. M. Davis to son, January 13, 1865. Malcolm Letters. UG. Barrett, *Patterson*, 75, 77.

68 War Journal, February 13, 1862. Albert Moses Luria Papers. SHC. See also, E. W. Thompson to L. L. Polk, December 26, 1864. L. L. Polk Papers. SHC. Bell Irvin Wiley, ed., *"This Infernal War": The Confederate Letters of Sgt. Edwin H. Fay* (Austin, 1958), 92, 302. Reading this correspondence, one gets the impression that Fay was disappointed that his wife never did request his desertion.

69 Harry Lewis to Mrs. John E. Lewis, August 9, 1862. John Lewis to Mrs. John E. Lewis, June 10, 1864. Harry Lewis Papers. SHC.

70 J. C. Salter to sister, July 11, 1864. Confederate States of America Archives; Army-Miscellany. Officers and Soldiers Letters. DUKE. Bailey Diary, December 18, 1863; January 24, 1864. Louisiana Historical Association Papers. TULANE.

71 Manning P. Alexander to Pellona David Alexander, August 27, 1864. Manning P. and Pellona David Alexander Papers. UG.

72 Joseph Williams to Boby, April 11, 1865. Adams Collection. UG.

73 Charles A. Wills to Mary J. Wills, Mary 13, May 18, May 24, May 28, 1863. Mary J. Wills Papers. WM.

74 John Barfield to wife, December 9, 18[63]. EMORY. J. S. Gooch to father, February [1], 1864. Confederate Papers (Miscellaneous). SHC.

75 Joseph Williams to Destamona Williams, May 22, 1864. Robert Williams Collection. UG. W. A. James to wife, June 29, 1864. Confederate States of America Archives. Army-Miscellany. Officers and Soldiers Letters. DUKE.

76 William U. Morris to Josiah Staunton Moore, June 23, 1865. Josiah Staunton Moore Papers. VHS. "All interpretations of the defeat of the Confederacy fall into two broad categories: those that stress the South's physical handicaps, and those that stress human failings." Kenneth M. Stampp, *The Imperiled Union: Essays on the Background of the Civil War* (New York, 1980), 247. See also Gaines M. Foster's fine essay, "Woodward and Southern Identity," in *Southern Review* (April 1985), 351–60.

77 See Stampp, "The Southern Road to Appomattox," *The Imperiled Union*. For planters and the war, see James Roark, *Masters without Slaves* (New York, 1977) and Lawrence N. Powell and Michael Wayne, "Self-Interest and the Decline of Confederate Nationalism," in Harry P. Owens and James J. Cooke, eds., *The Old South in the Crucible of War* (Jackson, Miss., 1983.); for yeomen, see Bell Wiley, *The Plain People of the Confederacy* (Baton Rouge, 1943), and Escott, *After Secession;* for slaves, see Leon F. Litwack, *Been in the Storm So Long* (New York, 1980).

78 E. B. Long, *The Civil War Day By Day: An Almanac, 1861–1865* (New York, 1971), 704–712.

79 See Leonard P. Curry, *Blueprint for Modern America: Nonmilitary Legislation of the First Civil War Congress* (Nashville, 1968).

80 Ella Lonn gives the number of deserters from the Confederate army as 103,400, from the Union army as 278,644. *Desertion,* 231, 233. (Elsewhere, however, she estimates the Union total as 200,000. E. B. Long agrees with this lower figure. *The Civil War Day By Day,* 714.) Figures for both armies are unreliable. Confederates had little opportunity to go bounty-jumping since their government relied primarily on conscription rather than on cash inducements to volunteering.

81 Lonn, *Desertion,* particularly page 229.

6. THE END OF THE WAR

1 Lewis J. Martin to Mrs. C. E. Martin, April 28, 1861. Lewis J. Martin Letters. SCHOFF. Levi Kent Diary, October 13, 1861. SCHOFF.

2 John Franklin Smith to Justina Rowee, June 28, 1862. John Franklin Smith Letters. UT.

3 Matthew Bone to William Bone, October 23, 1861. Adams Collection. UG. John C. Holwell to wife, May 2, 1862. John C. Holwell Papers. CHS. Shepherd Green Pryor to Penelope Tyson Pryor, July 25, 1861. Shepherd Green Pryor Papers. UG. Wm. H. Bradbury to wife, December 12, 1862. William H. Bradbury Papers. LC. J. McCall to father, January 12, 1863; J. McCall to father, February 9, 1863. J. McCall Letters. United Daughters of the Confederacy Collection. AHS. Abram F. Conant to wife, December 15, 1862. Abram F. Conant Papers. LC. Hezekiah Rabb to wife, May 14, 1863. EMORY.

4 See, for example, James T. Binion to sister, June 8, 1862. EMORY.

5 William P. Andrews to friend, August 21, 1863. Confederate Miscellany. EMORY.

6 Daniel Faust to brother, May 7, 1863. Harrisburg Civil War Round Table Collection. USAMHI. Faust goes on to say, "and another thing it is for is to distroy slavery." But slavery seems to be something apart from the "national sin." Benjamin F. Ashenfelter to mother, May 10, 1863. Harrisburg Civil War Round Table Collection. USAMHI. See also "A Discourse Delivered in Bennington, N.H., August 16, 1863 Occasioned by the Death of Lieut. Edmund Dascomb," Harrisburg Civil War Round Table Collection. USAMHI. See the previous chapter for a discussion of simliar Confederate attitudes. See also Richard Henry Watkins to Mary Watkins, July 8, 1861. Richard Henry Watkins Papers. VHS.

7 Orra B. Bailey to wife, February 16, 1863. Orra B. Bailey Papers. LC.

8 Andrew J. Sproul to Fannie, December 3, 1862. Andrew J. Sproul Papers. SHC. Burrage Rice Diary, October 6, 1861. NYHS. Charles Wellington Reed to Helen, January 9, 1863. Charles Wellington Reed Papers. LC. John Harmer to Mrs. Eveline Harmer, August 5, 1864. Harrisburg Civil War Round Table Collection. USAMHI. See also Louis Rowe to Abbie, May 27, 1864. Civil War Miscellany. USAMHI.

9 Albinus Fell to wife, April 9, 1862. Civil War Miscellany. USAMHI.

10 Richard Webb to Jennie, April 25, 1864, February 25, 1865. Webb Family Papers. SHC. H. C. Kendrick to parents, January 6, 1863. H. C. Kendrick Papers. SHC.

11 "While Northerners looked to the future with grave misgiving, morale in the South reached its apex for 1864 in August. The mood among Southerners was not one of militant determination to prosecute the war but rather a feeling that their desperate prayers were soon to be granted. Confederates fervently desired and needed an end to the slaughter and destruction of the long war, and they thought they saw indications on the Northern horizon that the enemy was faltering." Larry E. Nelson, *Bullets, Ballots, and Rhetoric: Confederate Policy for the United States Presidential Contest of 1864* (University, Alabama, 1980) 98–99. Tip to sister, October 27, 1864. B. P. Gandy to sister, June 4, 1864. Civil War Miscellany. UT.

12 James B. Rounsaville to mother, September 25, 1864. Civil War Miscellany. USAMHI. See also David M. Ray to mother, October 8, 1864. David M. Ray Papers. UT. Other Confederates were more prescient: "The Chicago Convention attracts great attention now, but I have little confidence in its Peace inclinations—or rather that they want peace on any terms." John Warwick Daniel Diary, September 1, 1864. VHS.

13 Oscar Cram to Ellen, September 11, 1864. Civil War Miscellany. USAMHI.

14 David Seibert to father, September 10, 1864. Seibert Family Papers. Harrisburg Civil War Round Table Collection. USAMHI. Seibert also predicted "by election time it will be too cold for coppersnakes." David Seibert to father, October 17, 1864. Seibert Family Papers. Harrisburg Civil War Round Table Collection. USAMHI. John Griffith Jones to brother, September 20, 1864. John Griffith Jones Papers. LC. Byron Parsons Diary, November 8, 1864. LC.

15 Edward A. Wild to Edward W. Kinsley, October 27, 1864. Edward W. Kinsley Papers. LC.

16 Wimer Bedford Diary, September 19, 1864, February 23, 1865. LC.

17 Thomas Skinner to friends, October 29, 1864. Civil War Miscellany. USAMHI.

18 For an example of the importance of voting to the men in the army—this time in a state election—see the diary of an Iowa captain. "Thanks for the glorious privilege of franchise. Franchise extended to the soldier even down in Ark. far away from home. Iowa is a jamspunky fine little state. Tomorrow we vote for governor, other state officers, and county officers. Bully for the men who made that law." Miller Allen Woods Diary, October 12, 1863. LC. Illinois did not allow its absent soldiers to vote; according to one Illinois soldier, its regiments therefore took little interest in the election of 1864. Jasper N. Barritt to brother, September 14, 1864. Jasper N. Barritt Papers. LC.

19 Howell and Elizabeth Purdue, *Pat Cleburne, Confederate General* (Hillsboro, Texas, 1973), 454–61. Wirt Armistead Cate, ed., *Two Soldiers: The Campaign Diaries of Thomas J. Key, C. S. A., December 7, 1863–May 17, 1865, and Robert J. Campbell, U. S. A., January 1, 1864–July 21, 1864* (Chapel Hill, 1938), 16–18.

20 Douglas J. Cater to Fannie, February 11, 1865. Douglas J. and Rufus W. Cater Papers. LC. Franklin Setzer to Caroline Setzer, February 19, 1865. Franklin Setzer Papers. UV.

21 Jacob Seibert to father, February 24, 1865. Seibert Family Papers. Harrisburg Civil War Round Table Collection. USAMHI.

22 James R. McMichael Diary, April 9, April 26, April 27, May 7, 1865. AHS. Abbie Brooks Diary, May 24, 1865. AHS.

23 *A Sermon Preached Before Brig-Gen Hoke's Brigade at Kinston, N.C., on the 28th of February, 1864.* . . . *Upon the Death of Twenty-Two Men Who Had Been Executed in the Presence of the Brigade for the Crime of Desertion* (Greensborough, N.C., 1864). John Paris Papers. SHC.

24 Diary, April 9, 1865. John Paris Papers. SHC.

25 David M. Ray to mother, May 15, 1865. David M. Ray Papers. UT.

26 Gen. Thomas T. Munford to Lt. Col. Gus. W. Dorsey, April 28, 1865. Louisiana Historical Collection. TULANE.

27 Ashley Halsey, ed., *A Yankee Private's Civil War By Robert Hale Strong* (Chicago, 1961), 15–16. Margaret Brobst Roth, *Well Mary: Civil War Letters of a Wisconsin Volunteer* (Madison, 1960), 56–57.

28 Richard White to cousin, April 23, 1864. Ross Family Correspondence. VSL. George Bates to William Bates, April 21, 1864, June 19, 1864. George Henry Bates Letters. SCHOFF.

29 Edward W. Kingsley to Sergeant Major, June 30, 1864. Edward W. Kingsley Papers. LC.

30 Benjamin F. Ashenfelter to mother, May 1, 1863. Harrisburg Civil War Round Table Collection. USAMHI. Felix Brannigan to sister, July 16, 1862. Felix Brannigan Papers. LC. George O. Jewett to Deck, July 18, 1863. George O. Jewett Papers. LC. Hugh Roden to George Roden, Sr., February 16, 1863. Roden Brothers Letters. SCHOFF.

31 James T. Miller to Jane and George, April 25, 1864. Miller Brothers Letters. SCHOFF. E. H. C. Taylor to Lottie, April 1, 1863. E. H. C. Taylor Papers. MHS.

32 George C. Chandler to uncle, November 5, 1864. Civil War Miscellany. USAMHI. J. Henry Beatty to sister, July 26, 1863. Civil War Miscellany. USAMHI.

33 John W. Bates Diary, June 2, June 12, 1864. Civil War Miscellany. USAMHI. Diary, January 5, 1865. George C. Lawson Papers in the Robert Shaw Collection. AHS. Samuel Storrow Papers. MHS. See also William G. Hills Diary, March 3, March 7, 1864. LC.

34 Charles M. Maxim to Mrs. Marcus Maxim, March 22, 23, 1864. Charles M. Maxim Letters. SCHOFF. Lucien P. Waters to parents, February 22, 1865. Lucien P. Waters Papers. NYHS. Dayton E. Flint to father, June 20, 1864. Civil War Miscellany. USAMHI. See also George Bates to William Bates, June 19, 1864. George Henry Bates Letters, SCHOFF.

35 Orra B. Bailey to wife, March 13, 1863. Orra B. Bailey Papers. LC.

36 George A. Hudson to folks at home, February 19, 1865, April 10, 1865. George A. Hudson Papers. LC.

37 See Thomas Reed Turner, *Beware the People Weeping: Public Opinion and the Assassination of Abraham Lincoln* (Baton Rouge, 1982) for a thorough discussion of the assassination and the trial of the conspirators. One soldier who was in the audience at Ford's Theatre when Lincoln was killed later bought a picture of John Wilkes Booth as a souvenir. Adelbert D. Baughman Diary, April 14, 1865; May 16, 1865. MHC.

38 Leslie W. Dunlap, ed., *"Your Affectionate Husband, J. F. Culver"*: Let-

ters Written During the Civil War (Iowa City, 1978), 435. William H. Bradbury to wife, April 20, 1865. William H. Bradbury Papers. LC.

39 Christopher H. Keller to George and Esther Keller, June 13, 1864, April 27, 1865, May 10, 1865; to Caroline M. Hall, May 5, 1865. Christopher H. Keller Letters. SCHOFF.

40 Wayne C. Temple, ed., *The Civil War Letters of Henry C. Bear: A Soldier in the 116th Illinois Volunteer Infantry* (Harrogate, Tenn., 1961), 47. Roth, *Well Mary,* 148. See also Alva Griest, *Three Years in Dixie,* April 24, 1865. Harrisburg Civil War Round Table Collection. USAMHI. John H. Francis to William E. Conrow, April 28, 1865. John H. Francis Letters. Conrow Collection. NYHS.

41 C. C. Enslow to wife, May 1, 1865. C. C. Enslow Papers. LC. Cf. William Pegram on the death of Stonewall Jackson. "But it seems a great pity that we should have lost Jackson, and that his brilliant career should have been stopped. I have no doubt however, but that 'all things are for the best.' Some of our troops made too much of an Idol of him and lost sight of God's mercies." William Pegram to sister, May 11, 1863. Pegram-Johnson-McIntosh Papers. VHS.

42 George Tobey Anthony to Benjamen Anthony, April 21, 1865, May 31, 1865. George Tobey Anthony Letters. SCHOFF.

43 Mother to son, May 2, 1865. David M. Ray Papers. UT.

44 Diary of prisoner at Johnson's Island, April 15, 1865. Louisiana Historical Association Collection. TULANE.

45 Francis A. Boyle Diary, 42. UG.

46 Roth, *Well Mary,* 143–44. Charles M. Maxim to Marcus Maxim, May 21, 1865. Charles M. Maxim Letters. SCHOFF. Additional recommendations of Davis's hanging can be found in Abram Verick Parmenter Diary, November 9, 1865. LC; Henry Pippitt to Rebecca Pippitt, May 30, 1865. Henry Pippitt Letters. SCHOFF. C. C. Enslow Papers, May 14, 1865. LC.

47 Diary, April 20, 1865. Howard Smith to Mary, April 23, 1865. Howard Malcolm Smith Papers. LC.

48 Henry Rinker to Mary, June 15, 1865. Harrisburg Civil War Round Table Collection. USAMHI.

49 David Nichol to sister, April 29, 1865. Harrisburg Civil War Round Table Collection. USAMHI. Charles M. Maxim to Marcus Maxim, May 21, 1865. Charles M. Maxim Papers. SCHOFF. Henry Pippitt to Rebecca Pippit, May 21, 1865, July 4, 1865. Henry Pippitt Letters. SCHOFF. One Union soldier explained his reluctance to stay in the South during the summer of 1865 was because there were too many blacks living there. Marshall M. Miller to wife, April 28, 1865. LC.

50 Henry W. Gay to father and mother, August 11, 1865. Civil War Miscellany, USAMHI.

51 Christopher H. Keller to George and Esther Keller, May 10, 1865, May 21, 1865, June 18, 1865. Christopher H. Keller to Caroline M. Hall, May 21, 1865. Christopher H. Keller Letters. SCHOFF.

52 Eric L. McKitrick, *Andrew Johnson and Reconstruction* (Chicago, 1960), 153–58, discusses the South immediately after the end of the war.

53 Norman D. Brown, ed., *One of Cleburne's Command: The Civil War Reminiscences and Diary of Capt. Samuel T. Foster, Granbury's Texas Brigade, C.S.A.* (Austin, 1980), 170–79.

54 Cate, *Two Soldiers,* 215.

55 J. W. Ward to father, May 17, 1863. Confederate States of America Records. Case III. UT.

56 Diary, April and May 1865. E. N. Gilpin Papers. LC. The chaplain of the 30th North Carolina Infantry noted another one of the costs of the war on his roll. A total of 358 soldiers of the 1552 thousand who had been in the regiment had died during the war. Of these fatalities, 114 had been husbands and fathers, who left behind 114 widows and 249 fatherless children. Chaplain's Roll, Alexander Betts Papers. SHC.

57 Alva Griest, *Three Years in Dixie,* May 14, 1865. Harrisburg Civil War Round Table Collection. USAMHI.

58 James A. Congleton Diary, June 15, 1865. LC.

59 William H. Barber to aunt, May 29, 1865. William H. Barber Papers. SCHOFF. John W. Bates Diary, May 24, 1865. Civil War Miscellany. USAMHI. Allan Nevins, ed., *A Diary of Battle: The Personal Journals of Colonel Charles S. Wainwright, 1861–1865* (New York, 1962), 527.

60 Charles M. Maxim to Marcus Maxim, April 28, 1865. Charles M. Maxim Letters. SCHOFF.

61 James M. DeHaven to mother, June 14, 1865. Civil War Miscellany. USAMHI.

62 William T. Sherman, *Memoirs* (Bloomington, Ind., 1957), II, 380.

63 For a discussion of the role of the Union soldier in postwar America, see Mary R. Dearing, *Veterans in Politics: The Story of the G. A. R.* (Baton Rouge, 1952). David Herbert Donald analyzes the relationship of the wartime experience to Southern politics at the end of the century in "A Generation of Defeat," in Walter J. Fraser and Winfred Moore, Jr., eds., *From the Old South to the New: Essays on the Transitional South* (Westport, Conn., 1981).

Bibliography

PRIMARY SOURCES: ARCHIVAL

ATLANTA HISTORICAL SOCIETY
Atlanta, Georgia

Abbie Brooks Diary
Richard M. Campbell Papers
George Hewitt Daniel Papers
D. G. Godwin Papers
Cornelius Redding Hanleiter
    Collection
George C. Lawson Papers (in
    Robert Shaw Collection)

J. McCall Letters
    (in United Daughters of the
    Confederacy Collection)
Capt. James R. McMichael Diary
Joshua M. Mitchell Papers
Underwood–Key Family Papers

THE COLLEGE OF WILLIAM AND MARY IN VIRGINIA
Williamsburg, Virginia

Jubal A. Early Papers
Forbes Letters

Mary J. Wills Papers

CONNECTICUT HISTORICAL SOCIETY
Hartford, Connecticut

Albert A. Andrews Papers
John S. Bartlett Papers
Caleb Blanchard Papers
John Crosby Papers
John C. Holwell Papers
Frederick Hooker Papers

George Kies Papers
Kies Family Papers
John E. Morris Papers
Henry Snow Papers
George Wetmore Papers
William L. Winship Papers

DUKE UNIVERSITY
Durham, North Carolina

CSA Archives—Miscellany
Nancy H. Cowan Papers
C. William Fackler Papers
George W. Jones Papers
William E. McCoy Papers
John Singleton Mosby Papers

William H. Nugen Papers
Helen and Mary Shell Papers
Snow Family Papers
John C. Van Duzer Papers
William Whitehead Papers

EMORY UNIVERSITY
Emory, Georgia

Confederate Miscellany

HISTORIC NEW ORLEANS COLLECTION
New Orleans, Louisiana

Samuel Gault Diary
John Hart Diary

Francis Dunbar Ruggles Papers
Walton–Glenny Papers

LIBRARY OF CONGRESS
Washington, D.C.

Jabez Alvord Papers
John Anglin Papers
John Carvel Arnold Papers
J. J. Asbill Papers
Alfred M. Badger Papers
Orra B. Bailey Papers
Jasper N. Barrit Papers
Wimer Bedford Diary
Joshua Taylor Bradford Diary
William H. Bradbury Papers
Felix Branigan Papers
Silas W. Browning Papers
Douglas J. and Rufus W. Cater
    Papers
William P. Coe Papers
William M. Collin Diary
Abram F. Conant Papers
James A. Congleton Diary
Samuel Henry Eells Papers
Charles Calvin Enslow Papers
Thomas Evans Papers
Thomas L. Feamster Diary,
    Feamster Family Papers
Lewis R. Fenton Papers

Wilbur Fisk Papers
Jacob J. Frank Papers
Thomas Francis Galwey Papers
S. J. Gibson Papers
E. N. Gilpin Papers
William J. Gould Papers
Henry I. and Robert Greer Papers
Isaac Hallock Papers
William Hamilton Papers
William G. Hills Diary
Lyman C. Holford Papers
Charles Wesley Hoshmer Papers
Charles Crook Hood Papers
George A. Hudson Papers
John Hughes, Jr., Papers
George O. Jewett Papers
John Augustine Johnson Papers
W. C. Johnson Papers
John Griffith Jones Papers
Keidel Family Papers
Edward W. Kinsley Papers
George F. Laird Papers
Allen Landis and Family Papers
Joseph Lester Papers

Jeremiah T. Lockwood Papers
John Wesley Marshall Papers
William C. McKinley Papers
Rufus Mead, Jr., Papers
James Burtis Merwin Papers
Allen Woods Miller Papers
Marshall Mortimer Miller Papers
James H. Montgomery Papers
John Singleton Mosby Papers
Peter H. Niles Papers
William W. Old Papers
Abram Verrick Parmenter Papers
Byron Parsons Papers
Albert Quincy Porter Papers
Richard Henry Pratt Papers
Charles Wellington Read Papers

Edward Paul Reichhelm Papers
David A. Rice Papers
Charles H. Richardson Papers
Josiah W. Ripley Papers
Patrick Ryan Papers
Bela T. St. John Papers
M. Shuler Diary
George Boyd Smith Papers
Howard Malcolm Smith Papers
William R. Stimson Papers
Aaron B. Tompkins Papers
John Whitten Papers
Frederick H. Wight Papers
Henry Wirz Papers
Thomas L. Wragg Papers

LOUISIANA HISTORICAL CENTER
LOUISIANA STATE MUSEUM
New Orleans, Louisiana

C. C. Bier Memorandum Book
Briant Family Papers
Florian Octave Cournay Papers
James R. Currell Papers

Mansfield Lovell Diary
Dr. William S. Mitchell Papers
George Moss Papers

MASSACHUSETTS HISTORICAL SOCIETY
Boston, Massachusetts

John E. Bassett Papers
James Beale Papers
Failing-Knight Papers
Fiske Family Papers
Holmes Family Papers

Thomas S. Howland Papers
Charles F. Read Papers
P. J. Revere Papers
Samuel Storrow Papers
J. C. Warner Papers

NEW-YORK HISTORICAL SOCIETY
New York, New York

"A Stirring Incident of the Federal
   War"
William H. Aldis Papers
E. DeLoss Burton Papers
William S. Cain Diary
Erving-King Papers
John Fleming Papers
Charles G. Folger Diary
John H. Francis Letters (in Conrow
   Collection)

Isaac Comstock Hadden Papers
James E. McBeth Letters (in
   Conrow Collection)
Henry O. Perry Diary
Rudolphe Rey Papers
Burage Rice Diary
Edward H. Sentell Diary
Alfred Baker Smith Papers
Lucien P. Waters Papers

PRINCETON UNIVERSITY
Princeton, New Jersey

John S. Copley Papers
Albert S. & Samuel S. Ely Papers
James Fenton Diary

Henry S. Sherman Diary
Paul Ambrose Oliver Papers
Charles W. Reed Letters

TULANE UNIVERSITY
New Orleans, Louisiana

W. B. Bailey Diary
Civil War Miscellaneous Series
Stonewall Jackson Papers (in the
George H. and Katherine M.
Davis Collection)

Ker-Texada Papers
Kostmayer Collection
Louisiana Historical Association
Collection

UNITED STATES ARMY MILITARY HISTORY INSTITUTE
Carlisle, Pennsylvania

Civil War Miscellany

Harrisburg Civil War Round Table
Collection

UNIVERSITY OF GEORGIA
Athens, Georgia

Adams Collection
Manning P. & Pellona David
Alexander Letters
John R. Binnon Letters
Francis A. Boyle Diary
Hambrick Civil War Letters

G. M. Hanvey Papers
Malcolm Letters
O. W. Low Letters
Francis H. Nash Diary
Shepherd Green Pryor Papers
Robert G. Williams Collection

UNIVERSITY OF MICHIGAN
Ann Arbor, Michigan

Michigan Historical Collection
Bentley Library

Schoff Collection
Clements Library

Calvin Ainsworth Diary
C. Emerson Allen Diary
Adelbert Baughman Diary
Frederick W. Bechtold Diary
William J. Carroll Diary
John R. Morey Papers
Jacob Preston Papers
Silas Sadler Papers
Edward H. C. Taylor Papers

George Tobey Anthony Letters
William Harrison Barber Letters
Numa Barned Letters
Charles M. Barnett Diary
George Henry Bates Letters
Andrew Brockway Letters
Thomas B. Byron Diary
Lucius W. Chapman Diary
Clark-Whedon Letters
Adam Cosner Letters

James Gaunt Derrickson Diary
William G. Dickson Letters
Reuben Smith Goodman Journal
Griffin Letters
James Henry Hall Letters
Lewis Hickok Diary
John R. Hunt, Jr., Diary
Henry J. Johnson Letters
William Ellis Jones Diary
Christopher Howser Keller Letters
Levi E. Kent Diary
Josiah Edmund King Letters
William Kossak Journal
Krewson Letters
Sidney O. Little Letters
Henry Grimes Marshall Letters
Lewis J. Martin Letters
Charles M. Maxim Letters
Calvin Mehaffey Letters

Miller Brothers Letters
George Hale Nicholls Letters
Frederic S. Olmsted Diary
Bryan Densmore Paddock Diary
Simon Peterson Letters
John Pierson Letters
Henry Pippitt Letters
Point Lookout, Maryland, Prison
    Camp Records
Albert R. Robinson Diary
Roden Brothers Letters
George Schubert Letters
Henry H. Seys Letters
William Henry Shaw Letters
Starbird Brothers Letters
Vandergrift Letters
Edward Hitchcock Wade Letters
Albert Wilder Letters
John Darragh Wilkins Letters

UNIVERSITY OF NORTH CAROLINA
Chapel Hill, North Carolina

North Carolina Collection

Newton Wallace Diary

Southern Historical Collection

Isaac Alexander Papers
S. G. Barnard Papers
J. Kelly Bennette Papers
Alexander Betts Papers
Francis Boyle Papers
Confederate Papers (Miscellaneous)
Joseph Cotten Papers
Dial Letter
Samuel W. Eaton Papers
Franklin Gaillard Papers
James E. Green Papers
Charles Fenton James Papers
Kenneth Rayner Jones Papers
H. C. Kendrick Papers
Harry Lewis Papers
Albert Moses Luria Papers

Mrs. Thomas Chalmers McCorrey
    Papers
Capt. William Randolph McEntire
    Papers
Neill McLeod Papers
John S. R. Miller Papers
Leroy Moncure Nutt Papers
John Paris Papers
Leonidas Lafayette Polk Papers
Theodore Mead Pomeroy Papers
Isaac C. Richardson Papers
Iowa Michigan Royster Papers
James M. Skelton Papers
Joseph W. Smith Papers
Andrew J. Sproul Papers
P. H. Turner Papers
Achille James Tynes Papers
Paul T. Vaughan Papers
Webb Family Papers
Asa J. Wyatt Papers

UNIVERSITY OF TEXAS
Austin, Texas

George H. Allen Diary
Civil War Miscellany
W. R. Coffee Diary
Confederate States of America
  Records
Edmund R. Crockett Diary
George W. Guess Letters
Thomas B. Hampton Letters

Lee Collection
G. W. Raines Papers
David M. Ray Papers
James W. Redding Family Papers
Maurice K. Simons Diary
John Franklin Smith Letters
Francis M. Troth Papers

UNIVERSITY OF VIRGINIA
Charlottesville, Virginia

Holladay Family Papers
John Singleton Mosby Papers

Micajah Woods Papers

VIRGINIA HISTORICAL SOCIETY
Richmond, Virginia

Frederick Fillison Brown Papers
Bryan Family Papers
Francis West Chamberlayne Papers
Cocke Family of Portsmouth,
  Virginia, Papers
John Warwick Daniel Papers
Edward Samuel Duffey Papers
Harlow Family Papers
Watkins Kearns Papers
Keith Family Papers
Osmun Latrobe Papers

Lomax Family Papers
McCarthy Family Papers
Hunter McGuire Papers
Meade Family Papers
Josiah Staunton Moore Papers
Gustavus Adolphus Myers Papers
Pegram-Johnson-McIntosh Papers
John Simmons Shipp Papers
Henry M. Talley Papers
John McLeod Turner Papers
Richard Henry Watkins Papers

VIRGINIA STATE LIBRARY
Richmond, Virginia

Ross Family Correspondence

PRIMARY SOURCES: PRINTED

Ambrose, Stephen E., ed. *A Wisconsin Boy in Dixie: The Selected Letters of James K. Newton.* Madison, 1961.
Anderson, Mary Ann, ed. *The Civil War Diary of Allen Morgan Geer, Twentieth Regiment, Illinois Volunteers.* New York, 1977.

Barrett, John G., ed. *Yankee Rebel: The Civil War Journal of Edmund DeWitt Patterson.* Chapel Hill, 1966.

Barrett, John G., and Robert K. Turner, Jr., eds. *Letters of a New Market Cadet.* Chapel Hill, 1961.

Boney, F. N. *A Union Soldier in the Land of the Vanquished: The Diary of Sergeant Mathrew Woodruff, June–December, 1865.* University, Ala., 1969.

Brown, Norman D., ed. *One of Cleburne's Command: The Civil War Reminiscences and Diary of Capt. Samuel T. Foster, Granbury's Texas Brigade, C.S.A.* Austin, 1980.

Carter, Capt. Robert Goldthwaite. *Four Brothers in Blue: Or Sunshine and Shadows of the War of the Rebellion, a Story of the Great War from Bull Run to Appomattox.* 1913. Reprint: Austin, 1978.

Cash, William M., and Lucy Somerville Howorth, eds. *My Dear Nellie: The Civil War Letters of William L. Nugent to Eleanor Smith Nugent.* Jackson, Miss., 1977.

Cate, Wirt Armistead, ed. *Two Soldiers: The Campaign Diaries of Thomas J. Key, C.S.A., December 7, 1863–May 17, 1865, and Robert J. Campbell, U. S. A., January 1, 1864–July 21, 1864.* Chapel Hill, 1938.

Coe, David, ed. *Mine Eyes Have Seen the Glory: Combat Diaries of Union Sergeant Hamlin Alexander Coe.* Rutherford, Madison, Teaneck, N.J., 1975.

Cummer, Clyde Lottride, and Genevieve Miller, eds. *Yankee in Gray: The Civil War Memoirs of Henry E. Handerson With a Selection of His Wartime Letters.* Case Western Reserve University, 1962.

DeForest, John William. *Miss Ravenel's Conversion from Secession to Loyalty.* 1867. Reprint: New York, 1955.

———. *A Volunteer's Adventures: A Union Captain's Record of the Civil War.* New Haven, 1946.

Dennis, Frank Allen, ed. *Kemper County Rebel: The Civil War Diary of Robert Masten Holmes, C.S.A.* Jackson, Miss., 1973.

DeRosier, Arthur H., Jr., ed. *Through the South with a Union Soldier.* Johnson City, Tenn., 1969.

Donald, David Herbert, ed. *Gone for a Soldier: The Civil War Memoirs of Private Alfred Bellard.* Boston, 1975.

Dowdey, Clifford, and Louis H. Manarin, eds. *The Wartime Papers of R. E. Lee.* Boston, 1961.

Dunlap, Leslie W., ed. *"Your Affectionate Husband, J. F. Culver": Letters Written During the Civil War.* Iowa City, 1978.

Durkin, Joseph T., ed. *Confederate Chaplain: A War Journal of Rev. James B. Sheeran, C. Ss. R., 14th Louisiana, C.S.A.* Milwaukee, 1960.

Erickson, Edgar L., ed. "Hunting for Cotton in Dixie: From the Civil War Diary of Captain Charles E. Wilcox." *Journal of Southern History,* IV, #4 (November 1938): 493–513.

Fatout, Paul. *Letters of a Civil War Surgeon.* Purdue Universities, 1961.

Ford, Worthington Chauncey, ed. *War Letters, 1862–1865, of John Chipman Gray and John Codman Ropes.* Boston, 1927.

Halsey, Ashley, ed. *A Yankee Private's Civil War by Robert Hale Strong.* Chicago, 1961.

Hammond, Mary Acton, ed. "Dear Mollie: Letters of Captain Edward A.

Acton to His Wife, 1862." *Pennsylvania Magazine of History and Biography*, LXXXIX, #1 (January 1965): 3–51.

Hassler, William W., ed. *The General to His Lady: The Civil War Letters of William Dorsey Pender to Fanny Pender*. Chapel Hill, 1965.

Howe, Mark deWolfe, ed. *Touched with Fire: Civil War Letters and Diaries of Oliver Wendell Holmes, Jr., 1861–1864*. Cambridge, Mass., 1947.

Jackson, Joseph Orville, ed. *"Some of the Boys. . . .": The Civil War Letters of Isaac Jackson, 1862–1865*. Carbondale, Ill., 1960.

Kirwan, A. D., ed. *Johnny Green of the Orphan Brigade: The Journal of a Confederate Soldier*. University of Kentucky, 1956.

Loving, Jerome M., ed. *Civil War Letters of George Washington Whitman*. Durham, 1975.

McDonald, Archie P., ed. *Make Me a Map of the Valley: The Civil War Journal of Stonewall Jackson's Topographer*. Dallas, 1973.

McGuire, Kate Flanagan, ed. *McGuire Papers*. Tusquahoma, La., 1966.

Nevins, Allan, ed. *A Diary of Battle: The Personal Journals of Colonel Charles S. Wainwright, 1861–1865*. New York, 1962.

Nichols, George Ward. *The Story of the Great March*. New York, 1865.

Olmsted, Frederick Law. *A Journey in the Back Country 1853–1854*. New York, 1970.

Partin, Robert, ed. " 'The Momentous Events' of the Civil War as Reported by a Confederate Private–Sergeant." *Tennessee Historical Quarterly* 18 (1959): 69–86.

Pierson, William Whatley, Jr., ed. *Whipt 'em Everytime: The Diary of Bartlett Yancey Malone, Co. H., 6th N.C. Regiment*. Jackson, Tenn., 1960.

Ransom, John. *John Ransom's Diary*. New York, 1963.

Roark, James. *Masters without Slaves*. New York, 1977

Robertson, James I., Jr., ed. *The Civil War Letters of General Robert McAllister*. New Brunswick, N.J., 1965.

Roth, Margaret Brobst, ed. *Well Mary: The Civil War Letters of a Wisconsin Volunteer*. Madison, 1960.

Rugeley, H. J. H., ed. *Batchelor-Turner Letters, 1861–1864: Written By Two of Terry's Texas Rangers*. Austin, 1961.

Sherman, William T. *Memoirs of General William T. Sherman*. Bloomington, Ind., 1957.

Shuffler, R. Henderson, ed. *Decimus et Ultimus Barziza, The Adventures of a Prisoner of War, 1863–1864*. Originally published anonymously, 1865. Austin, 1964.

Silver, James W., ed. *A Life for the Confederacy: As Recorded in the Pocket Diaries of Pvt. Robert A. Moore*. Jackson, Tenn., 1959.

Stauffer, Nelson. *Civil War Diary*. California State University, Northridge Libraries, 1976.

Taylor, F. Jay, ed. *Reluctant Rebel: The Secret Diary of Robert Patrick, 1861–1865*. Baton Rouge, 1959.

Temple, Wayne C., ed. *The Civil War Letters of Henry C. Bear: A Soldier in the 116th Illinois Volunteer Infantry*. Harrogate, Tenn., 1961.

Thompson, D. G. Brinton, ed. "From Chancellorsville to Gettysburg: A Doctor's Diary." *Pennsylvania Magazine of History and Biography*, LXXXIX, #3 (July 1965): 292–315.

Truxall, Aida Craig, ed. *"Respects to All": Letters of Two Pennsylvania Boys in the War of Rebellion*. Pittsburgh, 1962.

Walton, Clyde C., ed. *Private Smith's Journal: Recollections of the Late War.* Chicago, 1963.

Walton, William, ed. *A Civil War Courtship: The Letters of Edwin Weller from Antietam to Atlanta.* Garden City, N.Y., 1980.

Wiley, Bell I., ed. *Francis W. Dawson, Reminiscences of Confederate Service, 1861–1865.* Baton Rouge, 1980.

——, ed. *"This Infernal War": The Confederate Letters of Sgt. Edwin H. Fay.* Austin, 1958.

Williams, Frederick D., ed. *The Wild Life of the Army: Civil War Letters of James A. Garfield.* Michigan State University Press, 1964.

Winther, Oscar Osburn. *With Sherman to the Sea: The Civil War Diaries and Reminiscences of Theodore F. Upson.* Bloomington, Ind., 1958.

SECONDARY SOURCES

BOOKS AND ARTICLES

Anderson, Fred. *A People's Army: Massachusetts Soldiers and Society in the Seven Years' War.* Chapel Hill, 1984.

Axtell, James. *The European and the Indian: Essays in the Ethnohistory of Colonial North America.* New York, 1981.

Barney, William L. *Flawed Victory.* New York, 1979.

Berwanger, Eugene H. *The Frontier Against Slavery: Western Anti-Negro Prejudice and the Slavery Extension Controversy.* Urbana, Ill., 1971.

Brock, William R. *Conflict and Transformation: The United States, 1844–1877.* Baltimore, 1973.

Brownlee, Richard S. *Gray Ghosts of the Confederacy: Guerilla Warfare in the West, 1861–1865.* Baton Rouge, 1958.

Cooper, William J. *The South and the Politics of Slavery, 1828–1856.* Baton Rouge, 1978.

Craven, Avery. *The Coming of the Civil War.* New York, 1942.

——. "Coming of War Between the States: An Interpretation." *Journal of Southern History* II, #3 (August 1936): 303–22.

Curry, Leonard P. *Blueprint for Modern America: Nonmilitary Legislation of the First Civil War Congress.* Nashville, 1968.

Davis, David Brion. *The Slave Power Conspiracy and the Paranoid Style.* Baton Rouge, 1969.

Dearing, Mary R. *Veterans in Politics: The Story of the G. A. R.* Baton Rouge, 1952.

Degler, Carl N. *The Other South: Southern Dissenters in the Nineteenth Century.* New York, 1974.

Donald, David Herbert. "A Generation of Defeat." In *From the Old South to the New: Essays on the Transitional South,* edited by Walter J. Fraser and Winfred Moore, Jr., 3–20. Westport, Conn., 1981.

——. "The Southerner as Fighting Man." In *The Southerner as American,* edited by Charles G. Sellers, 72–88. New York, 1960.

Douglas, Ann. *The Feminization of American Culture.* New York, 1977.

Escott, Paul D. *After Secession: Jefferson Davis and the Failure of Confederate Nationalism.* New York, 1976.

Foner, Eric. *Free Soil, Free Labor, Free Men: The Ideology of the Republican Party before the Civil War.* New York, 1970.

Forgie, George B. *Patricide in the House Divided: A Psychological Interpretation of Lincoln and His Age.* New York, 1979.

Foster, Gaines M. "Woodward and Southern Identity." *Southern Review* (April 1985): 351–60.

Freeman, Douglas S. *Lee's Lieutenants.* New York, 1942–1944.

Gates, Paul W. *The Farmer's Age: Agriculture, 1815–1860.* New York, 1960.

Genovese, Eugene. *Roll, Jordan, Roll: The World the Slaves Made.* New York, 1976.

———. "Yeoman Farmers in a Slaveholders' Democracy." *Agricultural History* 49 (April 1975): 331–42.

Glassie, Henry. *Pattern in the Material Folk Culture of the Eastern United States.* Philadelphia, 1971.

Hahn, Steven. *The Roots of Southern Populism: Yeoman Farmers and the Transformation of the Georgia Upcountry, 1850–1890.* New York, 1983.

Henretta, James A. "Families and Farms: *Mentalitie* in Pre-Industrial America." *William and Mary Quarterly* 35 (January 1978): 3–32.

Hesseltine, William B. *Civil War Prisons: A Study in War Psychology.* Columbus, Ohio, 1930.

Hofstader, Richard. *The American Political Tradition and the Men Who Made It.* New York, 1960.

Isaac, Rhys. *The Transformation of Virginia.* Chapel Hill, 1982.

Jackson, John Brinkerhoff. *American Space: The Centennial Years: 1865–1876.* New York, 1972.

Jennings, Francis. *The Invasion of America: Indians, Colonialism, and the Cant of Conquest.* New York, 1975.

Johannsen, Robert W. *To the Halls of the Montezumas: The War with Mexico in the American Imagination.* New York, 1985.

Lee, Charles Robert, Jr. *The Confederate Constitutions.* Chapel Hill, 1963.

Lee, Susan Previant, and Peter Passell. *A New Economic View of American History.* New York, 1979.

Leed, Eric J. *No Man's Land: Combat and Identity in World War I.* New York, 1979

Litwack, Leon F. *Been in the Storm So Long.* New York, 1980.

———. *North of Slavery: The Negro in the Free States, 1790–1860.* Chicago. 1961.

Long, E. B. *The Civil War Day By Day: An Almanac, 1861–1865.* New York, 1971.

Lonn, Ella. *Desertion During the Civil War.* Gloucester, Mass., 1966—reprint of the 1928 edition.

McCardell, John. *The Idea of a Southern Nation: Southern Nationalists and Southern Nationalism, 1830–1860.* New York, 1979.

McCoy, Drew. *The Elusive Republic.* Chapel Hill, 1980.

McDonald, Forrest, and Grady McWhiney. "The South from Self-Sufficiency to Peonage: An Interpretation." *American Historical Review* 85 (December 1980): 1095–1118.

McKitrick, Eric L. *Andrew Johnson and Reconstruction.* Chicago, 1960.

Malone, Bill C. *Southern Music, American Music.* University Press of Kentucky, 1979.

Matthews, Donald G. *Religion in the Old South*. Chicago, 1977.

Mayfield, John. *Rehearsal for Republicanism: Free Soil and the Politics of Anti-Slavery*. Port Washington, N.Y., 1980.

Merrill, Michael. "Cash Is Good to Eat: Self-Sufficiency and Exchange in the Rural Economy of the United States." *Radical History Review* 4 (Winter 1977): 42–71.

Meyers, Marvin. *The Jacksonian Persuasion: Politics and Belief*. Stanford, 1957.

Moorhead, James H. *American Apocalypse: Yankee Protestants and the Civil War, 1860–1869*. New Haven, 1978.

Nelson, Larry E. *Bullets, Ballots, and Rhetoric: Confederate Policy for the United States Presidential Contest of 1864*. University, Ala., 1980.

Nichols, Roy Franklin. *The Disruption of American Democracy*. New York, 1948.

Noblin, Stuart. *Leonidas Lafayette Polk: Agrarian Crusader*. Chapel Hill, 1949.

Nye, W. S. *Here Come the Rebels!* Baton Rouge, 1965.

Oakes, James. *The Ruling Race: A History of American Slaveholders*. New York, 1982.

Owens, Harry P., and James J. Cooke, eds. *The Old South in the Crucible of War*. Jackson, Miss., 1983.

Owsley, Frank. *States Rights in the Confederacy*. Chicago, 1925.

Palludan, Phillip Shaw. *Victims: A True Story of the Civil War*. Knoxville, 1981.

Potter, David M. *The Impending Crisis: 1848–1861*. New York, 1976.

Powell, Lawrence N. *New Masters: Northern Planters during the Civil War and Reconstruction*. New Haven and London, 1980.

Purdue, Howell and Elizabeth. *Pat Cleburne, Confederate General*. Hillsboro, Tx., 1973.

Ringold, May Spencer. *The Role of the State Legislatures in the Confederacy*. Athens, Ga., 1966.

Royster, Charles. "Founding a Nation in Blood: Military Conflict and American Nationality." *Arms and Independence: The Military Character of the American Revolution*, edited by Ronald Hoffman and Peter Albert. Charlottesville, Va., 1984.

———. " 'The Nature of Treason': Revolutionary Virtue and American Reactions to Benedict Arnold." *The William and Mary Quarterly*, 3rd Series, XXXVI (April 1979): 163–93.

———. *A Revolutionary People at War: The Continental Army and American Character, 1775–1783*. Chapel Hill, 1979.

Shepard, Paul. *Man in the Landscape: A Historic View of the Esthetics of Nature*. New York, 1976.

Slotkin, Richard. *Regeneration through Violence: The Mythology of the American Frontier, 1600–1860*. Middletown, Conn., 1973.

Stampp, Kenneth M. *And the War Came: The North and the Secession Crisis, 1860–1861*. Baton Rouge, 1950.

———. *The Imperiled Union: Essays on the Background of the Civil War*. New York, 1980.

Taylor, William R. *Cavalier and Yankee: The Old South and American National Character*. New York, 1969.

Thomas, Emory M. *The Confederate Nation: 1861–1865*. New York, 1979.

Thornton, J. Mills, III. *Politics and Power in a Slave Society: Alabama, 1800–1860.* Baton Rouge, 1978.

Turner, Thomas Reed. *Beware the People Weeping: Public Opinion and the Assassination of Abraham Lincoln.* Baton Rouge, 1982.

Warren, Robert Penn. *The Legacy of the Civil War: Meditations on the Centennial.* New York, 1964.

Watson, Harry. *Jacksonian Politics and Community Conflict.* Baton Rouge, 1981.

Weisberger, Bernard A. *They Gathered at the River.* Boston, 1958.

Wiley, Bell I. *The Life of Johnny Reb: The Common Soldier of the Confederacy.* Indianapolis, 1943.

———. *The Life of Billy Yank: The Common Soldier of the Union.* Baton Rouge, 1983.

———. *The Plain People of the Confederacy.* Baton Rouge, 1943.

———. "Southern Reaction to Federal Invasion." *Journal of Southern History* XVI, #4 (November 1950): 491–510.

Wright, Gavin. *The Political Economy of the Cotton South: Households, Markets, and Wealth in the Nineteenth Century.* New York, 1978.

Wright, Gavin, and Howard Kunreuther. "Cotton, Corn, and Risk in the Nineteenth Century." *Journal of Economic History* 35 (September 1975): 526–51.

Zube, Ervin H., ed. *Landscapes: Selected Writings of J. B. Jackson.* Amherst, 1970.

DISSERTATIONS

Ford, Lacy K., Jr. "Social Origins of a New South Carolina: The Upcountry in the Nineteenth Century." University of South Carolina, 1983.

Jimerson, Randall Clair. "A People Divided: The Civil War Interpreted by Participants." University of Michigan, 1977.

Index